Travels in a Gay Nation

LIVING OUT
Gay and Lesbian Autobiographies

David Bergman, Joan Larkin, and Raphael Kadushin
SERIES EDITORS

Travels in a Gay Nation

Portraits of LGBTQ Americans

Philip Gambone

The University of Wisconsin Press

The University of Wisconsin Press
1930 Monroe Street, 3rd Floor
Madison, Wisconsin 53711-2059
uwpress.wisc.edu

3 Henrietta Street
London WCE 8LU, England
www.eurospanbookstore.com

1   3   5   4   2

Printed in the United States of America

Library of Congress Cataloging-in-Publication Data
Gambone, Philip.
Travels in a gay nation: portraits of LGBTQ Americans / Philip Gambone.
    p.   cm.—(Living out : gay and lesbian autobiographies)
ISBN 978-0-299-23684-7 (pbk.: alk. paper)
ISBN 978-0-299-23683-0 (e-book)
    1. Lesbians—United States—Interviews.
    2. Gays—United States—Interviews.
    3. Bisexuals—United States—Interviews.
    4. Transgender people—United States—Interviews.
        I. Title.   II. Series: Living out.
        HQ75.2.G36   2010
        306.76'6092273—dc22
                [B]
            2009041591s

For

my students

Getting used to one another is the way to move forward.

Kwame Anthony Appiah

There is only one subject: What it feels like to be alive. Nothing is irrelevant. Nothing is typical.

Richard Rodriguez

We are complicated and enormous.

Dorothy Allison

I hope to the outer edges of my soul that, at some point, books like these will just be records of good people in a very good world.

Scott Turner Schofield

Contents

Contents

Acknowledgments

This book would never have been written without the invaluable help of many people who offered me information, suggestions, leads, hospitality, and all manner of other assistance and encouragement.

First and foremost, I wish to thank the 102 persons who graciously and generously granted me an interview. In addition to the forty-four whose profiles ultimately were included in *Travels in a Gay Nation*, fifty-eight others deserve my recognition and deep gratitude. They are Franklin Abbott, Angel Abcede, Yolo Akili, John Amaechi, Don Bachardy, Tracy Baim, Kate Bornstein, Gary Burton, Alexander Chee, Alice Dan, Durk Dehner and Sharp, Lea DeLaria, Laura Esquivel, Kimberly Fisher, Rudy Galindo, Nancy Garden, Ann Giagni, Judy Grahn, Carter Heyward, Ray Hill, Alice Hom, Lucy Horne (Swami Dhumavati), Tonda Hughes, Kevin Jennings, Alice Kuzniar, Lou Lambert, Charles Leslie, Susan Love, Michael Lucas, Armistead Maupin, Tim McFeeley, Kathleen McGuire, Maura Melley, Charles Middleton, Tim Miller, David Mixner, Michael Nava, Thomas Pasatieri, Terri Phoenix, David Plante, Julie Rhoad, Jeffrey Roberson, Ned Rorem, Paul Rudnick, Alex Sanchez, Scott Turner Schofield, Mark Segal, Marc Shaiman and Scott Wittman, Bob Smith, Kennedy Smith, James Spada, Ross Terrill, Virginia Uribe, Patrick Webb, Ed White, and Bob Witeck. I hope many, if not all, of them will appear in a future volume.

For their kind hospitality while I was on the road, I wish to thank Jonathan Tucker, Kate Ritchie, Bryan O'Rourke and Alan Orenbuch, David McCarthy and Joe Ignatowski, Fred Fiandaca, Rob Andrews and Ron Shiloh, Tom and Betty Linker, Rodger Broadley and Joe Quinn, and Bruce Wile.

I also wish to thank Bill McLaughlin, Meg Connolly and Tom Saunders, AnnMarie Longobucco, Roger Savonen and Drew De-Rose, George Mansour, Steven Ralston, Ludwig von Hanh, Linda Dusman and Susan McCully, John Mitzel, Alan Rivera, Jack Gantos, Josh Bloom, Wendy Wheeler, Claudia Gonson, Marcie Richardson, David Imming and Dale Mitchell, Monique Truong, Ny Martin, Kelly O'Grady, and Chris Kennelly.

Special mention should go to those unsung heroes, the librarians at Harvard's Widener Library, Boston University's Mugar Library, and the Boston Public Library, whose guidance and professionalism on numerous visits I much appreciate. I also owe an enormous debt of gratitude to my two splendid IT guys, Geoff Greenberg and Bill Castell, who literally saved this book on more than one occasion.

Finally, very special thanks to six people who very directly made this book possible: Andrew Corbin, who provided the initial impetus for the project; Richard Marshall, who early on, when I was discouraged, told me the words I needed to hear; Jim Berkman, head of school at Boston University Academy, who awarded me the school's Metcalf Fellowship, which provided invaluable release time from teaching; Owen Andrews, who carefully read portions of the manuscript and offered keen feedback; Robert Allen, my agent; and last but by no means least, Raphael Kadushin, acquisitions editor at the University of Wisconsin Press. I am enormously grateful to his ongoing faith in my work and enthusiastic commitment to this book. Raphy is a gift to the world of LGBTQ studies.

Travels in a Gay Nation

Introduction

In David Moreton's wonderful film *Edge of Seventeen*, an unexpected summer romance with another boy throws high school senior Eric Hunter into a tailspin. When the object of Eric's affection—a blond big-man-on-campus type, with all the sensitivity of a bowling ball—returns to Ohio State (and another boyfriend), Eric is left to figure out how to get through high school, and life, with this new knowledge about himself.

Played perfectly by Chris Stafford, Eric begins to shed the trappings of his white-bread upbringing and goes in search of his true self. It's 1984. He starts wearing funky clothes. He finds the juvenile antics of his classmates tedious. One afternoon, he comes home sporting a shock of carrot orange hair. "It's getting a little extreme," his mother opines.

That night after supper, Eric is alone on the sofa watching TV. From the tube, we hear a voice ask, "How did you start wearing makeup?" and a male voice begins to answer just as Eric's dad comes in with two bowls of ice cream—a moment to bond with this son who is beginning to weird him out. "That is some hairdo," he chuckles nervously before spooning into his dessert. When his attention goes to the screen, a puzzled look comes over his face. "What are you watching?" This is clearly not the kind of program that a regular guy from Sandusky tunes into. "Oh, some interview show," Eric tells him with feigned nonchalance.

The purpose of the scene is clear. We're meant to see that Eric is moving away—one moment eagerly, one moment skittishly—from the Middle American dream his parents have laid out for him. But as I studied this scene more closely, I began to wonder why, specifically, screenwriter Todd Stephens decided to make the program that Eric watches a talk show. What are we being told here? Well, for one thing, in 1984 nascent gay and lesbian adolescents, especially those away from the big coastal cities, got information about their new queer world from whatever resources they could. (In an earlier scene, we see Eric furtively listening to an album by Bronski Beat, the slip jacket emblazoned with a pink triangle.) And what could be safer, less incriminating, than tuning in to "some interview show," innocuous enough to be broadcast on network television? It's just someone's story, he might have told his father.

I thought about Eric as I was reviewing what Gene Robinson, the first openly gay bishop in the Episcopal Church, told me the day I interviewed him: "We have come so far in this movement. It's hard for young LGBT people to imagine a world without *Will and Grace*, without Ellen, without Greg Louganis and Martina Navratilova. Or to remember back to what a hero Harvey Milk was." In a world without these superstars, Robinson turned to stories—in his case, biblical stories—to discover the version of his own queer narrative that made sense to him. "I kept recognizing myself as a gay man all through Scripture and learning, as all people on the margins have the opportunity to learn, that there is good news there."

Stories. Haven't they always helped us to learn who we are, whoever we are? Stories both anchor us in reality and inspire our imaginations and dreams. They remind us where we have been and hint at where we are going. Stories allow us to discover the common humanity in all people. Other stories initiate us into the culture of our tribe: *This is what it's like to come from our people, to belong to our people.* Stories give us vital information. They help us to make our own story stronger. They save lives. It's not far-fetched to suggest that the interview Eric Hunter listens to, even under the skeptical gaze of his father, helps to save his life.

Time and again, as I talked with folks during the two years of this project, I heard them tell me how important stories were in their own development as healthy, mature, vibrant persons. Books (from

4

Nancy Garden's young adult novel *Annie on My Mind* to James Baldwin's *Giovanni's Room*), magazines and newspapers, plays, poems, songs, hymns, movies, radio and TV shows, musicals. (How many readers of this book will smile understandingly when they come across Arthur Dong's recollections of seeing *Flower Drum Song* for the first time?)

Fiction and nonfiction, gay stories and straight ones. The importance of stories—hearing them, reading them, seeing them performed, and thrilling to what one is being told—is one of the few common experiences the forty-four people in this book seem to have shared as they were coming of age. I think, for example, of Lillian Faderman, who expresses profound gratitude to the social worker who gave her "books that enchanted me." Or playwright Jamil Khoury, who, at the end of our interview, noted to me, "Storytelling does indeed change the world."

Sadly, tragically, throughout much of our history, a lot of the life-changing stories that we LGBTQ folk might have heard never got told. Unlike any other community—ethnic, racial, religious, or cultural—we have, until quite recently, been raised in families, and taught by teachers, who were mostly ignorant of the stories of our people, stories that might have nurtured us in ways they often could not imagine. Our queer family was hidden from us, sometimes deliberately (think of those locked cages in the town library), more often because no one, even those most qualified to do so, dared to tell. (In our conversation, Jennifer Chrisler sadly noted how we LGBTQ people have historically been loathe, even afraid, to tell our stories.) In other cases, "our stories" were being told by people who had little authority to do so. As Frank Kameny told me, "It was my opinion that we gays alone are the authorities on ourselves and our homosexuality, and others should listen to us."

These days, of course, LGBTQ stories are everywhere. Is there an adolescent in America today who could arrive at the edge of seventeen and not know some gay stories? And yet the portrait of our community that emerges from this collective cornucopia of images and tales is often a sadly impoverished one. As Urvashi Vaid accurately points out in *Virtual Equality*, "While every gay, lesbian, bisexual, or transgendered person can proudly recite the names of music and film celebrities who are gay or lesbian, few can list the people who lead the political fight, behind the spotlight, to advance and promote gay and lesbian equality."

5

The queer stories that are out there—the ones getting the widest hearings, the ones given the imprimatur to inform the world of what being LGBTQ is all about—are too often the ones that many of us can least identify with: Technicolor stories of the big, loud, splashy celebs du jour whose lives and antics crowd the pages of the glossies, gay and mainstream. Of course, celebrities are a part of our community—in many cases an important part—but they by no means encompass the whole story of who we are and what we're up to.

It would be outrageously grandiose to suggest that *Travels in a Gay Nation* succeeds in telling that "whole story." It does nothing of the sort. But from the outset of this project my intention was to open up a much wider panorama—of faces, voices, stories, points of view—than the tiny, cramped window that currently looks out onto LGBTQ America. I wanted to shine a brighter light, cast a wider beam, on a world that I knew was richer, more interesting, and more extraordinary than the trivial, humdrum, and jejune gay world I was encountering in many of the mainstream sources of information.

Randall Kenan put it nicely when, in talking with me, he noted the "monodimensional" nature of most people's understanding of African Americans. "A lot of white Americans don't take much time to learn about black folk. They're satisfied with the received thing— what they get off the boob tube, the *New York Times*." No less so for queer folk. There is a similar received understanding out there about who we are. It's an understanding that's been manufactured, homogenized, and sold to us largely by the mainstream media, gay and straight. The word on the street is that we look a certain way, dress a certain way, think a certain way, consume a certain way. In most cases it's an innocuous enough image (as all lowest common denominators tend to be), one that has done some good in presenting queer people as just "folk."

The problem is that "folk" is not the full story. "We are complicated and enormous," the wise, wonderful Dorothy Allison told me the day we talked. Amen. And that is what I have tried to do in this book: let that complexity and that enormity speak loud and clear in the stories I've recorded here. My overriding concern was to assemble as diverse a list of interesting and extraordinary LGBTQ people as I could and then to invite them to tell me their stories. I tried for geographical and occupational diversity, ethnic and racial diversity, religious and ideological diversity, and generational diversity. (At the time I interviewed them, my subjects ranged in age from nineteen to eighty-four.) Some came from backgrounds of privilege; others grew up in poverty. Close to one third of the people in this volume are persons of color. Six were born outside the United States.

As *Travels in a Gay Nation* moved beyond an initial idea to the nitty-gritty of fieldwork, I deliberately avoided turning this book into a hagiography of gay and lesbian celebrities.

"Cultural icons are our heroes," writes Vaid, "but gay leaders who work in gay institutions (be they AIDS service groups, youth projects, community centers, or legal and political groups) are often vilified." Or, as the young adult novelist Alex Sanchez said to me in our interview (one not included in this volume), "Where are the stories about everyday gay and lesbian people who are heroes in their own right by virtue of just being themselves and being open and honest?"

I wanted to address those concerns directly. The more I met people—in the arts, the sciences, business, academia, medicine, sports, the military, religion, law, journalism—the more I understood what good, important, courageous, noble work they were doing, work that was enlarging the story of what it means to be an LGBTQ American. I had no intention of painting a complete or encyclopedic portrait of my subjects. Rather, I aimed to sketch out each life, capturing something of the personality, the voice, the passions. In the best sense of the word, I gave myself permission to be an amateur. Above all, I wanted to celebrate the humanity and dignity—and the complexity—in each.

Each portrait is based on a face-to-face interview, most of which lasted about an hour and a half, in some cases longer if spirit and stamina moved us. We conducted these conversations in coffee shops and bars, hotel lobbies and restaurants, homes and workplaces, painting studios and congressional suites, on porches and roof decks, in kitchens, classrooms, and conference halls. I arrived at each interview with a prepared set of questions, each set unique and based on my subject's work and what I already had learned about his or her life. If she was a writer, I tried to read as much of her work as possible before we talked; if a composer, I listened to as many recordings as I could find. I looked at movies, attended live performances, checked out YouTube clips. I read biographies, autobiographies, memoirs.

During each interview, I let the conversation meander as it might. On many occasions, ideas and topics I had not anticipated arose spontaneously, and I went with them. Q-and-A often gave way to dialogue and conversation, an easy, friendly give-and-take.

7

Many of the folks I spoke with were so garrulous, articulate, and thoughtful—so excited to tell their stories—that my script became superfluous. We just talked, and marvelous things arose. But no matter whom I was interviewing, no matter what their profession or circumstances, I tried to find the particular humanity in each. The anecdote, the telling detail, the special moment, the vivid memory— these more than a comprehensive life history were what I was after.

I was aware, too, that I was meeting my subjects at various stages in their own careers and lives. Some, like Russell van Kraayenburg and Chris Barnhill, had not yet finished college. Others were in mid-career. Still others had changed careers. A few were in semiretirement. And some averred that they would never retire! In short, what Studs Terkel identified as the core question that informed his own interviews—"What's it like to be a certain person in a certain circumstance at a certain time?"—became mine as well.

The subject of how my subject's sexuality informs his or her life and work often came up. Some had struggled long and hard in coming to terms with their sexual and affectional preference. For others (and there seemed to be no pre-Stonewall/post-Stonewall pattern here), their sexuality had been virtually a nonissue as they grew up and made decisions about their lives. For some, their identity as a sexual minority person was crucial to their life's work; for others, it was less so. But for each person in this book, there came a time in his or her life when, as Dorothy Allison once wrote, he or she "decided to live." That decision—to live honestly, openly, and fully—gave each of them the freedom to use their queerness as a base (here I'm borrowing from Urvashi Vaid again) from which to enter the world.

"Being gay," novelist Randall Kenan told me, "forced me to look at things theologically, sociologically, and artistically in ways that I wouldn't have otherwise. That was my path." As with all minority people, LGBTQ folk recognize that their standing in the world is always at a slant, always "not-quite," no matter how many political victories we win, no matter how assimilated into the mainstream we are. Admittedly, some people in this book have managed to construct for themselves lives as respectable and innocuous as those of their straight counterparts; others have embraced the identity of, to use Richard Goldstein's phrase, "unassimilable homos." But no matter what the case, it's fair to say that everyone in this book understands that at some level his or her life is imbued with an elusive quality that I've come to identify as "gay spirit."

At its core, that's what this book has come to be about: a series of friendly raids on that "gay spirit" through the life and work—the personalities—of some extraordinary LGBTQ Americans. I have been less concerned with defining this spirit than I have in letting it express itself through the words of the people who so generously and candidly talked to me during this project. With some I laughed and joked and told my own stories; with not a few, I cried. No matter the gender, the age, the profession, the particular life circumstances, I recognized—*we* recognized together—that something important was afoot here. I think of David Sedaris, who told me that his homosexuality has, "more than anything, affected my perspective, which is to be a watcher." Or Tico Valle, who says that what he likes about being gay is that it allows him to see the world differently and, consequently, "to appreciate differences in our world." "A claim to wholeness" is how the young black Atlanta poet Yolo Akili expressed it to me. I think in those conversations we came to be reminded once again that as LGBTQ people we participate in a sensibility—and create a culture—that, as Alison Bechdel told me, "makes the space bigger for everyone else."

One of the most interesting aspects of this project was to hear from the people I interviewed some of their own ideas of what this book was all about. Many reaffirmed the sheer importance of getting our stories out there: "It's good to be reminded," Alice Hom told me at the end of our conversation, "that our lives and experience need to be told." Others, like Jamil Khoury, saw it as a "forum for the riches of LGBT stories." Several told me the book would be an important archival document, one that would "capture our collective history," as Rachel Tiven put it. Others, like Kathleen McGuire, the first female conductor of the San Francisco Gay Men's Chorus, said the book would "inspire others to do great and important things with their lives" or, as Tammy Baldwin told me, "benefit generations to come."

For others still, the experience of being interviewed was intensely personal. "I feel like I've been through the most intense therapy session," P. J. Raval told me. Others, like Mark Segal, the publisher of the *Philadelphia Gay News*, found affirmation for his work: "We often question our contributions; the interview answered that for me." Laura Esquivel echoed this when she wrote to me, "Spending a lifetime of fighting to be heard (and seen) in so many ways makes me appreciate this [book] more than you can know."

9

Which brings us back to the point of stories in general: to give a voice to anyone who is "fighting to be heard."

Doubtless, each person who reads this book will sooner or later think of his or her own favorite candidates for "extraordinary LGBTQ person" who are not represented here. I have mine, too! Between July 28, 2007, when Tim McFeeley and I recorded our conversation around a picnic table in Provincetown, and June 29, 2009, when, at their kitchen table, I talked with Scott Heim and Michael Lowenthal, I interviewed 102 people for this project. There is not a single conversation that I would not have happily included in this volume. Alas, the various exigencies of today's book-making business limited the number of profiles I could tuck between the covers. I can only hope that in the near future a second volume will follow. There are too many more great stories I want to tell.

A word about the intended audience for this book. Anthony Appiah, whose own captivating story is included in this volume, once interviewed Fred Wilson about an installation that Wilson had mounted at the Maryland Historical Society. "How," Appiah asked, "do you create a show that anybody who comes in can make sense of without being alienated?" The day we spoke, I addressed a similar question to him: How do I put together a book so that anybody can find value in it and not be alienated?

"My instinct," he told me, "is to say you can't do that. I do think that getting used to one another is the way to move forward. A lot of that will require humanizing, that is, getting a sense of the human lives of people, not talking about theoretical matter, human rights, equality, all of which are important, but getting a sense of the texture of a life lived a certain way. Lived a certain way because it's the best way for that person to live according to his judgment or her judgment. Having a sense of a life as a *life*, as a thing that makes sense in its own terms, is very useful."

My hope is that *Travels in a Gay Nation* will give readers a sense of the texture of some forty-four distinct and extraordinary lives lived in ways that make beautiful, and inspiring, sense. Gay artist Patrick Webb told me that the Punchinello figure that is the subject of so many of his paintings—Webb calls him his "Everygayman"—is the *hero of his own life*. In this age where LGBTQ people are still coming under attack because their lives don't happen to square with other people's notions of what it means to be good and valuable and meaningful in this world, the men and women profiled here speak eloquently to the contrary. They have managed, despite everything—ignorance, oppression, fear, hatred, intolerance, injustice, violence, ridicule, or just plain indifference—to construct heroic lives for themselves. Splashy or quiet, center stage or behind the scenes, these are people all of us, queer and straight, should be paying attention to.

Dorothy Allison

In the spring of 1992, at the OutWrite conference for lesbian and gay writers, I heard Dorothy Allison give a stirring keynote address. "I believe in the truth," she told us. "I believe in the truth in the way only a person who has been denied any use of it can believe in it." Allison had just published her first novel, *Bastard out of Carolina*, and it was getting rave reviews. "As close to flawless as any reader could ask for," wrote the *New York Times Book Review*. She suddenly found herself being compared to the greats of Southern writing—Flannery O'Connor, Walker Percy, Tennessee Williams, Alice Walker, and William Faulkner. When she entered Boston's Park Plaza ballroom that March day in 1992, we greeted her like a conquering hero.

Sixteen years later, I catch up with Allison again, this time in New York, where she has just finished a weeklong visit, one that has included an appearance at the Brooklyn Book Festival and a presentation at Columbia University's Institute for Research on Women and Gender.

"I was in Shit Heaven!" she tells me.

Throughout our visit, Allison's language will roller-coaster between the earthy and the sublime, between raucous belly laughs and soft, sometimes painfully intimate speech. Between pork fat and red velvet cake, two of her favorite foods from childhood.

Born in 1949, two weeks past her mother's fifteenth birthday, Allison grew up "poor white trash" in Greenville, South Carolina. The country, she tells me, was "beautiful and empty and dangerous and scary. You love it, you want it, and you hate it at the same time. And you're mad as sin." The women in the family were waitresses, laundry workers, counter girls. In her memoir, *Two or Three Things I Know for Sure*, Allison writes that she was never allowed to be "beautiful and female, sexed and sexual."

"Beauty in the South has a particular design," she tells me. "It's about fragility and tenderness. The hard reality is that when you grow up poor, you grow up hard. You're not allowed to be tender; you can't afford to be. My mother was beautiful, astonishingly, heartbreakingly beautiful. But of course, she got pregnant with me. Pregnancy takes the beauty out of you pretty quick."

Allison never knew her father. He ran away. Her mother eventually married a "crazy, violent man" who railed against "niggers and Jew bastards." Her stepfather's vitriol sent Allison looking for "people to hang on to, people who would remind me what it is like to be human and alive and not a monster." She told herself that her stepfather might try to break her, "but he won't destroy me. I wanted to kill the motherfucker. Beating was such a ritualized practice in our house that none of my sisters or I questioned his right to do that. We thought it was normal. My mother didn't know he was fucking us."

At first, the girls protected their mother from that information. When Allison landed in the hospital with a fractured coccyx, her mother took her children and left.

"But then she would go back. I can remember him crawling across the floor on his knees, begging her forgiveness. By the time I left home and my sisters left home—and we got out as fast as we could—my mother learned a lot. I hit her with it in stories. I don't know how anyone who was raped as a child survives it. It inculcates such a deeply unending level of self-hatred that crops out in odd, terrible ways. Everything that I know, everything that I've done, everything that I understand—nothing fixes it. That's the most horrific thing I've had to realize. There's a lot of stuff you can do to make yourself an adult human being, to make yourself capable of relationships, to make sex not quite so impossible, but it never repairs the essential damage."

It wasn't until she was well into her thirties that Allison came to see the men in her family as "hurt animals. What shocks me is how

13

raw and tender boys are. I didn't know. I thought they were all animals. Christ, I should have known it. The men were all drunks. They were in pain. But boys can't say it. They don't get to collapse in a puddle and weep. The Southern culture colludes in keeping men in an infantile state."

When she was twelve, the family moved to Florida, a turn of events that provided Allison with "good solid schools, where you actually learned something. I was a compulsive reader and read every goddamn book in the library. I've been lucky. My addictions were books and writing, a much better solace than heroin or whisky."

From an early age, Allison was falling in love with girls. "I thought I was just weird, and essentially queer, meaning I did not want to marry. I did not want to be a woman like the women in my family. I did not want to be a slave, which is how I saw marriage and relationships. When I got to adolescence and realized there was lust on top of falling in love with girls, I was in big trouble!"

The first in her family to finish high school, Allison won a National Merit Scholarship, "partly on luck, and partly because I was desperately trying anything to get the fuck out. I'm a really good hustler. From a very early age I learned how to spot people who could be friends and who could help. A lot of queers have that ability to judge who you can trust, who you can ask help from."

At Florida Presbyterian College, she majored in anthropology. "I loved the idea of being the participant-observer, in which you observe a culture but only marginally participate. That's pretty much the way I've always felt as a queer: I'm not really in this thing; I'm only on the sidelines, watching you people dance and making notes."

Soon Allison discovered the women's movement but was reluctant to participate because, as a scholarship student, she feared "they'd find out I was a dyke and kick me out of school." It wasn't until 1973, when she began graduate studies in anthropology at Florida State University, that she joined a women's collective. During her two years in Tallahassee, she also edited a feminist magazine and helped found Herstore Feminist Bookstore.

"I became such an ardent feminist. It was a great way to meet women. A much higher class of girlfriend! I fell in love with a couple of girls from the women's consciousness-raising groups, but I was also dating rough trade from the pool halls." In an essay entitled "The Theory and Practice of the Strap-on Dildo," Allison recalled herself during those years as a "badly behaved femme slut."

"We pretty much created a movement of Slut Pride," she tells me. "I can remember dating a wonderful butch girl—*Jesus, fuck me*! (and she did)—but she strongly disapproved of the fact that I was not going to be faithful to her. I was emotionally faithful to her, but I fuckin' wasn't going to do her laundry and be a captive femme."

In the summer of 1975, Allison attended the Sagaris Institute, a feminist theory workshop in Plainfield, Vermont, where she studied writing with the lesbian novelist Bertha Harris. As a "dedicated politico," Allison had come to think of fiction writing as a "self-indulgent and trivial pleasure." The two-week seminar changed that.

"Bertha's writing class was remarkable. She talked about class— all that stuff that I knew but had no way of articulating. The scales fell from my eyes. It was the first time I could begin to talk about my real family and my real life experience with pride."

Allison stopped writing for six months. "I had to think. It scared me. And I was ashamed. I had so carefully obscured my family. I never took anyone home. I didn't talk about my family, or, if I did, I misrepresented them. Shame and anger—I had to work it through. It started the process of telling the truth."

By the midseventies, she was in Washington, D.C., working as the director of the Washington Area Feminist Federal Credit Union. She also put in time at *Quest*, a feminist quarterly, "writing direct mail letters to raise money. Nearly killed me. I was writing poems and stories in secret and feeling guilty because I should have been a revolutionary. Gradually, I realized that if I was going to do anything effective for the revolution, I'd be a hell of a lot better writing stories."

In 1979, Allison moved again, this time to New York, where she studied for a while at the New School for Social Research. More and more, writing was becoming the focus of her life. She started publishing pieces in the *New York Native* and "a bunch of other little things" and became "part of that whole wonderful New York queer writing community." While working at *Poets & Writers*, she met gay fiction writer Allen Barnett.

"Allen was such a gift to me. He grew up poor, too. He was the first gay man that I was friends with where we could talk about this stuff. Frankly, gay men wrote more in a way I could relate to than a lot of lesbians. The standards for lesbian writing were awful. Just the most trite, bad writing was celebrated. Jesus! There was this thing about 'authenticity.' And I'm like, Yeah, authenticity is important, but could we make it a little more readable?"

It was around this time that Allison began to use the word "queer" to mean "more than lesbian." As she later explained in her essay "Sex Writing, the Importance and the Difficulty," the word implied that "I am not only a lesbian but a transgressive lesbian." That notion found its institutional expression in 1981, when she helped organize the Lesbian Sex Mafia.

"It was essentially a club of lesbian perverts. The whole idea was to have meetings, share information, flirt with each other, and throw parties. Mostly it was leather dykes, a few bisexuals, a few fetishists. We had some really butch girls. Half of them were pre-op: they were planning to change genders. But what happened was they came to the meetings—we had all these high-femme, sweet pieces of trade— and they started dating. Almost all the pre-ops abandoned changing genders. They had thought they would have to become men to get the kinds of females they wanted. And we had bunches of really high quality, femme girls who were *thrilled* to see them come through the door and who did not require that they get reconstructive surgery."

Allison says that LSM was "a genuine challenge to the antipornography feminists, who had some simple-minded, doctrinaire notions. Didn't match my notions about what feminism was about. Big fight!"

The big fight reached a head in April 1982, when Allison, who had been invited to participate at the Barnard Conference on the Feminist and the Scholar, was vilified as an "antifeminist terrorist." She found herself accused of being "a pawn of the patriarchy, an antifeminist writer, and a pimp for the pornographers," as she later wrote in "Public Silence, Private Terror," an essay in her collection *Skin: Talking about Sex, Class & Literature*. Invitations to speak, publish, and edit were withdrawn. At her job, anonymous phone callers demanded she be fired.

"If a terrible moment in your life can be a gift, it was a gift because it sent me home." And there, after years of estrangement from her mother and sisters, Allison began the process of reconciliation. She sighs before she explains: "In the family, you're the brain. You go off to college. You meet the middle class. You look back at your family, and it absolutely cracks your life in half. I had such contempt for them. And then you go along, and your new family—the lesbian feminist movement—fails you utterly, kicks your ass—and there you are standing with your belly in your hands, wrecked and empty."

Most of the poems in Allison's first book, *The Women Who Hate Me*, published by Long Haul in 1983, were written in the aftermath of the Barnard Conference. The title poem, she later acknowledged, was "essentially aimed at the women I couldn't speak to at the Barnard Conference because they were screaming at me." She didn't even try to get the book published by a mainstream press. "I was active in the small press movement. I believed in the small press movement. I do even more so today. It's about making books that deliberately serve a community that wants them desperately and reaches that community. In the alternative publishing world, we weren't writing to make money. The biggest thing we wanted was the audience."

Over time, Allison began to favor prose over poetry. She started writing for M. Mark, the editor at the *Village Voice*. "She was a great editor. I had written this story that became the first chapter of *Bastard*. She did a really clean, professional edit on it. I had never seen that level of editorial work. Then she put me to work with Walter Kendrick, who became a great close friend and trained me in many ways as a writer. He was such a ruthless little motherfucker. He would suddenly declare that there were words I wasn't allowed to use. When you work with a great editor, everything changes. You can see these handicaps and tics and stuff. And you start getting rid of that shit. I did it."

Allison's second book, *Trash* (1988), was a collection of short stories. The subject matter is poor people, queers, and Southern women. "Most of what people think they know about us is derivative and small," she tells me. "We are complicated and enormous. We have a bigger role in shaping their culture than they understand. We are the *best* of this culture. We are the *best* of its literature, its politics. We are the best hope for this culture to be genuinely human." *Trash* won two Lambda Literary Awards and the American Library Association Prize for Lesbian and Gay Writing.

By the late eighties, Allison had moved once again, now to the Bay Area, where she worked as an editor for *Out/Look*, a lesbian and gay quarterly, and taught writing workshops. "The heart and soul of what I love best in American literature is queer, working-class writing. Read Randall Kenan, read Jim Grimsley, read Rebecca Brown! Wonderful work. Absolute, laser-pure rage."

For *Bastard out of Carolina*, Allison took that laser-pure rage and shaped it into a consummate work of art. Set in Greenville County,

South Carolina, *Bastard* is narrated by its protagonist, Ruth Anne Boatwright, called "Bone" — "nobody special . . . just a girl scared and angry." But Bone is also tough, honest, and "full of music," even as her childhood is brutally stolen from her. "I wanted the way I felt to mean something," Bone says, "and for everything in my life to change because of it."

Allison once wrote in an essay that writing *Bastard out of Carolina* became "the way to claim my family's pride and tragedy, and the embattled sexuality I had fashioned on a base of violence and abuse." What distinguishes the novel from her earlier story collection is her ability to temper her rage without invalidating it.

"I can look at my life now and see a story arc. It is necessary for my sanity that I learn forgiveness. It is necessary for my soul that I learn compassion. The big difference between *Trash* and *Bastard* is that I got farther along that road."

Bastard, which was published by Penguin, was one of five finalists for the National Book Award. "I didn't see it coming. It shifted my perceptions of the world. If you grow up as a writer in the alternative press movement, you have a profound critique of the above-ground press. I thought most of what they published was nonsense, not great writing. Suddenly, to be part of the world of great books puts you on different ground. I made a really deliberate choice to sell it to Penguin, partly because I was broke. I wanted to reach a wider audience than lesbians. That was hard. I believe in the small press, but I wanted every raped child to read this book."

One of the central issues of Allison's second novel, *Cavedweller* (1998), is her protagonist's struggle to forgive herself for getting out of a horrible marriage, in essence, to forgive herself for saving her life. I ask if self-forgiveness is something she herself has struggled with.

"How'd you know?" she chuckles. "That's the thing about being a writer—everybody knows everything." I ask if she's embarrassed by that struggle. "On some level, absolutely. My standards for myself are criminally high. It's the only way that people like me survive at all: to be better than everyone else in the room. And I will always be ashamed. Even if I do well, I always feel that I haven't done it well enough. That's the disease, that's the damage."

Allison lives in northern California with her partner of more than twenty years, Alix Layman, and their teenage son, Wolf. "I was a completely ignorant slut when I took on that task. How else does anyone agree to do such a stupid thing? Good God, all the girls in my family raised the younger ones. But I didn't know how it feels when you love them. I think I'm raising Vito Russo. He's got Vito's sense of humor. And the limp wrist—I don't know where he got that. He's being raised by two dykes!"

Allison has been a writer in residence at a number of places. "I love teaching. All the queer kids show up. All the working-class kids show up. At this moment in history, queer boys are more serious about writing or have a different concept of writing. It depends where you go."

How does she feel now that she has entered her sixties?

"I haven't quite accepted it. It hurts a whole lot more than I'm willing to acknowledge. And your body fucks with you. And lust changes. I don't approve. But meanwhile, my sense of humor is getting broader and deeper. There is so much stuff I know now. I'm kind of glorying in being an old fuck."

Dorothy Allison

Kwame Anthony Appiah

It was a privilege to grow up in a peripheral place. Because in peripheral places you *have* to know about other places."

On the day I visit Anthony Appiah, a professor of philosophy at Princeton University, I'm instantly aware of his deep appreciation for the "peripheral." With its typical gracious appointments, the Chelsea apartment he shares with his partner, Henry Finder, might be a typical English don's flat but for the fact that beautiful objects from non-Western cultures—African bronzes, miniature busts from ancient Gandhara—are on prominent display. Over coffee, Appiah and I talk for almost three hours. His conversation is reflective, precise, generous, and discursive. Frequently, he interrupts himself in mid-sentence to articulate another angle or offer a better example. An air of intelligent, relaxed courtesy prevails throughout our time together. Made to feel instantly at ease, I listen with invigorated attention. I suspect that's the experience of his students as well.

In addition to philosophy, Appiah has written extensively about African literature and culture. He has edited (with Henry Louis Gates, Jr.) *Africana: The Encyclopedia of the African and African American Experience*, coauthored (with his mother) an annotated edition of proverbs from Ghana, and edited (again with Gates) a number of volumes in the Amisted Press series on African and African American writers. He has also written three novels, including the mystery *Another Death in Venice*. Appiah has been the recipient of many honors, among them several honorary degrees and the first Joseph B. and Toby Gittler Prize for "outstanding and lasting scholarly contributions to racial, ethnic and/or religious relations."

Appiah's early philosophical work focused on such rarefied topics as semantics and theories of meaning, but his more recent books deal with "what makes human sense, and not in some theoretical way." In books such as *Color Conscious: The Political Morality of Race*, *The Ethics of Identity*, and *Experiments in Ethics*, he analyzes the world of human values, tackling the problems of race and racism, ethics, identity, cosmopolitanism, and homophobia.

Appiah is skeptical about the ability of logic and reason alone to move people toward good behavior. Instead, he espouses developing "habits of coexistence," an idea that found full expression in his 2006 book *Cosmopolitanism: Ethics in a World of Strangers*, which won the Arthur Ross Award of the Council on Foreign Relations. In that work, Appiah emphasizes what he calls "conversations across boundaries of identity"—the imaginative engagement with the experience and ideas of others—as a way to help people get used to one another and thus develop more harmonious relationships and happier lives. It's a notion that leads him to take a commonsensical approach to gay and lesbian liberation, namely, that over time and with exposure, people learn to live amicably with gay and lesbian people. Indeed, he says, because of the presence of openly gay people in the world, a "perspectival shift" occurs, one that breaks down old prejudices and barriers.

Appiah's affinity for cosmopolitanism has its roots in his childhood. Born in London of an English mother and a Ghanaian father, Appiah, whose full name is Kwame Anthony Akroma-Ampim Kusi Appiah, was raised in Kumasi, Ghana, the traditional royal capital of the Ashanti Confederacy. The family lived in a large "African bungalow" on a street within walking distance of the largest market in West Africa. It was a neighborhood populated by the new elite, the families of those who would lead the country after independence, which was achieved in 1957, three years after Appiah was born.

Each of his parents came from a prominent public family. His father was a lawyer, statesman, ambassador, president of the Ghana Bar Association, an elder in the Methodist Church, and a well-known figure in Ghana, who got into political trouble and, for a while, was imprisoned. His mother, from a privileged Gloucester-shire family, was a writer active in the cultural life of Kumasi. She hobnobbed with many important people all over the world.

His parents' interracial marriage in 1953 produced "a firestorm of comment in Britain and around the world." As a young boy, Appiah would flip through the family scrapbooks, in which were pasted clippings of the press coverage surrounding the controversy. "We went to England from time to time to see my grandmother. And the first question the British press always asked my mother was, 'So, have you left him?' Even friendly coverage tended to be a bit skeptical. The only press that was not skeptical was the African American press, like *Ebony*."

Appiah grew up speaking both English and Twi, one of the languages of Ghana. His early intellectual development, under the tutelage of his mother, was multicultural. He recalls that during vacations from school she would leave piles of books by his bed—James Baldwin, D. H. Lawrence, Spike Milligan (whose *Puckoon* impressed him because "it had the word 'fuck' in it"), the Koran, the Bhagavad-Gita.

Appiah was largely educated in Britain, first at Court Regis, a "pre-prep" school, where he rose to be the "first colored head boy," and later at Bryanston School, one of the country's Eton Group of preparatory schools. The curriculum was full of what Appiah once described as "texts that barely acknowledged the specificity of one's existence." The other texts—ones about his African heritage and, later, his homosexual identity—he had to find on his own. He remembers reading several of the novels that came out in the Heinemann African Writers Series. The first one he encountered was Chinua Achebe's *Things Fall Apart*, a novel set in colonial Nigeria.

"Even though it was set in Iboland, which is very different from us, the sense of village life, tradition and proverbs, eating with your hands, all of that seemed more like a life similar to ours. I probably read [these novels] on vacation. They wouldn't have been on any reading list in England in those days. I found *Giovanni's Room* for the first time intensely moving. This thing about men loving each other, which I hadn't read about before. Certainly, when the issue came up in my schools, the masters were keen that we not allow ourselves to be moved in those ways."

Until he was about seventeen, Appiah was a kind of "hippie, leftie evangelical Christian." He says, "I took seriously those parts of the Gospels that said you shouldn't judge people." When the time came, he declined to be confirmed "on the grounds that confirmation was a way of distinguishing between people who were in and people who were out. That struck me as unchristian."

This rebellious streak found another expression during Appiah's senior year at Bryanston. Despite the school's progressive bent ("there was no beating"), the student government was organized on "quite the colonial system." Senior boys who had distinguished themselves were "commanded to be the bosses" of the lower-form boys. Appiah wanted no part of this. He mounted a democratic student union and held a strike to demand that the school recognize the alternate form of government. "My parents were told that if I didn't stop this, I would be kicked out."

As for his homoerotic life during those years, Appiah says it was "imaginary, by and large," until his last semester. "I was at various points in love with various boys." Some of those boys were members of the independent reading groups he joined. "We read theologians like Barth and Bultmann, but also Sartre. For me it was all connected with these friendships, which were very intense." The discussions and the reading, especially Alfred Ayer's *Language, Truth and Logic*, which he found "absolutely, mind-blowingly liberating," began to challenge Appiah's religious convictions. A few years later, at Cambridge University, he experienced "an opposite moment to the one evangelicals have. I was playing a hymn at the piano and had this blinding moment where I suddenly realized, I don't believe in any of this. If I had stayed a Christian, I would have found a version that would have been nonhomophobic."

At Cambridge, Appiah had intended to study medicine, but after a few months, finding that he was spending all his time reading philosophy, he switched his major. In 1975, having scored the highest in his philosophy exams, he took his bachelor's degree and returned to Ghana, where he worked as a teaching assistant for a year at the University of Ghana. The next year, he was back at Cambridge to begin doctoral studies.

During the 1978–79 academic year, at the invitation of Henry Louis Gates, Jr., whom he met at Cambridge, Appiah became a special student at Yale. There he taught a seminar on Pan-Africanism. Initially skeptical about America, which he thought of as "a place full of racists and guns," he happily found that "all my assumptions were turned upside down immediately. My life was saved intellectually by the fact that I came to Yale through an interdisciplinary program in

African American studies. That broadened me a great deal. I was extremely lucky." He returned to Cambridge, where he had been awarded a research fellowship. By 1981, he was back in the States, now as a professor at Yale. Appiah has been in America ever since. He joined the Princeton faculty in 2002.

Appiah's signature book is *In My Father's House: Africa in the Philosophy of Culture* (1992). Part autobiography and part cultural history, it focuses on the role of intellectuals in the life of Africa. Among the book's many themes is Appiah's criticism of the notion of "race." He writes that race "disables us because it proposes as a basis for common action the illusion that black . . . people are fundamentally allied by nature and, thus, without effort; it leaves us unprepared, therefore, to handle the 'intraracial' conflicts that arise from the very different situations of black . . . people in different parts of the economy and the world."

How about the notion of "gay"? I ask him. To what extent does the label "gay" or "lesbian" disable us? My question elicits a long, careful, and partly autobiographical answer: a microcosm of the way Appiah does philosophy.

He begins by noting that at Cambridge—an essentially closeted world run by bachelor dons—his sexuality was well known even if he did not publicly identify himself as gay. He goes on to acknowledge that the gay liberation movement—and the outright use of a label like "gay"—made many more things possible for people who did not enjoy the privilege of the elite, homosocial milieus he enjoyed.

"I think that gay liberation was an enormously powerful and progressive thing as it developed. So was black power, so was black consciousness. These were all moments when it was more important to create the solidarity around an identity than it was to focus on the fact that every identity risks homogenization and the loss of the texture of each individual life. It's hard to explain to kids now how much things have radically shifted. I don't see how that could have happened without people actively identifying as gay and presenting themselves as gay. Gay visibility was crucial in that process.

"There is a very difficult theoretical point here: identities make things possible for people only to the extent that they have a structure. That means that if you attach yourself to an identity, it imposes things on you as well as making things possible. It can't make things possible without imposing things. There is always going to be some element of imposition.

"We are always struggling to reshape identities so that they fit us. How do I fit my sexuality into my life? Do you want to live your life in such a way that everybody responds to you, in every context, as a gay person? No, but then gay liberation wasn't about that either. Gay liberation wasn't about forcing everybody you ever meet to say, 'Hello, Gay Person.' But if you naturally reach out to hold your partner's hand on the street, gay liberation was about not feeling that you were going to be beaten up. Ninety-nine percent of the public social space is a space where it's still the case that you risk being beaten up for that. That seems a bad thing to me. To fight that, you have to make more and more visible the fact that people, like it or not, have gay neighbors and friends and family and that these dangers make their lives humanly less worthwhile."

Finding a balance between the competing claims to one's own truth is a major theme in much of Appiah's work. "You don't want to be in a world where everyone is the same," he tells me. "It's not interesting. It's also bad for knowledge. It's bad for moral knowledge. It's bad in lots of ways. But nevertheless, the more people are different from one another, the more there are challenges associated with that. We have to start out with the thought that diversity is a source of good things while at the same time recognizing that people who are different from one another have work to do to cohabit."

In a piece he wrote for the *New York Review of Books*, "How Muslims Made Europe," Appiah noted that during the era of Arab civilization in medieval Spain "Jews, Christians, Muslims, Arabs, Berbers, Visigoths, Slavs, and countless others created the kind of cultural goulash—a spicy mixture of a variety of distinct components—that would generate a genuine cosmopolitanism."

What then, I ask him, should be our proper response to those who today have no interest in making our civilization more cosmopolitan?

"Conversation is something that goes on between consenting adults. If you can't gain their consent, whatever you think you're doing, it is not a conversation. The first thing we have to do with people who most threaten us is to listen. You get used to one another, and then you see what you can figure out."

What does Appiah think is the value of being a philosopher?

"The primary obligation of intellectuals is to try to understand things and then to make that understanding available to others. The gift that intellectuals can give to nonphilosophers is the understanding of things." Nevertheless, Appiah has grown skeptical of the ability of knowledge alone to solve problems.

"I followed a path that's a bit like the one Du Bois followed: he thought that if you got people to see the truth about things, they'd behave better. In particular, he thought that racism would disappear in the face of knowledge. Eventually, he decided he was wrong: that the reason people treat each other badly is not mostly because of ignorance. I used to think you could carefully talk people out of certain kinds of bad behavior like racism, sexism, homophobia. However, it's not just that reason doesn't play as large a part in our lives as it might, but it's not clear that it would be better if it did. There are some things where it's more important to be clear that you shouldn't do them than it is to have the correct theory about why you shouldn't do them. I feel that I have offered people a way of thinking about identity and individuality that is actually useful for moderately well educated people in making their lives."

This is an idea that Appiah has articulated even more fully in his 2008 book, *Experiments in Ethics*. There he wrote, "Morality derives from an understanding of what other people are up to; it's not a system of arbitrary demands. . . . [W]e should expect to learn more from experiments in living than from experiments in philosophy."

Of his own "experiment in living," Appiah says he is most proud of his relationship of almost twenty-five years with his partner, Henry Finder. "It's the most important thing I have created or co-created." And this gets him back to what he calls the "privilege in not being normal."

"Perhaps the *one* insight in queer theory is that a gay person gets to see things that other people crawl through life without noticing. Those obstacles make you look. If you fit into all of the default modes of your society, great, but it means you don't have to think your way into an identity. For much of human history, human beings have lived with a very small range of default identities and had to make do. The great thing about modernity is that we've uncapped the limits. You can be a lesbian Republican poet. Hard, but it's an interesting challenge. We need to create societies in which people of different classes have the possibility of a dignified life. Everybody's entitled to it. We need an education system in which everybody gets what they need to make a worthwhile life."

Tammy Baldwin

Tammy Baldwin is the first woman from Wisconsin to serve in the House of Representatives and the first nonincumbent, openly gay person ever to be elected to Congress. She is a major proponent of universal health care, energy independence, renewable fuels, and family farm programs as well as a leading supporter of LGBTQ civil rights.

Baldwin was raised by her mother and her grandparents. In middle school, because of the encouragement of one of her teachers, she ran for student council. "Once I was involved, I was sold on it," she tells me the day we meet in her bright yellow office in the Rayburn House Office Building. "We engaged in meaningful projects." One such project was serving on the School Neighborhood Relations Committee. There Baldwin learned some valuable lessons about working with potentially hostile constituencies. "We invited the neighbors in to tell us how they liked being next to our school. There was an air exchanger in the industrial arts room that was quite loud. When the neighbors had their windows open, they'd hear this racket. We petitioned the school board to install a device so that it wouldn't be as loud and disruptive."

Baldwin says she was studious in high school but not allied with any one clique. "We weren't the jocks or stage crew crowd. I really enjoyed a variety of friends. For example, I served on the homecoming court but also participated on the math team—which would suggest a nerd of the highest order!"

Smith College, where she majored in government and math, was, she says, "a wonderful environment." The intimacy of the campus, which allowed for "enormous exposure to the faculty," was particularly important to her, as was the fact that every student leadership position was occupied by a woman. As a place for lesbian students, Smith could not have been "a more supportive environment, although we were far from where we are now in terms of discussion of diversity and acceptance." Despite "one or two workshops at our residence, where we talked about homophobia and issues like that," she remembers hearing "very strongly worded pushback" from some of the students who considered homosexuality wrong.

Baldwin came out during her junior year. On her Web site, she says, "When I came out, I searched for everything I could find to read that would give what I was going through some sort of social and historical context. I saw every movie (the few that there were). I think I watched *Before Stonewall* and *The Life and Times of Harvey Milk* at least a dozen times each." She also took inspiration from lesbian activists like Elaine Noble, Del Martin, and Phyllis Lyon.

"In coming out, I was immediately confronted with that jolt of, Oh, this might mean that I can't pursue the goals that I've dreamed about for so long, and then finding these inspirational figures meant, well, maybe there's an alternative. Maybe I can have both. I can be out and live a truthful, honest life and pursue these goals."

After she graduated from Smith in 1984, Baldwin interned for a year in the office of Wisconsin governor Tony Earl. She was part of a task force investigating pay inequities in female-dominated employment. Two years later, she won a seat on the Dane County Board of Supervisors, a position she held for four terms (1986–94). In part because of role models—there were two openly gay members of the Dane County board—the twenty-four-year-old Baldwin ran as an openly gay person. "There was no chance I was going to run and be in the closet." Ironically, during the campaign, the issue of her being a lesbian was never brought up, something that concerned her. "How could I be out if no one was raising the issue?" It wasn't until a few months into her first term in office, when the *Wisconsin State Journal* interviewed her for a piece on politics and the LGBT community, that Baldwin's name and the word "lesbian" appeared in print for the first time.

In the days before the article appeared, Baldwin wondered, "Whom have I not come out to, and what's going to happen to me when that paper hits everybody's doorstep? I was a little frightened about what that would mean. Then, when I actually lived through it, almost everyone who said anything to my face was supportive. I got one crank call in the middle of the night. And that was the worst of it."

During her stint on the Dane County board, Baldwin also earned a J.D. at the University of Wisconsin Law School, another step, she says, in her preparation for a career in politics. While she did practice law for a few years "to pay the bills," she was far more interested in learning how to craft laws. In 1992, during her final term as a county supervisor, she ran for and won a seat in the Wisconsin State Assembly. Baldwin credits gay Wisconsin assemblyman David Clarenbach, who was making a bid for Congress, with encouraging her to run for the seat that he was vacating. "He made it very clear that I could seek his wisdom in running."

Baldwin says there is a benefit to taking "the stepladder approach" to politics. "You can make your biggest mistakes on a smaller stage with a smaller spotlight and learn. I got to learn gradually in a setting where it didn't have as much of an impact."

It was another mentor, Paul Soglin, then the mayor of Madison, who suggested to Baldwin that she consider running for Congress.

"I was attending my first national convention, the 1996 Democratic convention in Chicago, as an elected delegate. It was thrilling, seeing all my political heroes. Paul took me aside and said, 'I want to bring you up to the Conference of Mayors suite.' I walked in. All these big-city mayors were there." Soglin sat down beside her and noted that the congressional seat for the Madison area would probably open up in a few years. "He looked at me and said, 'I want you to get ready.' My hair was standing on end! Boy, I took that seriously, and I took steps to expose myself to high-caliber training for the type of things that I would need to be good at in order to make that step."

Baldwin's candidacy was supported by both the Gay and Lesbian Victory Fund and EMILY's List, financial backing that she says "made a significant difference." The diversity of her district—one-third urban, one-third suburban, and one-third rural—also helped.

"In my first two congressional elections, I had huge percentages in the urban center, Madison. The suburbs split almost fifty-fifty, and I lost the rural areas big-time. All sorts of hard work has changed that. For years, I have committed myself to spending lots of time in the rural areas, building relationships, letting my constituents get to know me better. Now in the last three elections, I am beginning to break fifty-fifty in the rural areas."

In 2006, Wisconsin voters passed, by a fairly substantial margin (58 percent voted yes) an anti–gay marriage bill. What, I ask Baldwin, did that mean to her?

"It's hard." There is clearly pain in her voice, the first time during our conversation that Baldwin's characteristically chipper mood has flagged. "I found the passage of this constitutional amendment very hurtful and very, very disappointing. I don't know still if I can fully understand it. I always thought that Wisconsin would be different and better, *better* than the rest about it." Suddenly, her positive affect returns. "I know that struggles for full equality often take a long, long time. It's certainly going to be the case with this particular issue. I have to take hope from those who have been involved in these long struggles."

Baldwin fondly remembers the first time she met the gay and lesbian rights pioneers Del Martin and Phyllis Lyon. "At the first-ever lesbian summit sponsored by the National Organization for Women. I was so excited to meet them. What just took my breath away, they held each other's hand and started crying: 'Oh, we've been waiting to meet *you*. This is what our work was all about, that someone like you could get elected to Congress.'

"I often quote a line from a speech that Lucy Stone delivered in 1850 on women's suffrage and women's rights. She didn't live to see women get the right to vote. Seventy years after she gave that speech, women secured the right to vote in the United States. But, undaunted by that, she rode the circuit and gave speeches and tried to organize. She laid the groundwork. I actually do think that, not so much because of what is happening in Wisconsin, but because of what's happening elsewhere in the country, we'll see some rapid changes on the marriage issue in my lifetime."

In June 2008, Baldwin and fellow representative Barney Frank announced the formation of the House of Representatives LGBT Equality Caucus.

"The precursor to this was an ad hoc group of colleagues that I would bring together months before we expected consideration on the floor of legislation important to the community. We would convene, understanding that we needed to educate and persuade and provide political cover to members of Congress in order to build majorities."

No issue is more important to Baldwin than the passage of universal health care legislation. As a child, she experienced firsthand the inadequacy of the current system. "I had a very serious childhood illness. I was hospitalized for three months. My entire in-patient stay was not covered by insurance. My grandparents were able to pay the whole bill, but this would have devastated most families. I was uninsurable after this illness until I was a college student and was enrolled in a group policy."

Beyond her personal experience, Baldwin notes the suffering of many Americans as a spur to her passionate work on behalf of health care reform. "The American dream is a very powerful one. People really can achieve great things that would be improbable in other places. But you need a foundation of education and good health. With that foundation, so much can be achieved."

When I ask her about the responsibility she feels as a role model for LGBTQ people, Baldwin says, "Part of it is just remembering that, whether you meet folks or not, they're regarding you as a role model. You get surrounded by the complexities of your day-to-day life, and you forget that for somebody who is just coming out this is extremely important." She mentions a letter from a young person who wrote that he was interested in politics but, having just come out, hadn't thought he could pursue a career in government until he learned about her. "I get letters like that all the time."

So what's her advice for young LGBTQ people interested in politics?

"Go for it! Get in there. Observe, volunteer, break it down into pieces. I studied government as part of my formal education, but what was really powerful was just jumping in and getting involved—getting internships, volunteering on campaigns, joining a bunch of political organizations, going to hearings. It demystified the process. I remember my light bulb moment, sitting in the gallery watching the county board, thinking, These are just ordinary, hard-working human beings who are engaged in public service. I could do this! That was very empowering for me."

Baldwin and her partner, Lauren Azar, a public service commissioner in Wisconsin, have been together for more than thirteen years, sharing and renovating a Queen Anne Victorian house they bought together in 2000. "My service on the House Energy Committee means we'll have the nerdiest discussions over the dinner table." Do they appear in Washington as a couple? "Periodically. For big occasions. When I get sworn in every two years, she's flown in for that. The democratic caucus has an annual issues retreat. Everyone is encouraged to bring their families. Most years Lauren has been able to come. I think that's really important, for my colleagues to see us together."

Baldwin and Azar celebrate their anniversary on December 4. In 2006, the annual White House holiday party fell on that date. "So I got to bring her on our anniversary and say, 'Mr. President, you remember, this is Lauren. This is our anniversary tonight.'" There's a rascally tone in her voice. "We told everyone there, 'We're celebrating!'"

Christopher Barnhill

Christopher Barnhill calls himself "the voice of HIV-positive youth." Born in 1987 in Washington, D.C., Barnhill lost both his parents, who were heroin addicts, to AIDS before he was two years old. "I say, 'They died before I was born.' I don't remember them at all."

Taken in by an aunt, Barnhill grew up in a city where the HIV infection rate has reportedly risen to be the highest of any city in the United States. Barnhill, who is a care advocate/counseling and testing coordinator for Metro TeenAIDS, a health organization in D.C. that works with thirteen- to twenty-four-year-olds, has the statistics at his fingertips.

"One in a hundred youth in the D.C. area is positive," he tells me the afternoon I meet him. "That's like one child per every three classrooms."

A handsome, slight man in his early twenties, Barnhill says that Metro TeenAIDS, which provides care, counseling, and education on HIV prevention, sees between five hundred and eight hundred young people a year, the majority of whom, like himself, are African American.

"If you Google me, you will find articles about me. I've been on MTV, in *Metro Weekly*. Someone called me an AIDS celebrity. I was, like, an AIDS celebrity?" He laughs. "It is what it is."

From early on, Barnhill was pegged as a gay boy. Because he was shy and preferred the company of girls, his classmates called him Gay Chris. "I did pretty much all the things the girls would do. I hung with the girls, and the girls just loved me. I played with Barbie dolls. I did their hair. My uncles hated it. 'That's not right!' they told me. 'Be a boy!' So I would hide the Barbies. Looking back, I knew that there was something a little different about me. There's a uniqueness with gay people. We are special creatures. Being the smallest and the shortest guy, I always had the biggest mouth and the biggest attitude. People respected me for it."

From his middle school years and into his freshman year in high school, Barnhill "had girlfriends all the time. Later I found out all of them were lesbians." During his freshman year at Bladensburg High School in Prince George's County, Maryland, he came out.

"People told me I was going to hell. Guys would harass me and pick with me. I'd just give it right back to them, challenging basketball players who were six-three. There were three gay males in my high school who were out. Out of the three, I was the only one who never got into fights with anybody." When he came out to his aunt, she said, "We already knew you were gay, Chris. As long as you don't come in here dressed like a female."

Barnhill went through a period when he wanted the whole world to know he was gay. "You feel so liberated, you want to be the biggest, loudest queen ever. Tight jeans, slurring my words—I was crazy in high school. After a while, I started realizing that this feminine thing wasn't working for me. It took a five-year process to figure out what kind of gay I wanted to be. I still had my little sweetness, but not as syrupy sweet, not the kind to give you a sugar rush."

Barnhill tried to start a gay/straight alliance at Bladensburg, but "the parents had a problem with it." He got a better reception from his teachers, who, he says, respected him because he respected himself. As a member of the Air Force Junior ROTC he was worried about what his sergeant might do if he found out he was gay. "I thought he might be mean and cruel to me, but he wasn't. He was used to seeing gays. All the gays were in it. There is something about those uniforms!"

While he was still in high school, Barnhill was sexually active. "I loved older guys. I thought it was cute that older guys were interested in me. When I was sixteen, I had a twenty-one-year-old boyfriend. We were together nine months—in gay days that's a long time." Sex education? "Sure we had sex education," he says facetiously. "Three pages that talked about HIV/AIDS. The End. We saw videos from the 1980s."

Until he was sixteen, Barnhill did not know that his parents had died of AIDS. "I don't know why they call it sweet sixteen. That's the year I found out a lot about myself and my family." During that year, he started attending a black Pentecostal church. At a health fair sponsored by the parish, he was persuaded to get tested for HIV, the rapid test, "the longest twenty minutes of my life." The results revealed that he was positive.

"I wasn't upset, I wasn't crying. I felt relieved, because then I knew what I was put on this earth to do. I don't know if it's gay people or people in general, but some people are hand-picked to do certain things. When you find out what that thing is, a joy comes over you. You find your mission." It's the same message that Barnhill delivers in his HIV ambassador's video clip on the Web site Does HIV Look Like Me?

Once he learned his HIV status, Barnhill got to work making public appearances to speak about AIDS and safe-sex practices. "I was doing things to prepare myself to be a care advocate, putting my face out there." At an assembly on World AIDS Day, he came out to his high school as an HIV-positive person. Revealing his HIV status, he says, "is really helpful to the person you're trying to reach."

At first, Barnhill assumed that he had contracted HIV through sex, even though he had been practicing safe sex. But at eighteen, having gained access to his birth records, he discovered that he was born with the infection. He was baffled that his aunt and his grandmother had not told him. "I exiled myself from them. I didn't trust them. The doctor told me I should have been dead by then." That was also the year that one of Barnhill's friends died of AIDS. "It became more real to me."

Seething with anger, he began to withdraw. "My outlet was my walk-in closet. I had my TV in there, my cell phone. I used to write a lot—poetry, songs." After graduation, he walked out of his aunt's house and never returned. That summer, essentially homeless, he crashed in a friend's dorm room at George Washington University. When classes resumed, he moved out, bouncing from place to place. "I used to pretend to like guys I didn't like who were interested in me in order to get a meal or have a place to stay. I was really on my hustle in order to survive."

In addition to the work he did in order to pay his bills—waiting tables, telemarketing, cashiering at the National Gallery of Art café—Barnhill continued to speak at conferences and on the radio. "I used to go around the city talking to high schools and colleges about being positive. I even got on *Nightline*." Despite the publicly optimistic attitude he was taking, he acknowledges that he was one of "the walking wounded."

"Since I was not getting love from my official family, I tried to find love in the party-and-play family." By the time he was twenty, he was doing crystal meth. "Only every so often, but even every so often kept calling me back." About a year before our conversation, he realized that his vision for his life did not include addictions. "I was just repeating what my mother and my brother, who's addicted to coke, had done. I told myself, 'I cannot be a statistic.'"

During 2007–8, Barnhill served on the board of the Sexual Minority Youth Assistance League (SMYAL), a D.C. metro area service organization dedicated to supporting LGBTQ youth. When a full-time position at Metro TeenAIDS came up, he interviewed for the job and was hired in June 2008.

"It so happens that because we're based in Ward 6, one of the areas hardest hit by HIV, we deal a lot with the Afro American community. We're pretty much there for the initial diagnosis, helping them cope with their HIV-positive status. We're their friends—being there to listen, going to doctor's appointments with them—and their wardens when they need us to be on top of them. One of my clients is seventeen. Giving him that HIV-positive result was terrifying. Even now, he doesn't get that he's HIV-positive. I was like that. I had that numb feeling, too."

In August 2008, the CDC released a study that showed that the rate of HIV infections among gay and bisexual men of all ages has been increasing since 1990. What's going on?

"Yeah. When guys like you were growing up, you saw what AIDS was. You could tell who was HIV-positive. It was scary. I've seen it on old videos. You guys had an image. You had help for not getting it. Then when people saw that people weren't dying, they forgot about HIV."

Barnhill says that on a first date he always reveals his HIV status. "Most of the guys I date are negative. I work it right into the conversation. They don't freak out. They appreciate if you're authentic. If I had to give myself a title, it would be 'Authentic.' It's easier to tell the truth."

Barnhill has taped Internet videos for Metro TeenAIDS and recently started a video blog, available on YouTube, called Poz Lyfe—Christopher Barnhill. There he says that his whole mission is "to be that voice for the unspoken," a voice he describes as "open, transparent, fearless, and brave."

What's the one message he would like gay teens in D.C. to hear? "A lot of gay teens deal with a lot. Some are homeless, some go to prostitution, to drugs. I want them to know that if they want to get to a particular place in life, they should put themselves in a position to get there. Don't depend on people who are not beneficial to your development."

Barnhill, who at the time we speak is studying health education part-time at the University of the District of Columbia, says that in ten years he'd like not to be doing HIV work. "HIV is starting to get on my nerves. If HIV is nonexistent in ten years, I'd like to work with youth, maybe dabble in politics, be a D.C. council member."

We happen to be doing the interview during Washington's gay pride weekend. Barnhill has shown up to our meeting carrying placards for Metro TeenAIDS that he'll display as he rides on a float in the parade later today. So what exactly does gay pride mean to him?

"Community!" he fires back with a boyish smile. "Community, love, fellowship." He nods his head, assenting to his own succinct slogan. It's as clear and simple and beautiful as that.

Alison Bechdel

Alison Bechdel's comic strip, *Dykes to Watch Out For*, was one of the most successful LGBTQ cartoons ever published. The biweekly strip, which Bechdel once described as "half op-ed column and half endless, serialized Victorian novel," followed the adventures and misadventures of a group of friends through dating, love affairs, co-habitation, work, pregnancy and birth, child rearing, and ever more love affairs. Listed by *Utne Reader* as "one of the greatest hits of the twentieth century," *Dykes* was hilarious, poignant, sexy, incisive, brave, and scrupulously—and, on occasion, mockingly—politically correct. At the height of its popularity, the serial appeared in over seventy mostly gay and lesbian newspapers.

"I drew the first one in a letter to a friend of mine," Bechdel tells me as we settle down with mugs of ginger tea in the work studio of her home. The house, sunny, cluttered, and comfortable, sits on a plot of wooded land off a dirt road in central Vermont. "It was a single-panel drawing of this crazy lesbian holding a coffee pot. I titled it 'Marianne, dissatisfied with the breakfast brew.' And for some reason I gave it a subtitle, 'Dykes to Watch Out For, plate no. 27,' just as if it were an illustration in a textbook."

As she did more of these comic drawings of quirky, winsome lesbians, Bechdel's friends started encouraging her to submit them to the newspaper *Womannews*, where the twenty-three-year-old art school graduate was doing volunteer work. The editors liked what they saw and began to publish the drawings in the summer of 1983. Within a few years of its inception, Bechdel's playful jeu d'esprit, done "purely out of love and enjoyment, with no expectation of making money," became her full-time job.

At first, there was no ongoing plot or consistent set of characters, but within a few years Bechdel was introducing regulars into the series. Mo and her friends, she says, were not modeled after specific women she knew but only reflected different aspects of herself. She acknowledges two early inspirations: the comic strips of Howard Cruise, who was writing about openly gay material, and Armistead Maupin's *Tales of the City*.

In the early days of the strip, Bechdel caught a lot of flak for making so many of her characters butch or unattractive. "It's easy to make fun of all that earnest, youthful political correctness, but it *was* necessary. There was no way to move on without that kind of focus and nurturing attention. That's what my strip was about, to create this world where lesbians were subjects, where lesbians were universal, where lesbians were Everyman."

Bechdel's early followers—"a small but very loyal readership"—took to the strip and remained intensely passionate about it. "Which I think is because I never dumbed it down. I always felt committed to telling complicated stories, to not making easy gay jokes, to doing the best work I could about my lesbian world."

That commitment to complicated stories took Bechdel down a deeper, more complex, and more personally revealing path a few years ago when she published her graphic memoir *Fun Home: A Family Tragicomic*, her account of discovering, when she was in college, that her father had had several male lovers.

"The narrative," Bechdel acknowledges, "is pretty simple: my dad dies, probably a suicide, at the moment I realize I am a lesbian. That's all that really happens." But in her hands that story becomes an exquisite, brilliant exploration of family, identity, sexuality, and literary archetypes.

"I knew as soon as I started working on it that a simple chronological relation was not going to work. I also wasn't that interested in the story itself. What interested me more was ideas I had about all of these events."

If *Dykes* put Bechdel on the LGBTQ map, *Fun Home*, which

received widespread mainstream attention, made her a crossover sensation. It was named one of the best books of 2006 by several major publications, including the *New York Times* and the *Times* of London. *Time* magazine elevated *Fun Home* to one of its "Ten Best Books of the Year."

Bechdel grew up in Beech Creek, Pennsylvania, "a hardscrabble little farm town." Her parents were frustrated artists—her father a writer, her mother a painter and actor—whose dream had been to live in Europe. Instead, they settled in the central Pennsylvania heartland, where they had both been raised, and became teachers.

Bechdel's father was passionate—"monomaniacal," she says in *Fun Home*—about restoring their Victorian house. His enthusiasm for authentic details—antique furniture, gilt molding, heavy velvet drapes, flocked wallpaper, needlepoint—was so thoroughgoing that for all practical purposes the affection stopped being pretense and became real. "The house was some image of himself that he thought he could perfect, and it was never enough."

Bechdel's mother went along with her husband's "unwholesome interest in decorative arts," but a frosty antagonism developed between them. "They fought all the time. I didn't pick up on this as a child, but my father would go for weeks without speaking to my mother. He'd sulk and bear grudges. He was very angry. He wasn't leading the kind of life he really should have been leading."

She remembers that he groomed himself as a pretty boy. "He used bronzing stick. He had makeup. He had a tray with twenty different kinds of aftershave. He had a velvet suit!" She laughs. "He pushed it as far as he could in Beech Creek."

The absence of a strong masculine element in the household— she calls her father's mannerisms "nelly" and "sissy"—left Bechdel feeling as if she needed to compensate. She started acting more like a boy. The childhood drawings she did were only of boys, never of girls.

Bechdel, whose haircut and clothing tend toward the "gender nonconforming," says, "People ask me if I really wanted to be male; did my father really want to be female? I do often wonder, if I were twenty years old now, would I be transitioning like all these young women today seem to be. So much of who we are is generational. That's part of the story of my book: how different my life turned out from my dad's life, given these very similar circumstances."

In trying to piece together an accurate portrait of her father,

Bechdel looked for clues in her childhood diary, family letters, old photographs.

"It was a constant process of discovery. My dad led a very secretive life. I didn't have a lot of information. I tried to compensate for that with the archival record, which I now realize has its own distortions and lies. But I really believed as I was writing *Fun Home* that I could get to some sort of truth by looking at these external records."

In 1976, when she was fifteen, Bechdel's father took the family (minus the mom) to New York for the Bicentennial celebrations. It turned out to be quite a gay weekend. They went to the ballet, saw *A Chorus Line*, and even ended up at the apartment of a gay couple for refreshments. Bechdel says the homosexual element on the streets of the Village—she writes of "the arresting display of cosmetized masculinity"—caught her attention.

"It was so striking to see men so pretty. And then I realized what was going on: these were gay men. I didn't consciously associate it to my own homosexuality. Because they were men, it was enough of a remove that I didn't take it personally. But if I hadn't seen that I'm sure it would have been much more difficult for me to come to terms with my own self."

Bechdel attended Simon's Rock College for two years before transferring to Oberlin, where she majored in studio art. While most of the projects she did were conceptual pieces, she also started dabbling in narrative, storylike projects.

"I became a cartoonist because it was a way of flying under the radar of my parents' multifaceted, creative interests. It was a way for me to express myself creatively that they couldn't see, or judge, or have any aesthetic criteria for. I found a thing that was creative but that neither of them cared about."

At Oberlin, Bechdel immediately became aware of all the gay students. "It was right after that big march on Washington. Which I was clueless about. But I feel as if somehow that energy, or the exposure, spilled out, and a month after that I realized I was a lesbian."

The realization came about through reading. Bechdel laughs when she recalls this. "That's how I do things. I read about them first and then I do them." The book was *Word Is Out: Stories of Some of Our Lives*. "I don't know what possessed me to pick that up, but it was instantaneous: not just that I was a gay person, too, but that it was OK. Here were these nice people talking about it. It was like a bolt from the blue. And then it was just a matter of building up my nerve to actually go try having sex with somebody. That took four more months."

At first, Bechdel was scared of the gay kids she started meeting. "They were just so out there. The boys had drag names for one another, which was very off-putting. The girls were listening to Chris Williamson, which I didn't understand the appeal of. It made me question whether I was a lesbian." She pauses and smiles. "But I quickly warmed up to all that."

In part, the catalyst was her first lover. "Joan was a crash course. She was this total radical lesbian separatist-feminist. I knew I could never be as outrageous or out or confrontational as Joan, but I loved that she was. I always have deep respect for people who are willing to make the space bigger for everyone else. I would get involved with these very political women who were always getting arrested, organizing demonstrations. It was something I wanted to be a part of. Looking back, I think I did that in my own way. I do think the comic strip was a form of activism. I've always resisted saying that. I felt like it wasn't confrontational in the way activism should be. Now I see, of course, that it was a kind of confrontation."

Shortly afterward, Bechdel came out to her parents in a letter she wrote from college. Her mother wrote back: "I have had to deal with this problem in another form that almost resulted in catastrophe." Bechdel didn't understand.

"No idea. I wrote her, asking, What catastrophe? She called me back with the information that my father had male lovers. I felt like someone had hit me on the head with a baseball bat. I was already in this fragile state, assimilating my own homosexuality, revising my life story to accommodate this new information about myself, when all of a sudden I had to revise it all again. I was ripped out of every context, just floating."

Bechdel went home for a visit and tried to broach the subject with her father, who didn't open up until one night when, on their way to the movies, he told her about his first boyhood love affairs. "I'd never seen him like this. He was deeply, deeply shameful. It was like he was making this painful confession. He hated this about himself."

That summer, as he was crossing a road with an armload of gardening debris, Bechdel's father was struck and killed by a truck. As to whether his death was an accident or suicide, Bechdel says, "I made it more ambiguous in the book than I really feel about it. I guess I thought that would make a better story. But I feel as if it's something I know."

Bechdel returned to Oberlin to finish her degree and apply to graduate art programs, all of which turned her down. "I was a mess senior year. My dad had died, I had my first girlfriend, I was learning how to be a lesbian, I was having sex all the time." With a new girlfriend, she moved to New York, where, for the next four years, she worked at menial jobs, "deadly, mind-numbingly dull stuff." With a lot of time on her hands, she started drawing cartoons.

It wasn't until 1998—fifteen years after the first *Dykes to Watch Out For* appeared, eighteen years after her father's death—that Bechdel felt "able to untie that knot, to sort out what the fuck happened." That's when she started kicking around the idea for *Fun Home*. "I knew it was different from anything I had ever done. It became clear that it was going to be much more literary." The project took seven years to finish. At first, Bechdel didn't seek out a publisher, wanting the freedom to experiment with the project on her own. Nor did she tell her mother she was writing the memoir until she had been working on it for a year.

"I knew I would get easily scared off if she freaked out. So I had to feel like I was in too far to turn back." Eventually, she showed pieces of the manuscript not only to her mother but also to her brothers. Her mother suggested changes, some of which Bechdel incorporated into the final draft. Still, she says she feels that she betrayed her mother. "She had told me things in confidence, and I made them public. That's pretty inexcusable. My family is not happy about the book. I think they feel exploited, as I would if someone made me a character in their story and misrepresented my version of reality. Early on, I thought, This book is going to heal my family. We're going to take down our walls, and it's going to be beautiful. It didn't happen."

Bechdel speculates that, had he lived, her father might eventually have come out of the closet. "He might very well have come out with a little more something. Could I have provided that? I don't know."

Fun Home was a finalist for a 2006 National Book Critics Circle Award. It also won the 2007 Eisner Award for Best Reality-Based Work. The *New York Times Sunday Book Review* pronounced it "a pioneering work, pushing two genres (comics and memoir) in multiple new directions."

"It has taken two years for that to sink in," Bechdel says of all the accolades. "It was a good thing, but it was also traumatic. It was this totally queer story told in this idiosyncratic way. I was lucky that it caught this graphic novel wave at the right time."

These days, Bechdel is invited to speak in high school and college English classes and graduate art programs. "Literary audiences. It's so great. It's what I always wanted with *Dykes*—more serious attention—but I never got it. So this is very sweet."

Early in 2008, Bechdel announced that she was putting *Dykes to Watch Out For* on indefinite hiatus. "It was very, very difficult and painful. The strip has been, to an unhealthy degree, my identity, my self. And my income for a long time. But in order to move on, you have to bury the past, and I do want to move on."

Bechdel is proud that *Dykes* was "part of this huge cultural movement that made space for our queer stories to be visible. No one would have read *Fun Home* twenty-five years ago. No one would have been able to relate to a gay dad and his gay daughter. Nor would I have been able to tell it."

As our conversation wraps up, she rings a bittersweet note.

"It's always been ironic to me that the more progress we make, the more we erase our separate identity. And I mourn that. I loved the specialness of being queer. I loved the subculture and the separate, sort of invisible world. But of course I don't want those conditions to continue. Ultimately, the goal of all this is for people to do whatever they want without having labels. The categories are becoming vague for a good reason. But I can't help missing that moment when I knew who all the lesbians were and they were all reading my strip. It was all very cozy."

Mandy Carter

Mandy Carter's motto, one that has informed her career as a community organizer and coalition builder, is "Don't mourn; organize. If there's a need, fill it." The afternoon we meet, in a conference room at the Peace Farm in Voluntown, Connecticut, Carter reframes her motto with decidedly more agrarian imagery: "You only can take so much shit," she tells me, "but if you have enough of it, it *grows* things."

Carter, who has just finished a retreat and workshop at this rural education center for social change, has been growing good things throughout her forty-plus-year career as an activist. The efforts to which she has devoted her life seem impossible for any one person, even someone of her stamina and spunk. She has been the founding member of, worked for, or served on the board of countless organizations devoted to justice, nonviolence, and civil rights for people of color, LGBTQ folk, and women. In the political arena, Carter has been a member at large of the Democratic National Committee and a member of both the DNC Gay and Lesbian Caucus and the DNC Black Caucus. At the time I meet her, she has just been named to the Obama National LGBT Steering and Policy Committee.

"It's in my blood. I'm always looking for the next possible thing I can do. I can't be around people who are bringing me down. I've got an innate sense of the possible. If it's never been done, I want to be on the front line of that, to make a way out of no way."

Carter was born in 1948 in Albany, New York. When she was quite young, her mother "got up one day and left." She and her siblings became wards of the state, residents at the Albany Children's Home until Carter was eight years old, at which point a black foster family took her in. Her foster father, whom she calls "a real disciplinarian," used to beat her with goat straps. One Christmas, she got a lump of coal "for being a bad girl." When Carter reached puberty, the family sent her packing, fearing she would get pregnant. She returned to another orphanage, this time in Schenectady.

"What saved me was being in those homes. There we learned that it wasn't about you; it was about taking care of the unit. There was structure, security." Because most of the kids in the orphanages were white, Carter says she was slow to come to an understanding of herself as black. "In high school, I was one of the first black cheerleaders—almost unheard-of." When a schoolmate called her a nigger, she had no idea what the kid was talking about. "It wasn't something I had been ingrained with."

During her junior year, a member of the Friends Service Committee spoke to her social studies class about Quakerism and nonviolence, a "defining moment" in her early life. She says another defining moment was the year she flunked Spanish, which essentially ended her aspirations to attend a four-year college and started her on the path toward activism.

"I was living at the Y in Troy, attending community college. This was the Vietnam War era. There was such a sense of uncertainty. I began to think, What is the point?" She took off for New York City, where she again stayed at the Y. "I have this affinity for the Y," Carter chuckles. When she ran out of money, she slept in Central Park. Walking along the West Side one day, she stumbled across the League for Spiritual Discovery. "I didn't know it was Timothy Leary's place: LSD." In exchange for office work, they gave her a place to stay and free food.

Carter recalls that the LSD crash pad "was all about guys picking up young women. What was that 'hippie free love' stuff? They were just men trying to pick up girls. Guys would be down there like vultures every night." At the end of the summer—the 1967 Summer of Love—Carter took off with two friends for San Francisco. "It was just what people did in those days." They hitchhiked most of the way, hopping busses and trains in places where they couldn't get a lift.

When she got to San Francisco—"it smelled like incense"—Carter checked in at the Haight-Ashbury Switchboard. "They looked through their Rolodex and came up with Vincent O'Connor, a draft resister with the Catholic Peace Fellowship." O'Connor took her in, and Carter ended up volunteering for the CPF. In December 1967, she participated in a nonviolent sit-in at the Armed Forces Induction Center in Oakland. She was arrested and went to jail. "We told the judge that we knew exactly what we were doing," she once wrote, "and would do jail time rather than pay a fine and leave, all in the effort to underscore our commitment to end the war in Vietnam. It was jail, no bail."

Inspired by someone she met in jail who worked for the War Resisters League, Carter started volunteering for the organization. She recalls "the fierce, strong women of WRL. White women, but you didn't mess with them." By now she knew she was a lesbian, and "because there were so many gay people in the WRL," she came out to her comrades. "There was in me that kernel of trying to do the right thing."

In the summer of 1968 Carter attended a weeklong workshop in Carmel at the Institute for the Study of Nonviolence, "reading about Gandhi and hearing about these amazing campaigns in India, South Africa!" She began to understand that nonviolence was her deep-seated passion. That same summer, she took a bus with the Northern California contingent to the Poor People's Campaign. "I got arrested at the Housing, Education, and Welfare office as part of our nonviolent direct actions and spent a night in the Washington, D.C., Women's House of Detention."

The next year, when a staff position opened up at WRL, Carter took the job. Her salary was eighty dollars a month. "Home was a couch in the office and free dental. In those days it was Nirvana. If the phone rang at three in the morning—and it did—I was there."

Carter's adherence to nonviolence was tested by the Black Panther movement. "One of the big questions for those of us who were black was where we stood. As a pacifist I'd say, 'Pick up the gun, die by the gun.' But they were doing incredible things with breakfast programs in Oakland. That was really complicated for me."

Complicated, too, was her relationship with several of the black lesbians she met at Maude's, the lesbian bar where she hung out in

San Francisco. "They were trying to figure out where I was coming from: 'Mandy, you're not black at all,' they'd tell me. 'You don't talk black.'" One of her drinking buddies was Pat Parker, the black lesbian feminist poet. "Pat and I got into it all the time. Finally, we said, 'Can we just stop going on about who's blacker than who?'"

In 1974, the War Resisters League sent Carter to Los Angeles to direct an office there. The following year, when the Vietnam War ended, Carter did women's military counterrecruitment work, still focused on "the bigger vision of equality and justice." She was amazed at how many lesbians and women of color were signing up for the military. "WRL was on top of all that. That kept me in the flow."

By the time she returned to San Francisco in 1977, Carter was becoming more involved in the gay and lesbian political movement. She took on the task of organizing the first women's float at the San Francisco Pride Parade. "After we won a prize for our float, we got to thinking of all the other things we could do to mobilize and hook up with the gay male community. There were so many lesbians in San Francisco—just chuck full—that we could have organized a group of women who only wanted to knit with green thread on Thursdays."

This was the year that Harvey Milk won a seat as city supervisor. "You could see the city getting it! I was on cloud nine. To see it every day unfold before you. And to think about the possibilities. I was always thinking about what we could do next." Carter remembers the vigil following the murders of Milk and Mayor George Moscone. "That transformed the city. The gay men and lesbians looked at each other and said, 'Man, if we don't figure this out!' It galvanized our movements. People began to realize what a political force the gay community was."

Over the next several years, Carter worked for Rikki Streicher, the owner of Maude's and another bar, "doing a lot of organizing. Rikki was my mentor. She said to me, 'Mandy, what else can we do besides serving alcohol and having a softball league?'" When Tom Waddell, the founder of the Gay Olympics, was trying to get more lesbians on board, Streicher asked Carter to be the coordinator of outreach for the first games in 1982.

Later that year, Carter moved to Durham, North Carolina. "I needed to get out of San Francisco. I was drinking too much. It says a lot that the women's movement was based in these bars. I called up the War Resisters League and told them I'd take any job *east* of the Mississippi. I'd never stepped foot in North Carolina. My friends said, 'You're going *where?*'" She's been there ever since. "I love North Carolina. Jesse Helms did more to radicalize me and our state."

Carter helped organize the first gay pride march in Durham in 1986, an event that made the national news when the opposition mounted a campaign to recall the city's mayor, who had signed a gay pride proclamation. "What I saw was the beginnings of the radical Right coming after our community. We beat back the recall!"

Four years later, after a stint as wholesale manager for Ladyslipper Music, Carter became campaign director of Senate Vote '90, the LGBTQ effort to defeat Senator Jesse Helms. People told her she didn't have a chance, but she helped build a coalition of groups—she mentions blacks, gays, environmentalists—that had been adversely affected by Helms's voting record. "Black people came up to me and said, 'What's this gay thing, Mandy? You can leave that outside.' I said, 'No, you take all of me.' We came so close. That coalition still exists. Helms has come and gone. So, in fact, we won." For her work in attempting to unseat Helms, *Ms.* magazine named Carter one of its "Uppity Women" of the year.

In 1993, Carter helped bring the National Gay and Lesbian Task Force (NGLTF) Creating Change Conference to Durham. Inspired by that conference and subsequent conversations, Carter cofounded SONG, Southerners on New Ground, whose aim is to connect LGBTQ folks of all races in their struggle to combat the radical Right over a host of issues in the South.

"We made sure we talked about the connecting issues: race, class—which no one talks about—gender identity, culture. I've always been a bridge builder. Because I've developed such appreciation for my blackness and my lesbianism, I have the ability to be the face and voice for those who cannot."

In the midnineties Carter worked for the Human Rights Campaign, first as a public policy advocate and later as liaison to the National Black Lesbian and Gay Leadership Forum. "When I was working at HRC, I got a lot of grief. But I went with them because I knew I could be guaranteed a check. Back in those days, if you were an activist of color, where were you going to get a job?"

By the late nineties and into 2000, Carter was working on voter mobilization and registration in North Carolina and Florida. In 2001–2, she moved to Boston—the only time she has lived outside the South since moving to North Carolina—to work as a consultant during the same-sex marriage campaign. She recalls "sitting at a table, having this conversation about whether Marriage Equality has anything to do with black folk. Again, I had friends who said, 'Why are you bothering? It's not our issue.'" Carter stressed that "it wasn't about color; it was about whether you had access to resources. The fact that GLAD [Gay and Lesbian Advocates and Defenders] had faces of color in that suit was so critical."

After the Massachusetts Supreme Court decision that legalized same-sex marriage in the state, Carter was dismayed by the hostile reaction of some black ministers. "Every black community knows who's gay. They all know 'em, but their attitude is 'Don't name it, don't claim it, and we'll be fine.' How do we change that? One of the pieces of work we decided to focus on was how to have a dynamic conversation in our own black churches and community about how to address homophobia." Carter had observed, as far back as 1995, that within the black community there was "a movement just sitting there waiting to happen." Her vision came to fruition in 2003 with the founding of the National Black Justice Coalition, whose mission is to empower black same-gender-loving LGBTQ people in their struggle for "social justice, equality, and an end to racism and homophobia."

When she returned from Boston, Carter served as executive director of SONG from 2003 to 2005. During her tenure, she was nominated for the 2005 Nobel Peace Prize, one of the "1000 Women for the Nobel Peace Prize," which sought to recognize the contributions of thousands of women around the world in their work for peace. "I was humbled to say the least, but the scary part was they couldn't name some of the women."

As we wrap up, Carter has good news for me. The Evelyn and Walter Haas, Jr., Fund has recently announced that it will invest "several hundred thousand dollars" to fund pilot projects on "how we can engage nongay people, politicians, and institutions to have conversations about homophobia. I've been chosen to be part of this process." Never one to sit at home for very long, she's flying off to San Francisco to meet with the fund to start strategizing about black churches and to meet with an advisory committee on lesbian health. "They're meeting during Pride, which I'm happy about!"

Nowadays Carter's biggest frustrations are the dearth of people of color in the major LGBTQ civil rights organizations and getting black people to come out. "I can count on one hand the number of black gays and lesbians who are out. A lot of black lesbians ain't gonna look to white lesbians. So can you see the quandary? We need more black lesbians as elected officials. And when are we going to have our first black out lesbian in Congress? There are several high-placed black lesbians—no names—that you see every day. What role could they have played if they had come out? It frustrates the hell out of me."

What has been most important to her, being gay or being black? "Let's put it this way, I encounter more with my blackness than with my gayness. The things I bump up against are always about skin color, because you can see it. On the other hand, it's a gift I have, being a black lesbian in the South. How could I not use that opportunity? There's more of me than just me, but I wanna meet 'em!"

Mandy Carter

Jennifer Chrisler

On the 2000 census, one in three lesbian couples in the United States identified as raising a dependent child in their home; for gay male couples, the statistic was one in five. It's the kind of statistic that Jennifer Chrisler, the executive director of Family Equality Council, knows cold.

"And," she tells me the afternoon I meet her at Family Equality's offices in downtown Boston, "a lot of those children are asking, 'Why are they picking on us? Why do kids laugh at me in school? Why does my teacher do a family tree assignment with Mother and Father on the first two branches?' They want to know why the world has to be the way it is. No parent wants to see their children feel different."

With a constituency of 45,000 families, Family Equality Council is the largest organization in the country whose sole function it is to protect the rights of gay families. Founded in 1979, the council began as a loose network of gay fathers who had previously been in heterosexual marriages and for whom coming out had meant being cut off from custody and visitation rights.

"In the seventies and eighties," Chrisler explains, "the culture around being gay often did not support or include children. If you were LGBT, there was an automatic presumption that you weren't a good parent. These dads wanted to figure out ways around the system so that they could maintain a relationship with their children and find other dads who shared their values."

Over the years, Family Equality Council expanded to include a far broader and more political agenda. "At our core we're about LGBTQ parents, but we're also about single parents and grandparents and family constellations that don't fit the traditional heterosexist model of a married mom and dad raising their biological children."

The woman who has become the country's leading advocate for nontraditionally headed families was raised in upstate New York in an "all-white, pretty much all-Protestant, working-class community," a homogeneous world where weddings—heterosexual weddings— were a big deal. "My mother used to buy me wedding magazines. I would pore over them. I went through a phase in high school when I wanted to plan weddings. I was obsessed."

In 1988, when she entered Smith College, Chrisler supported— and here she lowers her voice to a whisper—George Bush. "It just goes to show that profound impact your parents have on you, your political views, your outlook on the world, your sense of what's out there. My worldview was so narrow." The quad where she lived was a bastion of "classic girls with their pearls." One of her dorm mates had a debutant ball—"coming out in a whole different way," Chrisler jokes. After an incident where Chrisler inadvertently made an ethnic slur—"I used a horrible, awful expression when I was talking about trying to knock down the price of something"—she began to question how educated she actually was.

During her sophomore year, a campuswide protest over a racial harassment incident began to galvanize Chrisler's thinking. "It absolutely changed me in terms of my views on social justice. I learned some fast lessons about privilege and race and religious discrimination." In a matter of months, she had become the chair of a group that developed programs for students to talk about diversity and how to break down racial tensions. In the process, Chrisler met and fell in love with her "first mad, wild crush, a very out, loud, proud lesbian." Though it was an unrequited love, she came out to her mother—and much later her father—"chipping away at who you know and having those conversations one by one by one." She says that Smith was a great place to come out to your friends. "It was very affirming, incredibly supportive. I swear, they throw a party every time someone comes out there: 'Ooh, another dyke on campus! Woo-hoo! Is she going to be a four-year kid or full-time?'"

After graduation, Chrisler stayed at Smith to complete a master's degree, after which, in the summer of 1993, she moved to Boston. Hoping to do policy work around educational issues, she took a job with state senator Cheryl Jacques, one of the first open lesbians to serve in the Massachusetts State Legislature. In the three years she worked for Jacques, Chrisler moved up the ladder, from office manager to staff director. She happily recalls "the incredible locus of events"—the same-sex marriage debates, the fight for a gay presence in the annual St. Patrick's Day Parade, the state's original Safe Schools Protection Act—that took place during her years working for the senator.

During her years with the Massachusetts Senate, Chrisler learned several valuable lessons in political astuteness. She singles out "being able to handle different constituencies and communicate with them in a way that is relevant and manages the varying levels of expectations." But perhaps the most salient lesson was that "people lifting their voice about legislation actually makes a difference. Of the hundreds and hundreds of bills that were debated every year in the Senate, it only took four or five calls to the office to get the senator's attention." At the end of 1996, about the time that Chrisler left her job working for Jacques, the two started dating.

For the next few years, Chrisler worked in corporate public relations and later for a small private venture fund. By then, Jacques had come out, run for reelection, and won by her biggest margin ever. When she decided to jump into a special election in the Massachusetts Ninth Congressional District, a seat left vacant by the death of Congressman Joe Moakley in May 2001, Chrisler quit her job and became Jacques' finance director, raising over 1.3 million dollars in just eight weeks.

After the election, which Jacques lost, Chrisler "took a big chunk of time off" to raise their twin sons, Tommy and Timmy, who were born in 2002. The couple moved to Washington, where Jacques took over as director of the Human Rights Campaign. It was, Chrisler says, "a tumultuous time" that included the defeat of John Kerry and "the awful, awful marriage bans" passed by several states. When the directorship of Family Equality Council (at the time called Family Pride) opened up, Chrisler, whose boys were then three years old, threw her hat into the ring. "Lo and behold, six months later, there I was starting a new job, having been out of the workforce for three years."

The political battles that the Family Equality Council has had to wage often center on narrow, entrenched notions of what constitutes a family. I ask Chrisler about James Dobson of Focus on the Family, who holds fast to the notion that the nuclear family is "supported by more than 5,000 years of human experience" and constitutes "the foundation on which the well-being of future generations depends." She is quick with a comeback.

"I'd love to know what anthropological history he's reading. The reality is, in society after society, the idea of the nuclear family is the furthest thing from how the vast majority of children have been raised. If you look at anything other than modern Western European notions of what a family is, it directly controverts what Dobson says. It's just ridiculous."

Chrisler is fired up now, and she has plenty more to say about the James Dobsons of the world.

"The classical heterosexist notion of a nuclear family headed by Mom and Dad is a *great* system by which to perpetuate the power structures that exist in this country. Of course, it would behoove James Dobson, a white, straight, heterosexual male, to perpetuate that myth in order to extend his political power. It's because the notion of not needing two parents, not needing men in order to procreate, taps into some of the deepest notions of how power works in this country. It's counterintuitive to everything they uphold in order to subordinate women, to subordinate families, to subordinate race, to subordinate class in order to perpetuate their power."

Moreover, Chrisler emphasizes, more than twenty-five years of research have shown that children raised by same-sex parents do equally well in the traditional measures of children's health and well-being. "The only thing that shows up between our kids and kids raised by straight parents is that they tend to have a more open worldview and aren't so rigid about their own identity. And I think those are good things!"

Chrisler is proud that Family Equality Council has "put the power and passion of our families to work" to make schools safe for kids of same-sex parents and to help defeat anti-LGBTQ family legislation, particularly antiadoption initiatives. Despite the fear that these families experience in the wake of proposed discriminatory legislation, many have been "brave enough and strong enough to show up and testify and let themselves be heard."

Jennifer Chrisler

She also points to "the huge victory" represented by hundreds of LGBTQ families who, through the organizing efforts of Family Equality Council, have participated since 2006 in the annual Easter Egg Roll, the largest public celebration sponsored by the White House "to show *this* president in particular"—she's referring to George W. Bush—"that you don't have to have a mom and a dad to have a family that participates in great American traditions."

As the lives of gay people and their families have gained visibility, is the average American growing less panicky about same-sex parenting? Chrisler's answer vacillates between caution and optimism.

"For as far as we still have to go as a movement, we have come so significantly far in terms of the level of visibility, the conversation about who we are, what our rights should be, how human we are in the grand scheme of things. I think there has been a growing acceptance that we are a part of the American fabric. At the same time, we shouldn't underestimate or diminish the fact that the vast majority of Americans are still inherently uncomfortable with the idea of gay people parenting.

"And yet parenting is in some ways our most common denominator with the larger American public. Parenting is a universal experience that transcends a lot of differences—race, class, religious background—and it can transcend sexual orientation and gender identity, if people open up their hearts and minds enough to let it. Most parents can connect on the common understanding of the love of a parent for a child, which is a pretty powerful thing."

Chrisler says that the vast majority of Family Equality Council's constituency uses the organization as an on-line resource. Other parents avail themselves of the community events that the council sponsors, like Family Week in Provincetown and smaller regional gatherings. Still others, she says, "look to us for nothing other than to be their national voice, giving credence to the family structure that they're living in. They finally get to see their daily lives translated onto a stage where they feel that somebody is sticking up for them."

In 2006, in collaboration with the University of Pennsylvania, Family Equality Council put together a two-day symposium that brought together scholars, advocates, and direct service providers who work with same-sex-headed families. Aside from the opportunity for all these people to convene in one place, the summit was the inspiration behind an on-line database of information and articles for LGBTQ families. Chrisler points out that, until the symposium, most of the research was on lesbian moms. Family Equality Council has now launched a couple of large-scale research projects on gay fathers and the outcomes for their children.

"It's harder to be a gay dad because so much of child rearing is a mother-dominated world. You go to school, and you're the only dad showing up for PTA stuff. You're much more isolated as a gay dad. They have to navigate the gay piece as well as being dads in a traditionally female-dominated place."

On its Web site, Family Equality Council has published a guide for advancing the cause of same-sex parents called "52 Ways to Be OUTSpoken." But how realistic is it, I ask Chrisler, to expect parents, whose time is already stretched, to take on advocacy work, too?

"Parents are incredibly busy," she acknowledges. "They have lots of demands. Whether you're privileged enough to be of an economic background where your demands are T-ball and play dates, or you come from an economic stratum where your demands are three jobs in order to have health care for your kids, parent are busy, busy people. We try to think of ways that we can plug our parents into making change that fits those different levels.

"It's important to remember that the act of parenting as an LGBT person is political in and of itself. Just being a parent and telling the truth of your sexual orientation—that combination is going to make change in the world."

Chrisler believes in the power of public storytelling as a vehicle to inspire change in leadership. "We are loathe to tell our stories. We have been oppressed for so long that when our families say, 'Fine, we won't disown you, we won't shun you at family outings,' we're happy with that, and we're afraid to ask them to affirm us or support us or stand up for us." She notes that the younger generation of queer activists—"one generation removed from the level of shame that was once attached to being gay"—is asking far more of itself and others than what her generation learned to ask for.

Chrisler acknowledges that with all the recent attention on same-sex marriage and same-sex parenting, those gay people who have chosen not to marry or have families have sometimes been left feeling like second-class members of the community. Here, too, however, she remains sanguine about the future.

"Marriage is not the be-all and end-all of our civil rights movement. Our community has evolved. There is no longer the singularity of identity around LGBT sexual orientation that there used to be.

Jennifer Chrisler

We have much more complex identities now. Being gay is only one facet of who we are. We don't have to be all or nothing in order to succeed and achieve. While marriage is important, we need to look beyond marriage as we think about policies to support one another and to make sure that all LGBT people are protected in whatever way they need to be."

What advice does she have for same-sex couples considering parenting? "Make sure you and your partner have conversations about your philosophy on raising kids. Get lots of rest, go on dates, travel, do all of that before you have your kids, because once they come, the kinds of trips you're taking will be very different."

Beyond that, she counsels prospective parents to "look really deep at what little pieces of your own internalized homophobia you're hanging on to. It is unhealthy to have children and be closeted. When your kids blurt out in the grocery line, 'I have two moms,' you can do one of two things. You can respond, 'And isn't he lucky?' or you can stammer and say, 'Come on, Johnny, let's get out of here.' Each of those responses teaches a different message about how to feel as a child with this kind of family constellation. There is a strong urge on the part of many to look as hetero-normative as possible. It's very hard to be a child raised by a closeted parent. People have to make tough choices about when and how and where they come out as an LGBT parent, but when you choose to hide that part of your life, it sends very confusing messages to kids about keeping secrets and shame."

As for her own family life, Chrisler, who was legally married to Jacques in 2005, says that it's "really mundane. We do all the same kinds of things that many parents across this country do. We fight, we make up, we go to bed tired, we love our kids, we yell at our kids. One of the things I try really hard not to do is to overidealize our families, because the reality is we make the same mistakes every parent does. At the same time, I hope that we're teaching our kids to view the world with a little more compassion and concern for people who are at a disadvantage, who may not be getting a fair shake. I hope we create and nurture their sense of justice. Every day you have to be a watch guard for your family."

Beth Clayton
and
Patricia Racette

Beth Clayton and Patricia Racette are roasting a chicken. The savory aroma is the first thing I notice as they welcome me into their Upper West Side apartment. Located a few blocks from Giuseppe Verdi Square, the place seems a fitting address for America's first out gay or lesbian opera couple.

"We wanted a little piece of sky," Clayton explains when I remark on the spectacular view they enjoy.

"Our neighbors all know we're opera singers," Racette adds. "But we don't sing here. We're actually not here that often."

Turns out the New York apartment is just their pied-à-terre. Clayton and Racette make their primary home in Santa Fe, the city where they met over a decade ago and where, in 2005, they celebrated their commitment ceremony. But this week they're both in town together, a rare occasion, and a friend is coming for dinner. While we chat, one or the other of them gets up periodically to check on the chicken.

Now at the height of their careers (Racette has recently received a Lifetime Achievement Award from the Licia Albanese–Puccini Foundation), the two are in constant demand. A dramatic soprano with a penchant for Puccini ("I can't wait to do *Fanciulla*!"), Racette has, for the moment, racked up the bigger career, with appearances at the Met and the San Francisco Opera as well as at other opera houses in the United States and Europe. Arts critic Manuela Hoelterhoff has described her voice as "a steely core wrapped with silk." And Clive Barnes, reviewing Racette's performance as the abandoned Japanese bride in the Met's 2007 production of *Madama Butterfly*, called her "a dramatic soprano of the utmost subtlety and emotional power."

Clayton, four years younger and several inches taller (she's a six-footer), is a mezzo with a voice that is "warm, dark, round," according to the *New York Times*. "Sexy" is another adjective that frequently appears in reviews of her singing. One of Clayton's signature roles is Carmen. "Simply sensational" was the verdict of the *Chicago Tribune* about her performance in 2000. "A brazen seductress in love with love."

"My favorite role," Clayton tells me. "A role that is me."

Both Clayton and Racette come from small-town backgrounds. Clayton grew up in Arkansas. "The biggest town I lived in probably had ten thousand people." Racette, who was born in 1965, comes from a blue-collar Catholic family just outside Manchester, New Hampshire. She tells me her childhood was "very provincial. My father didn't even like to go to certain parts of Manchester because they seemed too busy."

From an early age, music figured in both their lives. Clayton started piano lessons around age five. With a Methodist minister for a father, she was active in the church, where she "did a lot of singing." She took roles in church camp musicals and school productions. "In high school, they would build musicals around me."

As a young child, Racette, too, loved to sing. On long weekend drives with her parents she'd stick her head out the window—"like a dog"—and belt out songs at the top of her voice. After an unhappy stint with accordion lessons—"the thing came up to my forehead"—she taught herself to play guitar. "And I started writing songs. Sad things about heartbreak. It was my survival. I'd spend hours in my room with my music. When I got to high school, the choir director asked me if I'd like to join the choir. 'Oh, no, no, no,' I told him. 'I only do this alone.' A diva in the making!" But she relented the next year and joined the choir, where the director introduced her to jazz, which she fell in love with. "I wanted to be in a Manhattan Transfer kind of thing." By her senior year, Racette had set her sights on a college where she could study jazz.

To help her prepare for auditions, she got a voice teacher, who told her that she would be better off singing the classical repertoire. "I cried for three days." Undaunted, she went to the University of North Texas, a college with a good vocal jazz department, paying for the tuition with money she had earned waitressing. Only after she got there did Racette discover that there was no major in vocal jazz. "I had to major in voice or music education. And in doing so, I had to take classical lessons."

Her earliest exposure to opera occurred freshman year, when she attended a performance of Bizet's *The Pearl Fishers*. "I left at intermission. If you're trying to get someone hooked on opera, that's not the way to go. If truth be told, I was annoyed by the whole form."

It was around this time that Clayton, still a high school student back in Arkansas, went to Little Rock to see a performance of Purcell's *Dido and Aeneas*. Her first experience with the art form was the polar opposite of Racette's. "I was gobsmacked. When Dido sang her 'Lament,' I couldn't get hold of myself."

Opera finally claimed Racette during her sophomore year at North Texas, when her voice teacher gave her a new piece to learn, "Senza mamma" from Puccini's *Suor Angelica*. "So I sit there on the floor of my apartment, listening to a recording—Renata Scotto—from beginning to end. I was completely, forever hooked."

Senior year, Racette auditioned for a coveted spot in the San Francisco Opera's training program, the Merola Opera Program, which has launched the careers of some of America's great opera stars. She won first prize. "I was so scared. It was such a big city." But she ended up staying. "I met someone," she explains. "We were there for ten years."

Meanwhile, in 1987, Clayton entered Southern Methodist University, double majoring in voice performance and music education, "to please my family." While at SMU, she sang in a few college opera productions. "Real jewels," she says facetiously. "*The Apothecary* by Haydn and stuff by composers in residence." And she, too, fell in love with a woman. "I was twenty, my first experience. As I look back, I think women had been drawn to me over the years. You know, you have your coach stories, your community theater things. I just kept thinking, Oh, whatever. That's not for me. We were together for almost seven years, until I was with Pat. I'm a real committed lesbian."

By now, Racette was touring with the San Francisco Opera's Western Opera Theater (WOT), giving, she estimates, seventy performances of *Madama Butterfly*. She also began singing on the main stage, at first in student matinee productions. Then in 1992, she took on the part of the maid in Rossini's *The Barber of Seville*, an event that many still remember. In her entertaining book *Cinderella & Company* Manuela Hoelterhoff recalled, "Racette caused such a diversion stripteasing as Berta, the maid, she jump-started her career."

"Things went very well for me," Racette admits.

That same year, Clayton finished at SMU and went off to New York, where she studied for two years with Mignon Dunn at the Manhattan School of Music. What did she learn from Dunn? "Just sing. Stop thinking about it. Simple is better." In the summer of 1995, she joined the apprentice program of the Santa Fe Opera. "I did my first *Carmen* outing there. Santa Fe concretized my career." Nineteen ninety-five was a big year for Racette as well. She made her Met debut on March 4, singing the role of Musetta in Puccini's *La Bohème*.

"I was psyched. A whole cross-section of my entire life was there—college people, high school teachers and friends, family, aunts and uncles. It was one of those great evenings." How did she take hold of her nervousness? Racette pauses. I see her weighing whether or not she will share this with me.

"I call it my nugget. It's this thing inside. It feels very private, very quiet. It's a very solitary thing, but it's why you're doing this, it's why you're living this life. There is something you feel you want from it and that you want to give to it. It aches if I don't get that opportunity to affect others."

She gets up to take a peek in the oven, and I turn to Clayton, asking about some of the major roles she has taken on. As a mezzo-soprano, she frequently gets "trouser roles," male characters sung by a female voice. "It's fun to be something completely opposite to what you are," she tells me. "I'm not a manly woman, but I feel that I can believably embody male roles without pasting it on."

Racette returns, holding a scrapbook, and shows me photos of Clayton playing Medoro in a production of Handel's *Orlando*. "Isn't she hot? Johnny Depp, sort of."

"My most convincing pants role ever," Clayton agrees. (One reviewer of this production noted her "smoldering androgynous athleticism.")

Racette chuckles. "I was actually confused. I told her, 'You look so hot as a guy.'"

One of opera's greatest trouser roles is Octavian, the young lover of the older, aristocratic Marschallin in Richard Strauss's *Der Rosenkavalier*. In 2005, Clayton sang Octavian opposite soprano Carol Wilson's Marschallin.

"During an early rehearsal, I asked Carol, 'Is it OK if I'm really kissing you?' She got a little concerned about her lipstick, but we were good to go. So we were getting ready for the final rehearsal, and Carol said, 'My husband is coming in for the opening. Is yours?' I thought, God, she really doesn't know? I said, 'Well, my partner is not able to come.' I could see this look on her face—registering 'Oh!'—and, *boom*, downbeat, and the rehearsal started. That was really fun."

Wayne Koestenbaum has written about the "lesbian regard for the mezzo voice." Does Clayton think lesbians are particularly attracted to the darker timbres of the mezzo register?

Racette doesn't give her a chance to answer. "Oh, come on! It's because they're in pants half the time! That's what it is!"

Clayton picks up the campy tone: "The lesbians have to balance all the queens who are screaming for the sopranos. For the guys, it's all about the high notes and the big tits."

Back to more serious stuff, I ask where each of them stands with regard to singing versus acting. Does it matter if an opera singer can act well?

Racette: "I cannot stand just getting up and singing. For me the theatrical aspect of opera is key. It's the arc of the evening that matters."

Clayton: "Why step on the stage if you're just going to shout? The only lessons I really learn are during a performance. That's my learning curve." She turns to Racette. "You've helped me realize that. To take a risk while you're performing is the biggest gift you can give yourself."

How do they keep infusing risks into operas they have sung a hundred times?

"That's even better," Clayton says.

Racette agrees. "That's when the spontaneity starts. It's what I love about this art form. Even if you repeat everything—cast, conductor—it's still going to be different. That's what I love about live theater."

Beth Clayton and Patricia Racette

What about the cult of the diva? Thumbs up or thumbs down? "Ah, yes," Clayton acknowledges. "We call it the 'diva hat.'"

"We're very down to earth," Racette explains. "I'm not the kind of singer that one might associate with the divas of decades ago. And when I have to take on the—how shall I put it?—the *visual* responsibilities of our profession, it's a big pain in the ass. I'm successful doing it, but give me a T-shirt and a pair of boxer shorts and I'm a much happier person."

Clayton tells me that because of her height and her looks (luscious and sultry are adjectives that would not be too far off the mark), she is often mistaken as the leading lady. "Meanwhile," interjects Racette, "I've just finished singing to four thousand people at the Metropolitan Opera, and someone will come up to me and say, 'Oh, were you on the crew or in the chorus?' Beth has a look, an 'I'm important' look. I have this girl-next-door look. It would be better if I showed up in the big hat and sunglasses."

She explains: "People would rather someone have a certain air about them—cool and bitchy—but I just can't check myself at the door anymore. I can't walk through this life and wait to rejoin myself when I retire. As a gay person, I think it's incumbent on the artist to be an honest person; otherwise there is something fraudulent about it."

"I feel," Clayton adds, "that I have been given a gift to own my lesbianism and my life through my art form, a gift that so many people don't get."

Racette and Clayton met in the spring of 1997. "At Francesca Zambello's house," Clayton tells me, referring to their friend, the international director of opera and theater.

"In fact," Racette adds, "if you look in Hoelterhoff's book, you'll see a photograph of me. And if you look closely, you'll see Beth's shoulder. That was the very night we first met."

At that party, Clayton says, the two of them were "paying attention to each other big time. The energy was palpable. We were looking forward to working together that summer in Santa Fe. It was genuine; it wasn't lascivious. It was my first big-girl contract. Being treated like a real artist and working with a fellow lesbian."

Clayton had been engaged to sing Flora Bervoix, the good friend of Violetta Valéry, the "fallen woman" in Verdi's *La Traviata*. "When we were going through rehearsals," Racette later recalled to the *Advocate*, "it was like the rest of the world ceased to exist."

The story of their "illegal kiss" during act 2 is now legendary. At one point in that act, Violetta is directed to swoon into the arms of Flora. This Racette did. "And then Beth just leans down and plants one on me!" She laughs. "I could still kick your ass for that!"

Racette later told Doug Tischler during an interview for AfterEllen.com, "I had to turn my entire body into her because I couldn't stop laughing when I was supposed to be passed out!"

"We were out of control that summer," Clayton agrees. "Madly, crazy in love."

Since then, the two singers have worked together on only a few occasions. In the summer of 2002, they were back in Santa Fe singing the two sisters, Tatiana and Olga, in Tchaikovsky's *Eugene Onegin*. "During the duet," Clayton recalls, "we were holding hands. With our backs to the audience, singing into that canyon, with the lights of Los Alamos in the distance."

Racette came out publicly, in print, in a 2002 cover story about her in *Opera News*. "It wasn't until the actual moment of the interview that we decided that this was something I was going to be honest and forthright about."

"We had never been closeted in our lives about it," Clayton explains. "In this profession we are blessed because there is so much more flexibility. But to put it in print! In earlier years, Pat had been very considerate. My career was just getting started, and I thought, Gosh, I don't need that adjective. It felt like extra baggage just when I was establishing myself. But now I'm very proud to embrace it. It doesn't define my career by any means. It's validating. We're living our truth."

"The biggest blessing I have is the life I have with Beth," Racette adds. "How can I possibly cover that up, like a dirty, nasty secret? I want to scream from the rooftops about it. Those who have been against our being open—and I've received some comments in that vein—say things like, 'How are we supposed to believe you're Mimì?' Well, when you thought I was straight, I was *still* acting. It's called theater art. Whether you're gay or straight, you can tap into passion."

The couple tells me that the biggest difficulty in being a two-singer family is that they don't get to spend enough time together. They often don't even get a chance to hear each other's performances. Otherwise, Racette says, "we're a really great team. We're nauseating for our friends. We've been together eleven years, and we're still very much in love."

"But there is no way I could be with another mezzo," Clayton jokes.

The chicken is almost roasted, and their guest will arrive shortly. But they graciously say there is time for a few more questions. Well, then, why does opera attract so many gay artists and spectators?

Racette hardly lets me finish my question. "The pageantry! There's something for everybody, something so magnificent and so overt about it. For those who choose, for whatever reason, to be closeted about their lives, there is something about the overt aspect of opera that is cathartic."

"And transportive," Clayton adds. "So many times in the past, and even today, gay people haven't had the chance to live out their lives and their love stories. So you can put yourself into the plot, into the situations, and let them be yours."

Indeed, Wayne Koestenbaum has called opera the "civilization of the closet." So as more and more gay people come out, will opera function less and less as an emotional surrogate for them?

"I would like to see the world *behave* as diverse as it actually is," Racette says. "I'd like to see just as many gay people only interested in sports as there are gay people only interested in the arts. I'd like to see straight boys falling in love with opera."

"We've built a lot of bridges that way," Clayton says.

"I'll never forget," Racette tells me. "I once sang with a very handsome partner. He was jaw-to-the-floor when I told him I was a lesbian. I said, 'I thought everyone knew.' And he nailed me; he said, 'That's very arrogant. Why should everyone know?' I said, 'Fair enough.'"

Kate Clinton

It's a few days before Christmas, and the lobby in Kate Clinton's Upper West Side building is decked out for the holidays. Nothing splashy—just an artificial balsam, festooned with lights and tinsel, tucked into one corner. Opposite, on the concierge desk, a flyer lists the names of the building's staff, a reminder to the residents that an end-of-the-year gratuity is appreciated. As I wait for Clinton to come down in the elevator, I try to square my image of her—the very funny, and very political, lesbian stand-up comic—with the understated gentility of the foyer. On her Web site Clinton describes herself as "a card," someone who "still believes that humor gets us through peacetime, wartime and scoundrel time." For the past seven years, the scoundrel time under her hilarious, hard-hitting attack has been the presidency of George W. Bush. If there are any Republicans living in this building, I'll bet she's let them have a piece of her mind.

Clinton comes down and we walk over to a café just around the corner. After putting in our orders, I begin by reminding her of something she told me when I first interviewed her back in 1993. "I'm not interested in becoming a lesbian fundamentalist," I quote her to herself. "I'm interested in sort of a radical middle." What about that "radical middle"? I now ask.

"You know, I was fascinated as a child by the notion of a happy medium. I struggle with it still; we all do: the public and the private, the professional and the amateur. The really radical thing is to be able to see both sides and navigate between. That's the hunger of people right now. We have been so divided, so partisan."

Over the years, Clinton's comedy has become more political, a turn that she freely attributes to the influence of her partner of twenty years, Urvashi Vaid, an activist and former director of the National Gay and Lesbian Task Force. "Whenever Urvashi goes to one of my shows, she says to me afterward, 'Well, you have to do more politics.' I tell her, 'People can't handle that, a steady diet of politics, like you can!'" Clinton's delight in the good-natured taunts of her "girl" is palpable. "It's a struggle to be really radical and, well, living on the Upper West Side"—she laughs—"in an essentially 'bourgie' life."

She becomes more sober now, a touch of the former English teacher in her voice. "It was always portrayed to me that serious is more real, more truthful, and that humorous takes the backseat. But humorous can carry the weight of serious better than serious can carry the weight of humorous."

Born in 1947, Clinton grew up Catholic. In grammar school her teachers were nuns. After high school, she attended Le Moyne, a Jesuit college outside of Syracuse, New York. "I never got excited by my religion classes, but the philosophy classes, the literary criticism classes. I remember reading Leslie Fiedler for the first time and being, *Oh, my God.*" For eight years after college, inspired by the Jesuit tradition of service to others, Clinton taught English. Then in 1979, she fell in love—with another female teacher. "There I was, walking around with a big smile on my face. I just wasn't interested in suffering anymore."

She began to think about doing something else with her life. Taking a leave of absence from teaching, Clinton signed up for a course at the Women's Writing Center in nearby Cazenovia. "They all thought I was some interloper from the suburbs. I mean, here I am surrounded by patchouli and Birkenstocks, and I had a green terry cloth shirt on. I had never, ever, taken women's studies, but I had always thought something was missing. So I went, and I was hooked. That year, I read like I had never read, and everything began to make sense to me."

At the workshop, encouraged by Adrienne Rich, Clinton wrote a critical essay about feminist humor. "I gave the paper to a friend of mine. I'll never forget: she looked at it and said, 'Well, it's good, but where are the jokes?'" That's when Clinton decided to write her first comic routine. Though she had never done stand-up comedy before, her years of classroom teaching had shown her "how to work the room." She also picked up some pointers by observing student readings. "I remember that we went to a nursing home once. We did this reading—it was just tortured poetry—and suddenly from the back there was this voice: 'Spruce it up, honey!' By the time they got to me, I felt compelled to make people laugh."

Eventually, one of Clinton's friends booked her at a women's bar in Syracuse. From the beginning, she worked in the lesbian angle. It was 1981, the year Clinton marks as her debut as a professional stand-up comic. "I was on fire that year. It was the heyday of the coffeehouse-festival culture. I was a lesbian talking about lesbian things. My idea was Mort Sahl—without the cardigan and the paper under the arm, but to be able to talk about what was happening."

And talking about what's happening is what Clinton has been up to ever since. In addition to playing scores of comedy clubs and festivals, she has emceed numerous fund-raising events, galas, and benefits; appeared on news and talk shows; performed at the opening ceremony of Gay Games VII; appeared in several documentary films; mounted a one-woman show; and hosted TV shows like *In the Life* and *The World According to Us*. Along the way, she has garnered some impressive accolades, including a Lambda Legal Defense and Education Fund Award. In 2007 the Gay & Lesbian Alliance Against Defamation (GLAAD) honored her with its Pioneer Award.

Clinton rattles off what she's been doing lately: her columns in the *Advocate* and the *Progressive*, a new book deal, a new CD, her ongoing video blog, more concerts, performances, conferences, even a part-time gig as a commentator on CNN before the U.S. invasion of Afghanistan. "*Before*," Clinton emphasizes. "When all of that went down, any kind of frivolous commentator was gone. It was the time for men to talk about war. The message was, 'We're serious now.' I was gone."

Clinton is acutely aware of the challenges and opportunities of mixing politics with humor. "I think that what I do is a sacred opportunity. I want to give my audience something to think about. In that way I don't let them off the hook." She tells me that she doesn't play gay pride celebrations anymore. In the old days it was "drag queens and amplifiers like you can't believe, and then there would be me, saying, 'Here's your medicine now.' And they'd be pretty much blasted sitting in the sun. One of the last columns I wrote for the *Advocate* was about alcoholism in the movement. I can't believe the level of alcoholism. It saddens me."

What else gets her dander up these days? Without missing a beat, Clinton fires back, "The Church. They haven't disappointed. I thank them for the twenty-six years of material they've provided me. I should put them on the payroll!"

In her second book, *What the L*, Clinton wrote, "Religion is the opposite of the people." How so? I ask.

"Christianity. Islam. Both religions really don't have a very high opinion of human beings. 'We are corrupted by sin; we're born this way.' What kind of opinion of human beings is that if that's your starting point?"

So why the enormous following that these sin-based religions attract?

"It's the vacuousness of materialism and capitalism. I'm not around malls and chains. But when I'm on the road, I find it appalling that this is people's lives. It's meaningless, and they're looking for meaning. It's a longing for community in a really atomized world. The fact is, megachurches look like malls, like entertainment complexes now."

In a 1995 interview with Roz Warren, Clinton noted that words like "penis" and "lesbian" were finally able to be spoken publicly. (Once she was nearly beaten up by "the oldest living lesbian in the continental U.S." for using the word "dyke" in a show.) Nowadays, I ask her, what are the words that are still difficult to speak?

"In a white audience, to bring up race makes people very nervous. I've been doing a line about Mary Cheney and the title of her book, *Now It's My Turn*. And I go, 'Oh, when wasn't it your turn, white girl?' You can just feel people get nervous. Another thing that got people really nervous recently was talking about trans issues. My attitude about it is different now. In the past if I did a transgender joke and it didn't go over, I would have just let it pass. Now, if it doesn't go over, I'll look at the audience and say, 'Oh, come *on*!'"

Can Clinton envision a time when her humor will not reference homosexuality?

"I hope I never lose it. The drive toward hetero-normativity and the mainstream is really boring. I love what Grace Paley once said, that the mainstream is wide and shallow and slow moving. It's the tributaries where the fun is. I want to be the headwaters of the mainstream!"

Since her twenty-fifth anniversary tour in 2006, one that took her to ninety cities, Clinton has tried to keep the traveling down to one weekend a month. Her daily life these days? "I get up and I make a delicious omelet for my girlfriend and we read the paper." Clinton shakes her head. "It is a contact sport—you should hear the scream-ing!" After Vaid leaves for work, Clinton goes to her desk, where she tries to write until noon. "Writing" can mean anything from draft-ing, to taking notes, to keeping up with her blog, which, she says for a laugh, "my slave-driving manager makes me write every week."

The composing process can often take Clinton in surprising di-rections. "Sometimes I do a show and I think, Oh, this would make a great column; and sometimes I write a column and I think, This would make a great five-minute sketch. I mean, I'll write a three-page thing that's fuckin' brilliant, and after two shows it will be down to one line. And then a throwaway line will really grow because of what you hear from the audience. It's a folk art. In that moment of laughing, you get to hear all those different ways that people are tak-ing it, and you'll think, Oh my God, I've never thought about it that way, and then you'll take it from there."

Clinton tests out new material with friends and, of course, with Vaid. "Urvashi will come home and I'll say, 'I want you to listen to his,' and she'll say, 'Could I take my coat off first?'" During July and August, Clinton performs most weekends at one of the clubs in Prov-incetown. "By the end of the summer, if I've been really disciplined, I have ended up with forty minutes of new material. That's critical if people are going to come back every year."

How has her comedy evolved over the years? "I have more confi-dence in it. I know what will work. Of course, there's a danger in that: the material may not be any better, but I know how to push it." Has the demography of her audience shifted? "Absolutely. This sum-mer the guy who runs the Crown and Anchor in Provincetown said to me, 'Are you going through a transition?' I said, 'What do you mean?' and he said, 'I've never seen more men here.' It's true. I've caught on. I'm an overnight success!"

In part, Clinton attributes her increased popularity with men to her appearances on Logo, the cable channel targeted to the LGBTQ audience. "Quite frankly, being on television confers upon you a certain cachet that you're real. I mean, I've been real for twenty-five years, but because it's on that box, it's believable, and it's accessible."

Over her career, the challenges of being a lesbian stand-up comedian have changed. These days it's the traveling, "the absolute critical killer! It's so unpleasant and undependable and inhuman. Circling Newark for four hours and you just think, What am I doing? I could just do a blog and they'd get it! And the junk you eat on tour—all those hamburgers!—the stress. I mean, I want to be in it a long time, but I can't keep up that pace."

Clinton takes pride in having been a part of the gay and lesbian movement for the past quarter century, "and my particular role in it, which has been to be sort of the court jester, reflecting who we are, making fun of ourselves, too. I don't think we're that precious that we can't make fun of ourselves. And, truly, I'm very proud of my relationship with my girl. We have weathered twenty years now. We're a great match. She says we're the marriage of comedy and tragedy."

Clinton has referred to herself as a member of the Gay Geezer Boomer Generation. When I ask her what it's like to be a "gay geezer boomer" now, she can't refrain from cracking another joke: "I should have been nicer to Barbara Gittings!" But then she gets serious. "The legacy of our generation was that it was a huge, massive coming out. The others wore their suits, and they marched and picketed, but AIDS just made it, like, 'We don't have time.' We were furious, we kicked the doors down. Sometimes I feel like Madame Defarge. I've watched the course of revolution.

"People say to me, 'When Bush leaves, aren't you worried about what you'll do for comic material?'"

I put my sandwich down, waiting for another kicker punch line. But all she does is look up, a mischievous smile on her face.

Judy Dlugacz

In *Listening to the Sirens*, her book about "homomusical communities," musicologist Judith A. Peraino notes that during the early 1970s feminists were turning to women-identified music as "the product of choice to initiate the real goal of feminist business." Among those pioneering feminists was Judy Dlugacz, one of the most successful women's music entrepreneurs of the seventies and eighties. A founding member and president of Olivia Records, Dlugacz guided and nurtured the company from its days as the brainchild of a lesbian-feminist collective.

"Going to school in feminism informed me," Dlugacz tells me the day we connect at her office in San Francisco. It has taken us a year to find a mutually convenient time to meet, for Dlugacz is a woman as much out of the office as in. Olivia Records may be no more, but its reincarnation as Olivia Tours has Dlugacz sailing off to distant and exotic ports, where she puts together vacation packages for travel-loving lesbians of all ages. But today she's back in town, happy to reminisce about her days with what Stephen Holden in the *New York Times* called "one of the record industry's most solid success stories."

With its egalitarian ideals, ethic of consciousness raising, and promotion of lesbian love and community, Olivia's discography—albums by Meg Christian, Chris Williamson, Linda Tillery, Mary Watkins, Teresa Trull, Deidre McCalla, and others—resonated with lesbians of all stripes. While the majority of independent record companies fail within their first year of operation, Olivia kept putting out highly popular albums for almost two decades.

"Here we were like the Little Red Hen," Dlugacz recalls. "We had to do everything ourselves—create the music, distribute the music, produce our own concerts—because no one would really help us. We helped create visibility. In the early days, visibility was everything. It created community. It saved lives."

Born in 1952, Dlugacz grew up in Queens and "farther out on Long Island when my parents had a little more money to invest in a house." Her father, of Polish Jewish extraction, was a CPA and a socialist; her mother, a teacher and union organizer. "We always had organizers in the house: everyone from Bayard Rustin to Norman Thomas, who ran for president on the Socialist Party ticket. All sorts of amazing people."

A self-described tomboy, Dlugacz remembers running around the neighborhood in a powder blue jean jacket, brandishing a cap gun. "My mother let me be exactly who I was. I was a fast runner and played sports. I wanted to slick my hair back like Elvis." In high school, she was editor in chief of the newspaper, a member of the student council, and a flautist in the band. And, she adds, "politically active even then." Inspired by her mother, who had led the first teacher strikes on Long Island, Dlugacz organized a march for Biafra. When she graduated, she got a scholarship "for being an iconoclast."

At the University of Michigan, where she majored in psychology, Dlugacz fast-tracked her way through in three years "so that my parents didn't have to spend a lot of money." On campus, she lived in a new residential college, which she calls "a think tank of radicals." Hearing about the existence of the Radicalesbians, a lesbian-feminist collective, she decided to check them out, justifying her interest because she was taking a "deviant behavior" class that semester.

"That was my cover. In that first meeting, I was sitting in a corner. My legs were tucked up to my chest, my arms were folded. I didn't want anyone to look at me. But what they said absolutely did me in: that not only was it OK to be a lesbian; it was *best* to be a lesbian. It was all about being a strong, independent woman in the world. I thought, Oh, my God. I can come out now." Dlugacz signed up, accompanying the Radicalesbians as they went around to colleges conducting coming-out groups for women.

"In those days, women could not even get a credit card without a man cosigning. When I went to college, the Left was completely dominated by men, and women were getting strong and angry. You saw this real shift. It was a magnificent time to be in school."

Dlugacz graduated in 1972 and moved to Washington, D.C., planning on attending law school the following year. She took a job as an electrical construction apprentice, the first woman in the D.C. area to do so. Evenings and weekends, she and other lesbian feminists, including some from the defunct Furies Collective, began to hang out together. "We thought that if every woman knew about lesbian feminists, they would all come out, and it would change the world."

The women decided that they needed an organizing tool to accomplish that mission. One member of the group, a lesbian singer named Meg Christian, was hosting a local radio show. On one of her programs, Christian interviewed another lesbian singer, Chris Williamson, who was beginning to have some success.

"The two of them started talking about how difficult it was for women to record in the music industry. Chris turned to Meg and said, 'Why don't you start a women's record company?'" Meg came back to the other women and pitched the idea: a national women's recording company. "Within a few minutes they had convinced us that we could do it. I dropped going to law school. I called my parents. They plotzed."

The first record that Olivia made, issued in 1974, was a 45 with Christian on one side and Williamson on the other. In a few months, the initial run of five thousand had sold out. With the profits, Olivia was able to make its first full-length album, Meg Christian's *I Know You Know*.

Christian's songs concerned lesbian relationships and struggles. "Her focus on explicitly lesbian concerns," writes Peraino, "clearly defined 'women's music' as 'lesbian music,' and lesbianism itself as political action." While Olivia's brand of feminism was sometimes criticized as centering on desire rather than the nitty-gritty of political oppression, Dlugacz's company had clearly found a responsive chord among its consumers. Christian's album sold about seventy-five thousand copies.

At the beginning of 1975, the Olivia collective moved from Washington to Oakland. "We lived together, we worked together, pooled our money. It was all just one foot in front of the other." Dlugacz says that the music Olivia put out in those years helped people come out. "It was the Internet of those days. Through our mail-order business, you could buy a record without identifying yourself as a lesbian." Christian's and Williamson's concert audiences started growing, from "fifty people in a church basement or the halls of college dormitories" to two thousand in major concert halls all over the country.

"We called it 'women's music' because we believed that women wouldn't accept it if we called it 'lesbian.' We were really very sharp in terms of all that. It enabled people to listen from their heart." The first time the word "lesbian" was actually used on an Olivia album cover was in 1977, when the company produced *Lesbian Concentrate* in direct response to the campaign by Anita Bryant to repeal a Dade County anti–sexual discrimination ordinance.

"It was one hundred percent undiluted lesbian. It meant that all of our recording artists had to come out. One or two changed their names to protect themselves. We were always asked by the press, 'How can you do this? Aren't you discriminating against men?' I would always sit there amazed. Almost every single band in the world is all men. I would say to the press, 'If you can name one female bass player, one female guitar player, one female drummer, one female producer, I will stop doing Olivia.' No one ever could. It made it so clear how ridiculous that question was."

In the eighties, Olivia began sponsoring concerts of women's music as well. The first one, at New York's Carnegie Hall, celebrated the tenth anniversary of the company. "Two shows in one evening. It turned out to be the largest-grossing concert at Carnegie to that date. The audience came to celebrate something. We helped create visibility. In the early days, visibility was everything. It said, 'We *are*!' We told ourselves that women must see each other in order to go back out into the world and be strong."

During the Carnegie concerts, Dlugacz was busy with logistics. "As I was walking around, checking on things, I thought, If I do nothing else with my life, this is the moment. When it was all over, I tried to get to the stage. I couldn't make it: there was too much excitement. People were screaming. The noise was so loud it almost pushed me over." The *New York Times* barely mentioned the show.

"Two inches. It was so sad. They would not give any space to us. We were scary to them."

In 1988, about the time that Olivia Records began to lose its appeal, Dlugacz started Olivia Tours. "Someone said, 'Wouldn't it be great to have a concert on the water?' I said, 'That's it! We can do these vacations for women. I can do that!' I knew it would work. I didn't even think about it." Why such confidence? "Because I was out of the closet my entire adult life, except on vacation. I knew how great it would be to be able to hold hands and to be able to . . ." Dlugacz exhales audibly, showing me the depth of relaxation she knew lesbians on vacation were looking for. "We had the full faith of our community, a community that loved us and that knew when we said we'd do something, we did. I just sent a letter to my mailing list for Olivia and said, 'Hey, I think you're going to love this.'"

Dlugacz's predictions were right. Six hundred women committed themselves to a cruise a year into the future. The cruise, with the Dolphin Line, which had already been hosting cruises for gay men, was so successful that she turned right around and organized a second one.

"Back to back. It was amazing. The enthusiasm was tremendous. What we did was magical. When you get to be yourself, even when you think you're out all the time, you have no idea what it's like to be in a world where you're in the majority. On these cruises, you're in the majority. For some of these women it's a life-changing experience."

At first, many of the women who cruised with Olivia were closeted, though that is far less the case today. Still, Dlugacz says, "Even if they're out to their families, they're not necessarily out at work. Women buy houses. They're in the suburbs. They're often very isolated." She emphasizes the "cross-generational" mix on Olivia's cruises. "We have women from twenty-five to ninety-five. Younger women sometimes think, Oh, I just want to be with my group, but when they come on a trip and they have this cross-generational trip, it's phenomenal."

Olivia has also designed cruises targeted for lesbians of color and their friends. "Our trips have always been about being all-inclusive. But we are now putting extra effort into saying, 'These trips are for you, too.' We're dedicated to making that happen."

While the cruises have always included some top-shelf lesbian entertainment (Melissa Etheridge, Lily Tomlin, k. d. lang, the Indigo Girls), Dlugacz and her company have also begun folding conferences into the packages: leadership summits, writers' and authors' conferences, culinary events, a film festival. And in 2008, when the California Supreme Court legalized gay marriage in that state, Dlugacz said, "Let's have weddings!"

"It was amazing. We had already planned this cruise to the Mexican Riviera leaving from San Diego. All of us—the entire Olivia crew—got licenses. We did a hundred individual weddings." The ceremonies took place on California soil, at the Hard Rock Hotel, the night before the cruise ship sailed. Dlugacz thinks that occasion marks the largest number of individual weddings done in a single place in a single day. "And the next day, we went on honeymoons!"

At the end of each trip she goes on, Dlugacz tells her passengers, "You thought you came here just to go on a vacation, but I hope, when you leave, it's been more than vacation. I hope you see each other as part of the same fabric."

Dlugacz lives in Marin County with her life partner of thirty years. Together they raised a daughter and now have a granddaughter. "Rebecca is ten. She's going to be the next generation of activist. We took her to see the film *Milk*. She came out of the film and said, 'You know, gay people are better. I can't believe this is rated R just because it's gay.' She immediately wanted to buy a gay flag."

Most recently, Dlugacz has turned her attention to writing a book about the last thirty years of lesbian history in this country told through the experience of Olivia. "I've got amazing stories to tell. We go around the world, and we become the ambassadors for lesbians, even where the word 'lesbian' never comes up. We don't announce we're coming—I don't go in and say, 'The lesbians are coming!'—but sometimes we get announced."

She tells me the story of an Olivia cruise to Turkey right after the war in Kosovo, when the economy was in bad shape. "We docked in Kuşadası. There were bargains to be had there. The women bought up all the leather goods and carpets they could find. The local newspaper came into town and interviewed some of them." Then the tour continued on—to Ephesus and Lesbos—and finally to Istanbul, where Dlugacz was "a little nervous about going to this large Muslim city." The advice to the passengers was that they should comport themselves in a low-key manner.

"Well, that morning, the AP of Turkey had spread the story that the women of Olivia had come into Kuşadası, spent half a million dollars, and saved the country's economy! So every major newspaper in Istanbul—*four* of them—ran the story. We're getting off the ship, and suddenly the paparazzi of Istanbul are there to meet us. The newspapers, the TV were all there. We go into the Grand Bazaar, and all the shopkeepers were shouting at us, 'Lovely lesbian ladies, come to my shop!'"

Dlugacz smiles. "So many stories."

Judy Dlugacz

Arthur Dong

Filmmaker Arthur Dong is perhaps best known for his documentary trilogy *Stories from the War on Homosexuality*, films that examine some of the institutions and cultural attitudes that have often been hostile—in some cases, brutally so—to gay men and lesbians. Dong had been making films for over a decade when the first of the trilogy, *Coming Out under Fire* (1994), based on Allan Berube's history of gays and lesbians in the military, secured his place as a major voice in documentary filmmaking. Described by Stephen Holden in the *New York Times* as "quietly devastating," the film earned the director several major awards. His subsequent films—one has appeared about every five years—have continued to win critical acclaim.

We meet at his home in the Silver Lake neighborhood of Los Angeles, a pleasant residential area known for its ethnic diversity and home to the city's largest population of same-sex couples outside of West Hollywood. Dong ushers me into his studio, which also serves as the play area for his young son. Tables of editing equipment agreeably coexist with a playpen and toys. Album covers—he's got over forty of them—from various LP recordings of *Flower Drum Song*— are mounted on the walls. It turns out that the film version of that Rodgers and Hammerstein musical, based on the novel by Chin Y. Lee, was the first English-language movie Dong ever saw in a theater.

"In Chinatown"—he's speaking of San Francisco, where he was born in 1953—"there were four theaters playing only Chinese-language films." It was in one of those theaters, when he was about eight or nine, that he first saw *Flower Drum Song*, a film he once described as "a refreshing change from the low-budget films from overseas that we sat through week after week." (Over forty years later, Dong was instrumental in getting the film accepted on the National Film Registry. "No film since," he wrote in his nomination statement, "has had such a major and lasting impact on projecting a three-dimensional portrait of Asia America.")

Hooked on American movies, Dong was soon a regular at the repertory houses in the city. "I was fascinated that you could watch a film made thirty or forty years ago. There is no doubt that I'm fascinated by history. I've always loved the movie *The Time Machine* because you could go back in time. I'd love to have dinner with Jean Harlow. That would be so cool."

In 1967, when he was thirteen, Dong saw his first documentary film, a CBS television special called *The Homosexuals*. "It was a slanderous portrayal. They showed the cheesiest, sleaziest images." But at the time, what he was primarily aware of is that much of the film had been shot in places he knew. He remembers thinking, Oh, is *that* where they are!

Bright and popular, in high school Dong was a cheerleader and boys' vice president. "All a façade. It was really hard for me to take gym classes, very difficult to be in that machismo environment." A high school art project introduced him to the world of filmmaking, giving him a medium to express his growing sense of alienation. His project, shot in his bedroom with a little Brownie movie camera, focused on the life of a five-year-old Chinese American boy confronting social mores and cultural bias. It took first prize in the California High School Film Festival, a prize that included a thousand-dollar award and a public screening. The evening the film was shown, Dong "just freaked out. The impact of watching my film—a very political film. I remember thinking, This is scary stuff. This isn't just about watching Greta Garbo or Nancy Wong."

It was about this time that Dong told his high school counselor that he was gay—he'd known since he was thirteen—and was planning to drop out. In response, the counselor arranged for Dong to complete his senior year without having to be on campus. Together with a female classmate, he took a studio apartment in the Tenderloin district. "We said we were common-law man and wife. It was preposterous, but we got away with it." Between his independent study classes, he worked at various jobs, which were credited as "work-study experience" on his transcript. Dong laughs as he recalls all this.

"A lot of people now ask me to speak to school groups. To the dismay of a lot of them, I tell the kids I dropped out of high school and college."

After high school, Dong went to San Francisco State. He started taking "really heavy-duty courses—film history, film criticism—that proved to be over my head. I was a working man by then. I had to make a living. I recognized that this medium is so important that I better not fuck it up." He dropped out, vowing that he'd give himself ten years "to go out and explore life a little more before I hit the books again."

During that decade, Dong "did things that any young gay man would do in the seventies." To pay his bills, he held a variety of jobs, eventually landing a position at a local television station. In his spare time, he studied ceramics and traditional Chinese music. In 1978, through his music teacher, he met his future husband, Young, to whom he was legally married thirty years later.

"Back then our gay brothers called us 'lesbians' because we were two Asians in love with each other. We were 'sisters.' We weren't supposed to love someone from our own race; we were supposed to love the white man. The erotic being was on the cover of *GQ*."

Not long after they met, he and Young took a two-month trip to China. Allowed to travel freely, Dong pulled out his camera and started shooting film. On the plane ride back, he began to edit the footage. "That's when I remembered that I wanted to be a filmmaker." The next year, he returned to San Francisco State to finish his degree. "Everything made sense to me. Even English 101 had a purpose. It was about constructing images. I understood that writing was like filmmaking."

In 1982, having earned his B.A., Dong went on to found Deep Focus Productions, his film company. At the time, he was filming *Sewing Woman*, his documentary about his mother's job in a sewing factory. Released in 1983, *Sewing Woman* touches on several issues—immigration, labor, women, ethnicity—with a grainy, homemade realism that earned it a nomination for an Academy Award in 1984. Only fourteen minutes long, it is still being shown in college film courses today, an example, Dong says, of what you can do for two thousand dollars.

Dong went on to the Director's Fellowship program at the American Film Institute, the "Juilliard for Filmmakers." In 1987, he shot a résumé film in Hong Kong, a short narrative called *Lotus*. Set in the last days of the Qing dynasty, the film used only Chinese actors, who spoke in English. Dong makes sure that I understand that these were the days before Chinese-born directors like Ang Lee and John Woo had risen to prominence.

"The studio heads and agents that I met said, 'There is nothing we can do for you. Obviously you're a talented director, but there is no place for you here.' They wouldn't say that today."

Frustrated by the lack of response to his narrative film, Dong returned to making documentaries. The result was *Forbidden City, USA* (1989), his film about Charlie Low's famous nightclub in San Francisco's Chinatown. Almost as soon as it opened in 1938, Low's cabaret, which featured Asian entertainers, became enormously popular with tourists and servicemen, perhaps the most popular among the dozen or so such clubs operating during the forties and fifties.

I ask Dong if the success of places like the Forbidden City had to do with its promotion of an exotic, differently sexualized image of Asians. Were stereotypes being perpetuated?

"Of course. It was marketing. Charlie Low was not stupid. He was using what he could to market his club. The performers put up with it. On the other hand, it exposed many Americans who had never seen Chinese as other than coolies or laundrymen or restaurant workers to Chinese performers. And it wasn't only the women who were hot. The men were hot too!" He pauses—there's something more on his mind.

"They're all dead now, so it's OK to say this. Forbidden City was so gay. There were certain stars on stage that the gay folks knew were gay, and that's where you hung out to meet them. It was a fun time for all. When I first met Allan Berube, I wasn't sure he knew who I was. He said, 'Of course I know who you are. I use your film in my Queer History class. It's the queerest film.'"

Dong's first explicitly gay film was *Coming Out under Fire*. When he first read Berube's book, he immediately thought of the imprisonment of Japanese Americans.

"That kind of violation, it still baffles me. I felt the same regard for gay and lesbian soldiers who had gone through the same experience. I immediately connected. I saw it clearly as a violation of civil rights within the context of a social structure, the military, that I had no regard for." He says that reconciling those two feelings was part of the challenge of doing the film.

The prevailing attitude during World War II is best summed up by one of Dong's interviewees, who says that being gay during World War II was all about "Be invisible and shut up." As a Chinese American, how did that notion resonate for Dong?

"We *can't* be invisible. We can shut up, and we do shut up, and we're forced to shut up, but we can't be invisible. We're always seen as the outsiders. I can still feel it. In certain situations I still feel like the outsider."

Berube's book revealed that military service had created opportunities for gay camaraderie, and Dong highlighted that aspect in his film. "We approached it as personal stories. Because of that, the harsh reality of their experience was tempered. Of course there were very tragic moments and tragic chapters. But the people we worked with were very resilient. That was very inspirational. For them what was joyous was coming out to friends and finding a community. Not that we don't want more progress, but we have to acknowledge that there is indeed progress."

In 1995, with a fellowship from the Rockefeller Foundation, Dong went to Tyler, Texas, to observe the trial of Henry Earl Dunn, Jr., an accomplice in the murder of a gay teenager, Nicholas West. "I wanted to know more about him." Out of that initial curiosity about "this good-looking black guy who was a murderer" came the idea for *Licensed to Kill* (1997), Dong's film about the murderers of gay men. The film presents several factors that shaped the psychology of these murderers—the influence of fundamentalist Christianity, child abuse, bullying, self-disgust, the feeling of disenfranchisement.

In her review for the *New York Times*, Janet Maslin noted the "bizarre civility" of the murderers and "the astonishing casualness and the shocking sense of entitlement with which they justify this brand of murder."

"That's what I wanted," Dong tells me. "One of the things I do well is to walk into an environment with a stranger and a crew and establish a sense of trust and comfort immediately. I was so filled with joy that these men were opening up to me. I knew I really had a film coming here. Every time we left the prison, my crew was yelling and screaming, 'Oh my God, how could you sit there and listen to that crap!' They could hardly contain it."

Of all the awards he has received—including three Sundance Film Festival Awards, five Emmy nominations, plus numerous awards from both the gay and Chinese communities—Dong says he may be most pleased with the OUT 100 Award. "They gave it to me for mounting a one-man campaign against gay violence."

License to Kill made many of Dong's gay viewers unhappy. "They wanted the victims' stories." He recalls the time an editor of one gay publication said to him, "Give me one compelling reason why I should cover this film." Dong shot back an angry response: "I'll give you a couple of reasons why you *shouldn't* cover it. It doesn't have naked boys; it doesn't have white pretty boys!"

Dong says that he makes films in order to learn. "When I approach a person to be interviewed, I hope they'll help me explore their point of view." His next film, *Family Fundamentals* (2002), did just that. It's about conservative Christian parents who have gay sons and daughters. Remarkably, the film eschews easy finger pointing.

"Yeah, people hate it," Dong says of his refusal to pummel his audience with a heavy-hitting message. "I wanted to produce a film about gay issues that those fundamentalist parents could actually sit through and appreciate. If the film had been full of heavy propaganda, they wouldn't look at it." Dong also provides study guides for his films that offer viewing suggestions and tips for encouraging dialogue rather than debate. An official selection at Sundance, *Family Fundamentals* went on to garner a "Top 10 Pick" designation in a number of publications.

With his next film, *Hollywood Chinese* (2007), Dong turned from homosexuality to the depiction of Chinese in American films. Much of the film focuses on stereotypes, like Charlie Chan and Fu Manchu, and the 1937 Hollywood version of *The Good Earth*, which was done primarily in "yellow face," a movie that, he says, "should have been our *Gone with the Wind*."

Dong is not as condemnatory of these images as, for instance, his contemporary B. D. Wong, whom he interviews in the documentary. "As offended as I might be by Charlie Chan, I have a swell time seeing his kids. Those kids are role models. They are having so much fun—talking jive, going to college, having a great time being Americans. Because I was brought up with a very strong foundation of seeing Chinese on the big screen, when I did finally did see, say, Luise Rainer in *The Good Earth* or Sydney Toler as Chan, it was more an intrigue and a novelty than an offense."

While he was making *Hollywood Chinese*, Dong learned of two surviving nitrate reels—"totally dangerous, but in almost perfect condition"—from the forgotten 1916 film *The Curse of Quon Gwon*. Directed by Marion Wong for the Mandarin Film Company in Oakland, California, it is the earliest extant example of Chinese American filmmaking. Dong used clips from the film in his documentary, but, even more important, he was instrumental in getting Wong's film accepted on the National Film Registry.

"It's one of the first features in the world made by a woman. The family had kept the film a secret because of its commercial failure. It caused their bankruptcy. It was a shameful, dark chapter in their lives that they wanted to put behind them. This is the kind of stuff I love. This is what I live for."

Does he feel more ghettoized as an Asian American or a gay person?

"I'm not really sure. I do know that if I did feel any marginalization from an outside source, it would be because, as an Asian American, I can't be invisible. Being Asian American you're not targeted as much for being gay because it's a 'white man's disease' in this country. It's hard to compare the two." What he does know is that he loves "being bold in both communities."

As for being a father, Dong says, "We've been embraced by the heterosexual community in ways we never thought we would. What's wonderful about living in Silver Lake, we can walk to school, and there are other same-sex couples. It makes it very natural for my son—he's three and a half now—to know that there are other daddies. He's cool."

Dong so enjoys being a "house dad" that he finds he is not staying as long at film festivals anymore—and sometimes even turns down invitations to appear—"because I want to get back home. What we teach a child has a big influence. I know this now. I'm very careful about what I teach my child."

Mark Doty

In the opening poem of *Fire to Fire: New and Selected Poems*, Mark Doty relates an incident that happened to him once in the English countryside. One evening, as he and his companions emerge from an inn, he catches sight of a bat, "an inky signature too fast to trace." The bat is an "emissary of evening," a "quick ambassador," a "fleeting contraption / speeding into a bank of leaves."

As they watch the "fluttering pipistrelle," the party discovers that only Doty can actually *hear* the bat, "a diminutive chime / somewhere between merriment and weeping." The poem continues, through "branching questions," to meditate on narcissism and self-consciousness, the making of poetry, and the divide between the human and animal worlds. But it's that phrase, "merriment and weeping," that most captures my attention, nicely pinpointing what Doty's poetic ear and his entire literary output—eight volumes of poetry and four books of prose—have always been attuned to.

"Partly, it's the pleasure of perception," he tells me the afternoon we sit down to talk. "The beauty and delight of the world make one not want to lose it. As Faust says, 'Stay! Stay!' And partly it's the other way around: the temporariness of things enables us to see their value. That little gyroscope is the energizing force of lyric poetry. Love and death, love and time, spinning us around and around. I don't reconcile them. I try to make something that contains both of them."

We're in the café of the Rubin Museum of Art, not far from Doty's apartment in New York's Chelsea. Amid the tinkling of cups and saucers, the music of a guqin, a classic Chinese zither, wafts through the room. It seems a fitting backdrop for a poet who reads Buddhist texts—"though I'm not a practitioner"—and tells me that his poetry is all about "a sense that the present is what there is."

As he once said of the poetry of Rilke—that it "exhilarates and saddens, enlivens and unsettles"—so, too, Doty's poetry takes the scintillant world (sheen and shimmer are everywhere in his work, not least in his many poems about drag queens) and both celebrates and pauses to consider—again I'm quoting from his essay on Rilke—"the pressing questions of evanescence."

Doty is one of our great writers about loss: the transitory world, the decay of beauty, the death of the beloved. His 1996 memoir, *Heaven's Coast*, about the death of his lover, Wally Roberts, is one of the outstanding monuments in the literature of AIDS. Indeed, if Doty had written nothing else, he would still have made a name for himself as a gay writer of signal authority and beauty. That he is also—indeed, primarily—an award-winning poet is a stunning testimony to his talent, vision, and courage.

On the day we speak, Doty has recently finished the manuscript for *Fire to Fire*. At the time, neither of us knows that he will be awarded the 2008 National Book Award for Poetry. In praising his "elegant, plain-spoken, and unflinching" work, the judges will note that his poems "gently invite us to share their ferocious compassion. With their praise for the world and their fierce accusation, their defiance and applause, they combine grief and glory in a music of crazy excelsis."

But that is a year away. For now, what's on Doty's mind is getting the book out. "It feels like a self-portrait over time. I feel like I'm making a sort of edifice that represents the last fifty-four years of living."

Doty grew up in Tennessee. The first language he can remember loving is the poetry of the hymns he used to sing in church, "sacred speech that was rhythmic and heightened." His grandmother used to read him Bible verses, "which didn't seem offered as spiritual instruction so much as an occasion for wonder: *listen to this!* Pretty early on, I developed the sense that the word was a means of access to the imaginative world, or the world inside the world. Being a kid who moved all the time, I was socially pretty isolated, but you could have a kind of intimacy with the characters in books that was more complete than anything that the external world could offer you."

In his 1999 memoir, *Firebird*, Doty wrote about his childhood, about the "intimacy without ease" in his relationship with his mother and his lack of connection with his father. We decide that for this conversation we do not need to rehearse the details of those years. For today, it seems enough to note that his mother's creative interests—she had studied painting with a student of Diego Rivera's—kindled his own interest in the visual world, a value, he tells me, that "has continued to shape my life."

"I loved the stuff of her paintings—the tubes of colors, the smells. And especially the names. They were so thrilling to me. If you have a word—like 'cerulean' or 'azure' or 'aqua' or 'indigo'—you're more likely to see something beyond 'blue.' The word helps to refine and complete the perception."

Doty did his undergraduate work at Drake University in Des Moines, after which he remained in the Midwest for most of his twenties in a heterosexual marriage. "I didn't *know*," he later wrote, "living as I did in a place and time where gay people were hidden, erased, what kind of life I could have." In 1980, after the "dizzying change" of his divorce and the beginnings of a gay life, he moved to Manhattan. Soon after, he met the man with whom he would spend the next twelve years, Wally Roberts.

From the outset, exile and loss were themes in Doty's work. As early as his first book of poems, *Turtle, Swan*, which he published in 1987, he expressed in radiantly assured stanzas both his delight in his boyfriend and his anxiety about "where these things we meet and know briefly, / as well as we can or they will let us, / go." Where, I ask, does that sensitivity to the evanescence of things come from?

"There is a kind of selfhood that is like the perpetual stranger or the exile who looks at the world without the usual degree of familiarity. That comes from lots of places. Certainly from queerness. As soon as we're exiled—in my terms because I'm homosexual—you no longer think of things as natural, as givens. There is another way of being, which is a movement toward freedom. But it is larger than circumstantial conditions. On some existential level, I feel like I always just got here."

Memory, too, is another theme that showed up early on in his work. *Turtle, Swan* includes a poem addressed to C. P. Cavafy—"the patron saint of all of us"—one of the great (and gay) poets of memory. In the poem, Doty watches a boy and his companions diving unselfconsciously from a raft. In making the poem, Doty recognizes that the boy, with all his erotic charge, "is a memory reinvented," something he, the poet, is "inventing as much as remembering."

"One of my favorite philosophers, Gaston Bachelard, says that at their root memory and imagination are the same things. The farther back we go, the more difficult it is to separate memory and imagination. I am not interested in getting at facts but in having facts *felt*: what it was like to be there. I do my best to tell the emotional truth."

By Doty's second book, *Bethlehem in Broad Daylight* (1991), the homoeroticism had become more explicit. Gay bars, drag queens, and porno movie theaters all make their appearance. In the third book, too, *My Alexandria*, which was published two years later, the ravishing self-invention of drag queens becomes "torch, invitation, accomplishment."

"I'm drawn to instances of performance, to the ways in which we make a self. So if you don't think your selfhood is something that is fixed, then taking power over that is a way of inverting the way the world exercises power over you. Any time you get a drag queen around, they are strong, fierce, authoritative. You don't mess with them. Why do they have so much power? Because they take the gender thing and invert it, take charge of it. That's energizing.

"People making their mark, making their world, I find that very beautiful. And that's what I've done with myself: make my own definitions of beauty and grace and artfulness and authority and style. The drag queens in the poems are very often either muses—representatives of the art of poetry—or stand-ins for me. That's who I want to be, that figure who's singing for the group out of the speechlessness of the moment."

By the early nineties, Doty and Roberts had settled in Provincetown, a place, as he later put it, "where our presence as a couple was both welcome and ordinary" and where Roberts's HIV diagnosis—it came in May 1989—"was nothing unusual." The town at the tip of Cape Cod, with its "light on the marsh, the incredible shifting weather and sky, the mutable visual world," served the poet for fifteen years as "an imaginative theater." It was a place where he once again discovered that "the world delivers itself to us freshly over and over again. And that is an invitation to attach oneself to it and to care about it." But increasingly, Provincetown was also becoming the place of wreckage. "I am thinking of my terror / of decay," he wrote in "Becoming a Meadow," one of the first poems he set in Province-town, "the little hell opening in every violated cell."

Roberts died in 1994. The next year, in *Atlantis*, a book of poems set mainly in Provincetown, Doty confronted the mystery and horror of death, the way things unravel, dissolve, come to disas-ter, vanish. Like the two ruined boats that provide the title for one of the collection's poems, Doty and Roberts are "twin points we thought fixed / coming all undone." In the book's title poem—and the longest—he writes, "We don't have a future, / we have a dog." That dog, a black Lab named Arden, and another retriever, a golden one named Beau that the couple got shortly before Roberts's death, were to figure prominently in a book Doty would publish over a decade later. In the meantime, in 1996 he brought out *Heaven's Coast*, his memoir about his and Roberts's last years together. His first book of prose, it was, Doty tells me, an attempt to capture "what it felt like to be in raw, inconsolable grief."

"Wally's death made poetry feel, for a time, unavailable to me—too contained, too limited. To write a poem, I would have to be able to draw a boundary around one part of experience. I couldn't. I just had this oceanic sense of grief that was uncontainable."

Doty says that after he finished the memoir he realized he had "something else I could do. I could make the more resolved, vibrating little poem, or I could have this much larger arena, where I could move more slowly through a constellation of event and feeling and idea, and build a different sort of architecture." Three more books of nonfiction prose have followed: the memoir of his childhood, *Fire-bird* (1999); a meditation on Dutch still life painting, *Still Life with Oysters and Lemon* (2001); and, most recently, *Dog Years* (2007), his remarkable memoir about his life with Arden and Beau. Interspersed with these works of nonfiction prose were three more books of poems.

"I felt my life opening after a period of constriction," Doty told Christopher Hennessy in *Outside the Lines: Talking with Contem-porary Gay Poets*. By 1998, when he published his fifth volume of poetry, *Sweet Machine* (1998), he had met his current partner, Paul Lisicky, a novelist and memoirist. The tone of *Sweet Machine* is one of rediscovered pleasure in a world that is all "shine / and seem." Joy is once again as immense as a whale; every sequin is "an act of praise."

"It's an act of praise for the vivacity and energy and variation of the world. I see it all as a kind of hymn to what is." When I note that this idea takes us right back to the hymns of his childhood, he says, "If my work is praising God, it's doing so indirectly; it's praising creation."

A more somber tone returns in *School of the Arts* (2005), the book of poems Doty calls his darkest. "It came out of a place of real depression. I wasn't kicking up my heels at all. It's not a camp book—none of that." There are poems about the two old dogs; about his anxiety on a subway platform in the face of an oncoming train; about the terror of a narrowly averted airline disaster. The book includes a sequence of poems, "The Vault," that are, he acknowledges, "very sexually open." Everything seems to be racing toward darkness. In the book's long title poem, Doty records how his beloved Provincetown is being bulldozed into oblivion—"scoured, knocked flat, torn down."

"When I finished that poem, I knew I was done with Provincetown. It was time for the next thing." The next thing was New York, where he and Lisicky still live. "Provincetown is a place of removal and retreat. New York is just the opposite, a city of immersion. Whatever is going on with you, New York is bigger than that. You can be in the blackest dumps and walk out and see life around you, which serves as such a contrast to where you are that it's energizing, strengthening."

Doty had been in New York only a short while when *Dog Years* came out. A valedictory tone—as much for Provincetown as for the dogs—permeates the memoir. "It's not a dog book," he agrees. "It's a book about love, time, language, and consciousness that happens to have some dog characters in it." Was he concerned that the book might become maudlin and sentimental? "Of course. I really loved those dogs. But I had already thought about these questions. How does one write about that which you feel very passionately about without sentimentality? I was attracted to that risk. That was an interesting challenge to take on."

In the book, Doty ponders what it must be like to experience the world as dogs do, without language. "My imagination is very drawn to the places where language fails," he tells me. "To go toward that which is 'unsayable' because it's emotionally intense, or because we don't have names for it, or because it exists wordlessly, as presumably animal consciousness does, is enormously compelling to me as a poet."

Doty says that it's just about impossible for us to imagine what it must be like to apprehend the world without language. "We as humans departed from that kind of consciousness long ago. It was both an entrance into the human world and profoundly traumatic. I believe we are surrounded by consciousness or sentience and that it takes many different forms. We might learn a great deal about what it is to be human by spending time with chickadees or golden retrievers."

It is getting late now, and we have moved on to a deli a few blocks away, but I have a few more questions I want to ask him. In *Heaven's Coast*, he wrote, "My dick kept me alive." What has he come to understand about the value of sex?

"If anything, I feel more compelled by sex now. What draws me to sex—it's not about orgasm, the biological imperative. It's about intimacy, energy, contact, celebration. It's about blurring boundary, dissolving the line or the space between bodies. I find myself seeking an encounter with masculine energy. If I had to say what that is, I couldn't do it, but nonetheless it's a really driving force for me.

"When I met Wally, that was my first real relationship with a man. I had very traditional ideas about what romance was, what marriage was. That has just turned itself inside out over time. Like lots of gay men now, I'm much more comfortable not thinking of sex and love as the same thing. I don't want everything from one relationship. Things like intimacy, companionship, connection, lust, friendship—that whole rich spectrum is appealing to me and has come into my life in many different people."

Of the new poems in his *New and Selected*, Doty says that it's a poetry "not very much concerned with my biography or my personality. I see the speaker, I mean me, as a kind of representative citizen. It's not so important what the poet's past is. There's a presumption out there that gay readers want to read about gay experience. There's probably some truth in that, but does that mean you only want to read about sexual experience, or that you want to read about lives that are just like your own? We did not go through a great struggle for liberation in order for somebody to tell us how to be gay. I dislike the idea that there is a right way to write gay books. I want to be able to address anything that interests me, to have that freedom of imagination. I don't want to feel that I have to leave my life out of it, but I'd also like to be able to turn wherever it is I want to go without feeling some social obligation."

There is still "gay content" in the new poems, but it often doesn't take center stage. "Theory of Multiplicity," for example, which is set in a laundromat on 16th Street is more concerned with the relativity of perspective. Doty emphasizes that no one reading of an event or scene is definitive. No one has "the entire vantage." And from that realization a kind of humble and quietly ecstatic sense of the unity of all things emerges:

> I felt in that moment
> not dissolved in anything, not selfless, but joined
> in a layering of singularities—a multiplicity
> not God, exactly, that theoretical viewpoint,
> but a satisfying gesture in that direction.

Now in his midfifties, Doty says he is "thinking about changes in one's own body and the bodies of people you care about. And trying to have room for that in the work. Back in the day when I was writing about Wally's illness and death, it was important for me to move toward some affirmation or resolution. But over the course of time, if you do that too much, you leave out a lot of the experience—you get a very reductive art. The only thing that really gives you power over the terror of decay is developing a sense of distance, which has to do with detachment, a sense of irony, the sense of the way things always are. That seems to be something that's happening more for me now."

Doty says that he loves meeting younger readers. "Part of that is about being visible as an adult gay person. If I go to a school and speak about my life, it turns out it's more powerful if that's not my official subject. If I'm invited as a visiting homosexual, gay people come; if I'm invited as a visiting poet, hundreds of people come. Something powerful happens when somebody is invited to imagine another person's life as real. I have had kids—gay kids, straight kids—say, 'It's made such a difference to me. I saw other possibilities. I felt affirmed. This really opened my eyes. I didn't know I could like a gay person.'"

I remind Doty of a question he asked in *Still Life with Oysters and Lemon*. In thinking about how the "I" of a painter ultimately becomes an "eye," he wonders, "What is left of Adriaen Coorte but this?" I turn the question to him: What does he hope will be left of himself?

"A voice. The voice will stick around. If I've worked hard enough or been lucky, that voice will be recognizable. A voice whispering in people's ear."

Zoe Dunning

According to a 2004 Urban Institute report, there are sixty-five thousand gays and lesbians serving today in the armed forces. Most, if not all, compromise their integrity daily in order to serve their country. Those who have taken the brave step of acknowledging their homosexuality—servicemen and women like Joe Stefan, Keith Meinhold, and Margarethe Cammermeyer—have had to endure disciplinary action, court hearings, expulsions, and the dishonor of discrimination.

"That's why I fight like hell," Zoe Dunning tells me the morning of our visit at her home in suburban San Francisco. She's wearing a T-shirt emblazoned in bold red-white-and-blue letters that say, "End Don't Ask, Don't Tell." Dunning served as an openly out lesbian in the Naval Reserve from 1993, when she publicly came out, until her retirement in June 2007. She remains the only gay person since the controversial Clinton compromise policy to be retained through military process, a two-year ordeal that put her in front of a military board of inquiry.

"Other ex-servicemen and women have come up to me and said with a lot of pain in their heart, 'How come you got to stay? I was a good soldier, sailor, marine, airman, too.' I've heard over the years thousands and thousands of heartbreaking stories about kids losing their career, losing their family, being investigated, threatened, harassed, discharged. It's not American. It's not why I signed up to serve my country. I signed up for the values it stands for—democracy, freedom, integrity, service—and not what I see in this policy."

Those values were at the heart of Dunning's upbringing. Born in Milwaukee, she grew up in a modest middle-class family, the youngest of seven children. Both of her parents served in the military during World War II. The "Midwest ethic," as she puts it—working hard, playing fair, making a contribution, minding one's own business—is one she closely identifies with. "My parents basically said I could do whatever I wanted to do. I wasn't limited by gender."

As a youngster, Dunning was "sort of a tomboy": the first girl in her neighborhood to have a paper route, the first to play trumpet in her school band, the first to take industrial arts instead of home economics. In high school, she played three varsity sports and served on the student council. A self-described math and science nerd, she says she was asexual. "I didn't know there were gay women, and I wasn't interested in dating boys."

In 1980, Dunning was selected to attend Girls State, the summer civics program sponsored by the American Legion, where she met a woman who had just finished her first year at West Point. Coincidentally, when she got home after the weeklong gathering, there was an invitation from the Naval Academy inviting her to apply. With family resources scarce, Dunning saw it as an opportunity to get an excellent, well-rounded education—sports, academics, leadership training—all paid for by the government.

"When I filled out the paperwork, one of the questions was, 'Do you have any homosexual tendencies?' I could honestly say *no*."

She arrived in Annapolis never having seen the place. "Everyone lives in the same dorm—all forty-four hundred students. There was no privacy. Everyone knew everyone else's business. You weren't allowed to lock your door. Anyone could walk in on you at any time; anyone could inspect your room, go through your mail. It's a very controlled environment."

It wasn't until her freshman year that Dunning started to find out about lesbians. She noticed that some of her basketball teammates seemed "awfully fond of each other." One girl trusted her enough to come out to her. That, in turn, opened Dunning's eyes to the witch hunts and investigations that were a routine part of Naval Academy life. She says the gay students were "petrified."

"There was so much at stake: a six-figure college education. You can't just come home early from this thing that you've dreamt about your whole life and say, 'Well, I quit.'"

Dunning herself had lesbian relationships during her years at the Naval Academy. "It scared the hell out of me. I dated men as a cover." When she graduated in 1985, she chose to serve in the Navy Supply Corps because she thought it would give her skills applicable in the outside world. She intended to stay in the navy only for her minimum five-year obligation, always maintaining a low profile. The strategy worked fine until, with two years left to serve, she was told she was being assigned to Naval Security. For that she would need a top-secret clearance.

"My jaw hit the floor. When they do a clearance, they talk to every neighbor, relative, coworker, friend, enemy. My experience of military investigators is that they take innuendo and report it as fact and try to get you to confess."

Sure enough, the investigators confronted her with allegations of homosexuality, though they wouldn't say upon what evidence. Dunning refused a polygraph test. Her clearance kept getting delayed. Finally, after a year on the job, she got the clearance. Under the Freedom of Information Act, she requested a copy of the investigation file. "Turns out the evidence they were using against me was, like, 'She seemed awfully tight with this girl' or 'She wore tailored shirts and baggy pants.'"

A year later, Dunning's military obligation was over. She had applied to and been accepted at a number of business schools. She chose Stanford. To defray the cost, she decided to remain in the military, this time, the Navy Reserve, a commitment of one weekend a month and two weeks per year. This arrangement, too, went along without a hitch until January 16, 1993, when Dunning appeared at a rally in support of Keith Meinhold, a sailor who had been kicked out of the navy for revealing that he was gay.

Originally, Dunning had intended merely to watch from the sidelines, but a few days before the rally, one of the organizers asked her to speak at the event. At first, knowing how risky that would be, she declined. "But over the next forty-eight hours that request kept spinning around in my head. I started composing a speech. If I could speak, what would I say? The policy was being fought by everyone but those directly affected. It frustrated me. And the issue was very focused on gay men. I wanted to bring attention on gay women, who were also serving very honorably. I called back and said I would like to speak. After all, I was a Naval Academy graduate with a flawless record. I had a Stanford MBA. I thought, If this doesn't demonstrate the ridiculousness of the policy, then I don't know what else will. So I spoke. I said, 'I am both a naval officer and a lesbian.' I was definitely nervous and scared."

The rally, which took place outside the front gates of Moffett Naval Air Station, was sparsely attended and covered only by the local media. There was a brief mention of it on the evening news. Dunning figured one of two things would happen: either she would get kicked out immediately or no one in the military would take any notice. Her biggest hope was that by identifying herself, she had brought some visibility to the issue to help encourage President-Elect Clinton (he would be inaugurated four days later) to push through his promised new policy with regard to gays in the military. The next weekend, when she reported for her monthly duty, Dunning was notified that she was being processed for administrative separation and was no longer welcome.

"I distinctly remember that day. It was a Saturday morning. I was wearing my certified navy khakis. I had no idea where to go or what to do. I remembered that NGLTF was having an organizing meeting about the policy. I showed up in my uniform. 'I just got kicked out,' I told them. 'What can I do to help?'"

It was the beginning of Dunning's unceasing fight to end discrimination against gays and lesbians in the military. She began giving interviews and appearing at speaking engagements. In April 1993, she went to the March on Washington, where she lobbied Capitol Hill. Later that spring, she spoke at a gathering of over a thousand people at a dinner given by the Human Rights Campaign. Eventually, the law firm of Morrison and Foerster took on her case, providing $300,000 worth of pro bono representation.

At her first hearing in June 1993, the Military Board of Inquiry voted unanimously to discharge her, but because the president was expected to announce a new policy with regard to gays in the military, Dunning's lawyers argued successfully that she be allowed to continue serving until Clinton made his decision. While she was on her two-week tour of duty, Don't Ask, Don't Tell was announced. At a hastily called press conference—out of uniform—Dunning diplomatically said she was "disappointed" in the new ruling. "He was my commander in chief, so I couldn't publicly chide him, but I was pissed."

During the many weeks that it took to write the policy into law, Dunning continued to serve. Technically, she had been convicted under a policy that was now obsolete. She had to be retried under the new policy. Since she had declared at the Meinhold rally that she was a lesbian, the prosecution's presumption was that she engaged in homosexual conduct. The challenge for Dunning's defense team was to rebut that presumption—in effect, to present "evidence" that she did not engage in homosexual conduct. Dunning and her lawyers argued that the statement she made at the rally was meant to create a presumption not of conduct but only of "status."

"There are some who said I took the stand and lied and said I was celibate. I didn't do that. I wasn't untrue to myself."

To most people's surprise, the status-not-conduct defense succeeded. The Military Board of Inquiry exonerated her, but immediately after the trial the navy declared that such a defense would never work again.

"When I won, I was absolutely shocked and somewhat disappointed because now I wouldn't have standing to go to federal court to challenge the policy. I lost the war in the sense that I couldn't go to federal court. But I'm proud of the fact that I came out on my own initiative. I did it out of a strong sense of integrity and justice."

After the trial, Dunning had to choose whether she would "continue to serve in an institution that didn't want me or to get out. I didn't need to continue. I'd gotten my MBA; I was making a reasonable amount of money. But all the arguments to prohibit gays from serving in the military said that the mere presence of homosexuals in a unit would ruin morale. I wanted to prove that that was not true." She decided to stay in. For the next twelve years—and with little harassment from others—she put her head down and did her job. She was promoted twice.

"I was really, really careful at first, and then later my attitude was 'I dare you.' I wasn't going to do anything stupid, but if my whole purpose for coming out was to live an authentic and intentional life and not to have to hide anymore, then I didn't want to live with those constraints."

In June 2007, after a total of twenty-two years serving her country, Dunning retired from the navy. With her partner, Pam Grey, accompanying her in the traditional "piping over the side" ceremony, she walked down a red carpet into civilian life, breathing "a huge sigh of relief."

In retrospect, what does she think of the Don't Ask, Don't Tell policy?

"In some ways the policy turned out to be worse than it was before. It does create a zone of privacy: if you just keep your business to yourself, then you're fine. But what people don't realize is that you can't tell *anyone*; otherwise it's considered a violation. In theory and on paper it looked like it gave you greater protection, but in reality it resulted in far more discharges. It institutionalized the closet. And it also took the policy and made it into a congressional law—it codified it—so the president couldn't just come in and sign an executive order anymore."

Dunning serves as vice president of USNA Out, a national organization of LGBTQ Naval Academy graduates, and on the board of Servicemembers Legal Defense Network, a watchdog and policy organization dedicated to ending discrimination against military personnel affected by Don't Ask, Don't Tell.

"The thing I'm the most proud of is that I haven't given up. I'm not going to stop until gays can serve openly without restriction. I do a lot of public speaking. I testify before any government organization that will listen to me. I've contributed thousands of hours and thousands of dollars to SLDN to pursue that mission. In every interaction I have, I try to spread the word to inspire and motivate folks to become more active in the issue. It comes down to this: if the government says gays can't serve in the military, how are we going to get any other rights out of our government? It's a basic litmus test for a country's willingness to accept gays fully for who we are and what we can contribute.

"The polls show society being more accepting of gays serving in the military. It's just a matter of getting the government to reflect the constituency. What we do now is lay the groundwork. We talk to and educate anyone who can have influence. Every NATO country but the United States and Turkey allows gays in the military. We can learn a lot from the British experience. They've had no problems, no issues. In fact, the British military now recruits at gay pride parades."

Does she take pride in having been a part of the military?

"Absolutely. Tremendous pride. It is a major part of my identity. I would like my legacy to be that I did all that I could to overturn the policy—to right what I thought was a wrong—and allow gays and lesbians to serve without fear. Every person you talk to about their experience of having to live under this policy says it has eaten away at their soul. They have a feeling of being 'less than.' Everything I believe about integrity and honesty is violated by this policy. The policy is not congruent with what the military espouses. I'm trying to protect the military from itself."

Dunning's civilian career continues those themes of authenticity and integrity in leadership. She runs her own consulting firm, which focuses on leadership development for small and medium-size businesses. "We look at how you create change without defensiveness."

One of her favorite consulting projects is at the Citadel, the Military College of South Carolina. "I spend a week every year working with their student leadership and residential assistants. We teach them about leadership development, emotional intelligence, active listening skills, counseling skills. It's so rewarding for me and at the same time so bizarre. It's like going back in time. They are literally twenty years behind the service academies in terms of integrating women. I feel really good and powerful about being able to challenge the men and be a voice for the women who can't speak up for themselves."

A few years ago, after she delivered the keynote address at the annual Reaching Out Gay MBA conference in Chicago, someone asked Dunning, "Do I go out and prove myself and make myself indispensable and then come out? Or do I come out immediately and find out what happens?" I ask her what her answer is to that question.

"For me personally, my checkpoint is, What would a straight person do? If, for instance, someone asked me a question, Are you married? Well, I could be factual and say no. Or I could not answer. Or I could say, 'No, because the law won't allow me to be!' There are twenty different options to answer that question. What I say is pretty much what a straight person might say: 'I'm in a committed relationship with my partner, Pam.' That's my touchstone to try to stay authentic. My passion, what drives me, is to influence the next generation of leaders. Authenticity, intentionality, integrity—if those are your guiding principles, then everything else falls into place."

Joe Eck
and
Wayne Winterrowd

I have been invited to spend the day at North Hill, the Vermont hillside on which Wayne Winterrowd and Joe Eck have, for over thirty years, tended a seven-acre garden, deemed one of the best in North America. A "vinous lunch" has been promised, then a tour, followed by our interview and dinner. The preliminary correspondence to arrange all this has been friendly, gracious, courteous. "Let us know approximately what time you will arrive, and we will have the upper gate open for you." But for the fact that the instructions come via e-mail, this could well be a sentence out of Jane Austen.

When I pull up, the two men, both in their sixties, are in a bit of a flutter. The bull has disappeared, so off we trek through forestland (in toto, North Hill comprises twenty-five acres) to the fenced-in pasture. Scots Highland cows look up, eyeing us suspiciously before returning to graze on the rocky terrain. The bull? Eck guesses that it can't have wandered too far. He suggests we tour the garden.

It's mid-July. A jaw-dropping profusion of varieties, colors, shapes, aromas, and textures greets me as we wander through each "room," horticultural lingo for an area of a garden designed to achieve a particular effect. When I exclaim that *everything* seems to be at its height of perfection, I'm politely corrected. There are about eight thousand species of plants at North Hill. I've already missed the spring and early summer delights—snowdrops and hellebores, the daffodil meadow, magnolias, lilacs, primroses, and the rare, "fabled" Himalayan blue poppy. And I must return in the fall for still more delights. All my research for this visit has not prepared me for the dizzying splendor of the real thing.

Eck and Winterrowd's books, written together or individually, have been described as "inspiring," "a gold mine of practical advice," full of "seductive beauties." "Funny, affectionate, wise and snobbish exactly when you want them to be," wrote Dominique Browning in her *New York Times* review of their most recent one, *Our Life in Gardens.*

"The point we would make about gardens," Winterrowd says as we head back to the house for lunch (homemade pizza laden with leeks, scallions, and black olives), "is that they're just like life. We can't talk about a garden without talking about life." We eat in the kitchen, which is dominated by an open-hearth fireplace and a Jacobean cupboard. Afterward, they invite me into the living room. Like the rest of the place, it speaks of a life richly, deliberately, and unabashedly led.

"Gay sensibility is not so very different from that of all the sensitive people I know," says Winterrowd, whose rakish head of blond hair, now tending toward gray, suggests he was once a young man of considerable visual appeal. "The real divide is not between gay and straight but between people who see their lives as a work of art and those who see it as merely a means to a great fortune."

Eck (shorter, shaved head, piercing blue eyes) politely suggests to his partner that there might indeed be something to the idea of gay sensibility. "One thing about being gay is the degree to which, because of the more exploratory and frequent nature of gay men's sexual experiences, we enter a great many lives that wouldn't normally be accessible to us. We all have the experience of loving people who differ from us in terms of class, race, language. And that is . . ."

Winterrowd comes on board: "The point is, you're open to the experience of so many people out of the desire to belong, to work your way in. As gay people we learn to value, love, eroticize, embrace an enormous range of humanity, and out of that grows a kind of cosmopolitanism that allows us to be comfortable with so many different kinds of men."

The afternoon will go on in this way, with stories corrected, embellished, continued by one or the other.

As young boys, Winterrowd and Eck, both lonely children, found safety and security in the world of plants. "The impulse to create a safe, harmonious, tranquil world is born of some kind of pain," says Winterrowd, who grew up in Shreveport, Louisiana, and still retains the soft, lilting cadences of the Deep South. By the age of three, he was puttering around the family garden. His interest in cooking arose shortly thereafter, inspired by "two amazing black women who let me experiment in the kitchen." He quotes the great gardener J. C. Raulston—the first of many literary allusions over the course of the day—to the effect that he began to grow plants as a child because "they wouldn't hurt him."

Eck, who hails from suburban Philadelphia, also sought solace in gardening and in reading and music, which were, he says, "a profound refuge for me." He would disappear into his room with "whole bunches" of records and listen for days. After high school, he entered a monastery, a decision he calls "largely aesthetic. Every shopping mall made me cringe. I wanted to get as far away from that as I could. The monastic life was so beautiful and elegant and deliberate." Within a month, he had fallen deeply in love—"one of the great love affairs of my life"—a situation that allowed him to claim his sexuality and, eventually, to leave the religious life.

"I wonder," he says, "if there isn't some connection between the pursuit of an aesthetic ideal and the renunciation of religious faith. Wayne and I bring to gardening, but also to all our domestic arrangements, a religious fervor. The almost sacramental rituals of domestic life are enormously sacred to us."

The two met in 1969 at a gay bar in Boston, where Winterrowd had moved after graduate school in order to take a teaching position at Tufts University. "Sporters," Winterrowd recalls, "the place you went if you were brainy." Eck, who by then had quit "trying to be straight," was in Boston studying at Northeastern University.

"I am nothing if not determined," Eck says. "I decided I was going to have a boyfriend. I went home with a different person every night. That started in September. On February 28, I met Wayne."

Winterrowd fleshes out the story: "I had just ended a disastrous love affair with a trucker who looked like the young Marlon Brando. Joe grabbed me by the sleeve and asked if I would have a cup of coffee with him. We walked around the Common again and again."

"It was very beautiful," Eck adds. "It had snowed the day before. We just talked." Until the subways closed. At which point,

Winterrowd spent the night at Eck's apartment on Beacon Hill. "Top floor, with a beautiful view of the State House dome," he reminisces. "Joe had the crappiest furniture. In the morning, I said, 'All this stuff is going out on the street.' That committed us, I guess. And then we went shopping." They spent the next two months painting and decorating.

"People bond on all kinds of levels," Eck observes. "Sex, or because they can talk, or common interests. Our common interests were all over the map: we both read; we loved music and poetry."

The initial romance lasted about four months. Then the two separated, though Eck kept showing up at Winterrowd's apartment.

"It was a shabby time in my life," Winterrowd explains, "a time when I felt I could be anything, have anyone. I wasn't sure I wanted to put a lid on any of that. I'm glad I did. A lot of folly and heartbreak and loneliness and empty old age would have resulted if I had pursued what, at that time, I thought I wanted. Eventually, I woke up one morning and said, 'OK, I give up.' I wanted to make a life with someone. Joe stuck around long enough to make me feel it would work with him. And it has."

They rented "the most impossibly elegant apartment you could imagine," one with parquet floors and marble fireplaces, overlooking the Boston Public Garden. And there, in a room that had been a ballroom, the two men began their other agrarian passion: raising animals. "We collected chickens—rare, ornamental bantams." Plus pheasants, quails, and a pig, which they kept in the bathtub. "When we moved," Eck says, "we had thirty-nine animals."

The couple next rented an eighteenth-century farmhouse in Pepperell, Massachusetts. Within a month they had 250 animals. And a garden, their first together. "We entertained a lot," Winterrowd says, adding that the house came with "five fireplaces and a great cook oven." They stayed two years, after which Winterrowd got a Fulbright to teach in Copenhagen. They did not take to Denmark. "It was the middle of the Vietnam War. We were both angry with our country. In Germany, all the boys we knew were articulate, left-leaning types who wanted to sit up until dawn talking. We didn't have that in Denmark."

Back in the United States, they spent a year in Boston casting about for where they would put down roots. A piece of south-facing property outside of Readsboro, Vermont, won them over. Studying USDA temperature reports, they discovered the village was the

Joe Eck and Wayne Winterrowd

warmest place in the state—"a little heat pocket" in Zone 4. The fact that they could also be an openly gay couple teaching in the same school district was an additional attraction. In their book *A Year at North Hill*, they praise Vermont, "a state that, for political, ecological, and social wisdom, is bettered by none in our nation." The only potential rival for their affections has been San Francisco. But they acknowledge that there they would not have been able to live a rural life. "And," Winterrowd adds, "we probably wouldn't have been together. Too many seductions. We'd be dead."

At first they didn't intend to build, but the houses to buy were out of their price range. And once they saw the North Hill property, they found it irresistible: beautiful hardwoods, a stream, a meadow in the back. And so they built—"a small, modest cottage," Eck calls it, "all that we could afford, but pleasant."

The original intention was to create "Williamsburgy gardens," but they changed their minds after a trip to California, where they went to look for plants "and go to the bars in the Castro." One of the nurseries they visited was owned by Lester Hawkins and Marshall Olbrich, whose gardens had become "immensely influential and famous." The two couples hit it off so well that Eck and Winterrowd returned to Vermont with a station wagon full of plants given to them by the older nurserymen. That's when their garden began to get serious.

"We were making it up as we went along, under Marshall and Lester's guidance," Eck continues. "We'd come home after teaching school, change into blue jeans, and work until dark. In the predawn of the morning, we'd get up to prepare for our classes. I don't know when we slept."

Winterrowd interrupts. "I know the end of this story." He excuses himself to go to the kitchen to prepare supper.

"Our hands got so black with the dirt! We went to graduation with these black farmer's hands. That went on for years. Every single species and cultivar, without exception, we planted; every single stone we laid ourselves. A wonderful family from the village helped out."

Over the years, other structures appeared—a greenhouse, a pig house, a barn, poultry shelters, and, nestled in the woods, the guesthouse and outhouse for visitors. But it was the garden that consumed them. They were intent upon folding it into the land in a way that made it seem completely the work of nature. "What is of interest to us," Eck says, "is the degree to which a garden must feel inevitable."

They began to experiment with how far north certain species—he mentions magnolias and stewartias—could be cultivated. "We have an enormous number of things that people at the Arnold Arboretum told us we would never grow in Vermont." Global warming has helped. "Things that we had to protect twenty years ago—hollies that we would winter over in great wooden boxes—we don't do that anymore."

We move into the kitchen to join Winterrowd, who is rolling out the crust for tonight's dessert, rhubarb pie. Crimping the pie shell, he continues the story.

"After a few years, we began to publish articles. Our only models were scholarly things. In truth, they were very dull. The editors wrote back, saying they needed things that were more personal."

Eck picks up: "In horticultural writing, it's too easy to lapse into 'This pretty thing and this pretty thing.' There are only two ways to give intellectual content to garden writing. One is to focus on design. The other is to write about gardening as the locus of a life, which is what we have done. If the writing can talk about more than the plant, more than the garden—if it can talk about the process of living a life, the loves you've had, the places that matter to you, the people who have passed on, the passions you still have—those things can vivify the writing."

As their work became known, Winterrowd and Eck began attracting clients from all over, to the point where they were able to stop teaching and devote themselves full time to their gardening, writing, lecturing, and design workshops. Meanwhile, the garden kept growing. In 1995, their twentieth year in Vermont, the two men published their first coauthored book, *A Year at North Hill: Four Seasons in a Vermont Garden*. In that book, sumptuously illustrated with photographs by Eck, they wrote, "All gardens must be at once very serious and very playful, for they represent simultaneously a near approximation of the sublime and also the preservation of the child within."

Eck tells me a story to illustrate. "Two days ago, when we were resetting the perennial bed, we were tearing things out, cutting them down, fetching up trays of annuals from the stock yard behind the greenhouse. It was a marvelous day playing in the garden. We were completely joyful. But it's also very serious work. We can't move through the garden without attending to the litany of tasks in front of us—deadhead that rhododendron, stake up that hollyhock, weed that patch of poppy."

Other books followed: Eck's *Elements of Garden Design* (1996); another joint book, *Living Seasonally: The Kitchen Garden and the Table at North Hill* (1999); Winterrowd's *Roses, a Celebration* (2003); and his *Annuals and Tender Plants for North American Gardens* (2004). Winterrowd points out that all their books are "a very personal witness to the life we've lived here."

"We've been unashamed of our life, always," Eck says. When a reporter for the *New York Times* interviewed them for a piece she was writing, the two "insisted that it be made very clear that we are a gay couple. We think it's politically helpful." As soon as Vermont allowed civil unions between same-sex couples, Eck and Winterrowd had one, "because it would be good for the neighbors to read about that in the public record." That sense of social responsibility led them to host an annual garden party for the AIDS Project of Southern Vermont. In seventeen years, they raised over $175,000 for the agency.

North Hill is not just about flowers. "The original purpose of the land is nourishment," Winterrowd says, slipping the pie into the oven. "All the gardens we've ever designed, except one, include a vegetable garden. Gardening is no good unless it puts you deeply in touch with your most elemental experiences and roots."

By now it's six-thirty, and Winterrowd suggests another break. "We have animals to feed, and *you* have peas to pick if you want supper." Eck leads me to the vegetable garden. Half an hour later, our baskets full, we head back to the house, where the aromas of a savory stew permeate the kitchen.

Winterrowd's thoughts turn to their final years at North Hill. "How one sees one's life at the end of it and after it is over becomes a problem as we get older. People who have children can say, 'I am not here alone. There is something that will come after me.'" Eck finishes the thought: "It's important in the achievement of adulthood to live for a creature other than yourself. You can get awfully precious and self-cultivating if there is nothing but a pretty little house and a pretty little garden." Which brings them to tell me about their "adopted son," Fotios.

In 1992, at a party in New York, the two men met a nineteen-year-old European student who immediately won them over with his eagerness to learn all he could about the world of culture. They started inviting him to North Hill for weekends and introduced him to classical music, poetry, and gardening. "He gave us something that very few gay men get," Eck says, "the chance to give someone else a world."

As the relationship grew, Winterrowd and Eck became ever more involved in Fotios's life, helping to pay for his studies and engaging a lawyer to resolve his immigration status. Now in his thirties and a senior designer for a major fashion company, Fotios is their family. "When we introduce him to someone, we say, 'This is our son.'"

Because Fotios has taken little interest in the physical aspects of gardening, Eck and Winterrowd, who have willed their estate to him, hope that, upon inheriting it, he will quickly sell the property.

"Do you know Browning's 'A Toccata of Galuppi's'?" Winterrowd asks. "'Dust and ashes, dead and done with.' I guess that's how we see it." Eck explains: "A garden let go is a nightmare." They recount for me stories of other great gardens that were plowed under when the owner died. "We don't have the right to make that choice for Fotios, but we have lined our friends up to talk to him about why it should be so."

With the waning light and this talk of death, a somber spirit has descended. Eck picks up on it: "Like every thinking person, we are filled with dread and sadness as we contemplate what we, as a species, are doing to the place where we live. I think it's irreversible. We've spoiled our nest." He says he takes some comfort in contemplating the geologic evolution of the earth, "the rise and fall of physical features and species, and how the planet renews itself. That perspective so comforts and reassures us."

Winterrowd adds, "What is most important is to realize that the time we had here was really, really wonderful. It's had its arc. Right at the moment it's at its highest point. We're famous. We're healthy. That's enough. It's here, it's now. It's right now."

Lillian Faderman

When she was in the tenth grade, Lillian Faderman got a C, three Ds, and an F on her report card. Fifty-plus years later, this "overachiever," as she calls herself, enjoys a reputation as one of the premier scholars of gay and lesbian history, having published eight books and numerous articles on the subject. The array of awards she has won—the Stonewall Book Award, a Lambda Literary Award, Yale University's James Brudner Prize, the Bill Whitehead Award, the Monette-Horwitz Trust Award—attests to a life dedicated to the highest standards of scholarship.

The afternoon we meet, Faderman has just come in from a morning walk through the walnut orchards and lupine fields near her home in Fresno, California, a city she has lived and worked in for more than forty years. As we sit over a lunch of grilled cheese sandwiches and the biggest, most luscious dates I have ever eaten, she doles out carefully considered responses to each of my questions.

Faderman did not begin life with any foretokens of success. Born in 1940, she was raised in a cramped Bronx apartment by her unwed mother and her aunt, Jewish immigrants from Latvia. Her mother suffered from mental illness, a fact that "affected me profoundly as a kid. I had to parent her a lot. But there was no doubt that I was really loved by these two women."

In the spring of 1948, the three moved to Los Angeles, where Faderman, inspired by the movies, soon took up acting classes and began modeling. "In the movies I saw people who were successful and affluent and had a life that as a kid I would have considered exciting. I didn't quite get that the illegitimate kid of working-class immigrants wasn't supposed to see herself in those terms."

Faderman fell in love with the female director of her acting school. "I didn't see it as lesbian. I don't think I even knew that word. It was just so powerful, so overwhelming. I would go to the library and get these psychology books and find out that it wasn't abnormal to have a crush on someone of the same sex when you're a kid."

Faderman's education about homosexuality took a more worldly turn when a neighborhood friend, "a very pretty boy," offered to take her to gay bars. "He found a phony ID for me. And then he said, 'There are girls' bars like this, too. Do you want to go?' He took me to the Open Door in Los Angeles. It was absolutely amazing. Suddenly, I saw that this is what I wanted my life to be. Of course, now I look back on it and I'm horrified at the kind of place it was. But what I saw was that you could make your life with women. It made absolute sense to me."

Faderman says that fifty years ago, when she came out, life for lesbians was "underground" and "scary." She was always afraid of being busted, not only because she would have gotten into trouble herself but because it would have meant the end of the owners of the Open Door, "a little immigrant couple with Yiddish accents" who, having spotted her as Jewish, were kind to her. "The bar was my lifeline."

Through her acting classes, Faderman fell in with a gang of friends, all older, aspiring actors, with whom she would stay out late, talking and dreaming about being discovered by the big studios. She began to cut her high school classes. And she posed for the girlie magazines. Years later, she published some of those photos in her 2003 memoir, *Naked in the Promised Land*. Faderman chuckles, recalling the decision to include the nude shots in her book.

"I talked to the editors. We agreed that the story was so incredible that, if I didn't, people might not believe it. I was sorry I did it. It was so distracting for reviewers. That was the first thing they mentioned. Often the review would have a headline: 'Stripper Becomes Professor.' But there was no other way to write the memoir. It was a part of my life."

As her life began spinning out of control, Faderman started thinking of herself as a juvenile delinquent. She ended up in counseling with a man named Maurice Colwell (an "honorary Jew," she calls him), who convinced her to finish high school and go to college. "I can't imagine what would have happened to me if I hadn't met Maury. It was the summer I turned sixteen. He asked me, 'What do you like to do?' Well, what I liked to do was mess around with the women I met at the Open Door. But I knew that wasn't a good answer, so I said that I liked to read plays. He was so clever to immediately pick up on that and give me books that enchanted me. He was a very skillful social worker for a kid like me."

Colwell inspired Faderman to imagine a world of greater possibilities for herself. From the example of her mother's sorry plight, Faderman had already come to understand that "self-reliance was absolutely crucial" if she were to embrace a life beyond that of her adolescent fantasies. It was Colwell who gave her the formula to make all that happen: not only the practical tips, but also "how you could be a lesbian, rely on yourself, and be OK."

Before she had graduated from high school, Faderman married a gay man, a "lavender marriage," not at all unusual in those days, that lasted less than a year. "There were a lot of front marriages in the 1950s and earlier. I needed to get away from home. My mother would have been so upset if I had left to go to college. She could understand leaving to get married, but not for any other reason. And I was so impressed by Mark. He had a lot of savoir faire. He took me to concerts and plays. He had wonderful books. We genuinely liked each other, at least for a while."

In 1958, Faderman got into UCLA on a scholarship. Her student job at the university library paid so pathetically that she soon quit and returned to pin-up modeling on the weekends. One night at a bar she met a woman—called Sabina D'Or in her memoir—who became her lover. At the end of her freshman year, the two moved to San Francisco, and Faderman enrolled at Berkeley. To support the two of them—D'Or, an artist manqué with a compulsive disorder, couldn't hold a job—Faderman worked as a cocktail waitress and stripper at the Hotsy Totsy Club.

"I was hardly at Berkeley. I took my classes, then went to work as a waitress." She knew no other lesbians or gay men on campus. "I actually did run into one woman who was very butchy. She agreed with me that we must be the only two lesbians! I assumed all lesbian life was butch-femme life, that butches always had a huge struggle with the world and couldn't find a job. I thought that that was the only story there was."

On the Web site of the June Mazer Lesbian Archive, Faderman writes, "The lesbian world that I first came into, here in Los Angeles almost forty years ago, seemed to me to exist only in darkness. Our world seemed to have been invented in that moment of time. We had no past—or, if we did, no one knew or could tell me about it. Because we had no knowledge of those who came before us, our isolation and loneliness felt tragic and inevitable."

Does she think that experience of having "no past" propelled her into a career as an historian?

"Oh, absolutely. What I most wanted to do when I started doing lesbian history was to show young lesbians that, yes, we do have a past and it's a really nice past. It's not at all what the sexologists and psychiatrists were writing about. I would have loved books like I write to have been published when I was a teenager. It would have made such a difference to me."

Faderman graduated from Berkeley in 1962. She had been accepted into the graduate English program at UCLA, but countless voices were telling her she couldn't do it: *Strippers don't get Ph.D.'s*, she told herself. Her aunt admonished her, "Why do you want more school? The head uses up the blood you need to have babies."

Despite the odds against her, Faderman persisted. Five years later, in the spring of 1967, she finished her doctoral dissertation and passed her defense. Still, she wondered whether being a stripper was a better, more lucrative way to make a living than taking a mediocre academic position, which was all that seemed available to a female Ph.D. With the support of her then lover, Barbara Bradshaw ("Binky" in the memoir), Faderman took a position at Fresno State College, the only woman in the department. In 1969, she and Bradshaw published *Speaking for Ourselves: American Ethnic Writing*, one of the first multiethnic college texts. A second anthology, *From the Barrio* (1973), a collection of Chicano writing that Faderman compiled with Luis Omar Salinas, followed.

"All my work has been about being Other, whether ethnically or sexually different from the majority. It's not surprising that I did multiethnic studies in the sixties. I would have loved to do gay stuff, but it wasn't an option. As soon as I felt it was an option, by the mid-seventies, that's where most of my energy went."

Faderman published her first lesbian article, a reconsideration of Radclyffe Hall's *The Well of Loneliness*, in 1976. "Suddenly I came alive with this stuff." In the space of two years, she published several more articles based on her research into lesbian history. "I thought, Nobody here is going to read those things, and they didn't." By then she had broken up with Bradshaw, met her current lover, Phyllis (they've been together over thirty years), and had a baby. "I was the first lesbian to do donor insemination. I understood from my personal life that there was no reason why I couldn't."

After a sabbatical in the midseventies, Faderman wrote a paper on early-twentieth-century lesbian magazine fiction, subsequently published in the *Journal of Pop Culture*. She delivered the results of her research in a public lecture at Fresno. "I was very nervous about it. There weren't many women in the department even then. All the guys were there. I didn't know what they would think." In fact, the reception was surprisingly supportive. "The guy I was most worried about said, 'That's exactly the kind of scholarship we should be doing.' He didn't mean gay scholarship; he meant serious scholarship."

Nevertheless, she was concerned that what would pass muster in an academic journal might elicit hostility if published in a full-length book. That book, *Surpassing the Love of Men: Romantic Friendship and Love between Women from the Renaissance to the Present* (1981), was a groundbreaking piece of scholarship. No one had written this kind of thorough and meticulously researched lesbian history before. The critical reception was glowing. Not only was there a "huge, wonderful review" in the *Atlantic Monthly*, but her department nominated her for the university's Outstanding Professor Award. The city of Fresno got into the act as well, declaring May 1, 1981, Lillian Faderman Day. "I don't think the mayor had any idea what the book was about!"

Faderman's best-known book is *Odd Girls and Twilight Lovers: A History of Lesbian Life in Twentieth-Century America* (1991), the definitive study of lesbians from the "romantic friendships" at the end of the nineteenth century through the sex wars of the 1980s. Remarkable in many ways, Faderman's research relied not only on published documents but also on scores of interviews with lesbians across the country. "I used the snowball technique: you find one person in one area, and you ask them to introduce you to others."

Greenwich Village, the book reveals, was one of the first places in the United States where a lesbian subculture emerged. "It was long an artists' place," Faderman tells me. "Morality was looser. If you wanted to live a gay life, that was the place to go. Some of those artists had experiences in places like France, where things were certainly much more open, and they brought that influence to Greenwich Village."

Faderman's book came out in the wake of the lesbian-feminist revolution of the 1970s, which criticized gay men's ignorance of the deeper political issues surrounding male power. However, Faderman says that it wasn't her purpose to be polemical. "I wanted to record a history of lesbian life and not to take a single position. I've never been taken up by political correctness or any extreme political position, ever. There were things I loved about lesbian feminism, but I was always troubled by its lack of subtlety, its inability to examine the human psyche. What they wanted was so ideal, so perfect in conception, they never lived it. It was never like that in reality."

Faderman's pride and delight in Los Angeles, her teenage home, comes through in what she says may be her last gay-themed book, *Gay L.A.: A History of Sexual Outlaws, Power Politics, and Lipstick Lesbians* (2006). Coauthored with Stuart Timmons, the book reveals that, historically, "more lesbian and gay institutions started in Los Angeles than anywhere else on the planet."

"Everyone would have guessed New York or San Francisco. But it's not true! The very idea of a gay center—and the one in L.A. is huge now—goes back to the late 1960s. The first gay organization in the United States started in L.A. Maybe it's because there was such a possibility of anonymity in Los Angeles." While gay men and lesbians often moved in separate circles, Faderman and Timmons opted to deal with them in a single book. "Historically, gay men and lesbians saw themselves as very much alike. They had the same enemies; they suffered from the same kind of discrimination. I wanted to treat them in one book because I thought that that was historically accurate."

Faderman acknowledges that the "generational differences" between her and Timmons—he's seventeen years younger than she—presented challenges. "My tendency is to look at where things were when I came out in the 1950s and where things are now. I can't believe how fabulous things are now! Stuart thinks everything is crummy. I wanted to say, 'Yes, but.'"

As she considers her career, Faderman says she is "proud to have produced the kind of work that I would have wanted to see. I did what I really think I needed to do. I've been so blessed to go from a time when it was really scary to be a lesbian to a time when I can be open and write what I want to write. That's been delicious. It's such a legacy for us to be collectively proud of."

Barney Frank

One day, back in the late sixties, when Barney Frank, fresh from a stint at the John F. Kennedy School of Government, was working as an assistant to Boston mayor Kevin White, a man came into the office complaining about police brutality at a gay club called the Punch Bowl. Frank, whose job it was to act as the mayor's liaison with the police, told the fellow to come back with a few of the others who had witnessed the alleged incident. "I figured it was a twofer," Frank recounts on the afternoon I meet him in his district office in Newton, Massachusetts. "I'd be able to do my job *and* meet some other gay men. He never came back."

Some forty years later, and now a congressman from Massachusetts and chairman of the House Financial Services Committee, Frank has no problem meeting other gay men. They come flocking to see him. As one of the very few openly gay members of Congress, Frank has been an intrepid fighter for gay and lesbian rights. He filed his first gay rights bill almost forty years ago, in 1972, when he was a maverick legislator in the Massachusetts House of Representatives and a closeted gay man.

"I remember the first time I testified on behalf of gay rights legislation. I was terrified that they would ask me if I was gay." In the years since then, Frank has witnessed the emergence of what he calls

"one of the most important movements in the history of the world."
Moreover, he promises, "in the next twenty, thirty years, you're going
to see fully legal and social equality for gay men and lesbians in this
country. But it's going to be a fight." A fight, one among many, that
the feisty, brainy Frank is only too willing to take up.

As he stated at the outset of his 1992 book, *Speaking Frankly*, Barney Frank is in the business of "trying to translate progressive ideas
into actual public policy." Representing the Massachusetts Fourth
Congressional District, the liberal core of a liberal state, Frank has,
since his election to Congress in 1980, achieved a dazzling reputation
for intelligence, honesty, wit, and pugnacity. He also has an indefatigable commitment to getting things done. "He decided the way to
be most effective was being a powerful insider," David Mixner once
wrote. "In many ways he was right."

Frank's lifelong embrace of progressive issues, his unwavering
faith that there will always be broad public support for those causes
"when they are properly understood" by American voters, and his
consummate talent for articulating his views fairly, clearly, and force-
fully have made him one of the most effective Democratic leaders in
the House. Fellow congressman Ed Markey has called him "the
smartest and funniest member of Congress." With a "nuclear power
plant for a brain" (Markey again), Frank is considered the best floor
debater in the House today and, according to *The Almanac of American Politics*, "one of the best of all time."

Nobody is neutral about Barney Frank. His constituency has
consistently reelected him by wide margins. Writing in the *New Re-
public*, political commentator Morton Kondracke once noted that
Frank was "an almost universally acknowledged legislative superstar,
and a national treasure, who ought to be preserved." He has been
called "political theorist and pit bull all at the same time" (*The Almanac of American Politics*); "an equal opportunity curmudgeon" (CBS
correspondent Leslie Stahl); "saber tooth" (George W. Bush). Nevertheless, many of Frank's opponents tip their hat to him. "He over-
whelms you with rapid rhetoric," Rep. Henry Hyde, a Republican
from Illinois, once said, "but there is usually substance behind it.
He's a fearsome adversary."

The man whom *Out* magazine named to the "number one spot"
in its third annual "Power 50" list, Frank tells me the time has come
for major advances in gay rights: a hate crimes bill, an end to employment discrimination (including discrimination against transgender

people), and the repeal of "Don't Ask, Don't Tell." "Those of us," he wrote toward the end of *Speaking Frankly*, "who believe that America is good and just but capable of being better and fairer have a decided political advantage over those who view our society as a mean and selfish one in need of radical surgery."

Frank grew up in Hudson County, New Jersey, "a very corrupt political machine in those days—Mafia, corrupt longshoreman's union, corrupt teamsters." From an early age, he was fascinated by politics. At ten, he was glued to the family's first television set, watching the Kefauver hearings on the Mafia and the 1952 presidential campaign. "By 1954, I found myself drawn into politics." Frank also began reading the *New York Post*, "a very good newspaper with a lot of good liberal reporting." He remembers being especially riveted by the murder of Emmett Till, a black teenager from Mississippi. "He was my age, fourteen. I was so outraged by this."

Frank did his undergraduate work at Harvard. Of those years, he says that "the notion of ever having any kind of active gay life . . . well, I didn't even meet anyone who was gay. My freshman year, there was a guy to whom I was attracted who was coming on to me. At the time I thought he was probing. I recoiled. Not in a negative way. I just shut down." Frank tried dating women. "Agonizing times. It became clear to me that I had no sexual attraction to women."

By his senior year, with his growing passion for politics but well aware of his homosexuality, Frank assumed he would "probably need some shelter." He decided he would go to graduate school in political science, get a Ph.D., and enter academia. "The best way to do politics would be to teach about it, write about it." After a stint as assistant to the director of the Institute for Politics at the JFK School, Frank went to work for Kevin White, Boston's new mayor.

"White was a very modern guy. He embraced the sixties. We boycotted grapes for Cesar Chavez. He put women and blacks in power. He was one of the first to break out of his mold to embrace environmentalism, women's rights."

During the three years that Frank was with White, he remained "very closeted, very eager to meet people, physically and emotionally, and having a very hard time doing it." It was in the middle of his tenure as the mayor's assistant that the Stonewall riots occurred, an event that Frank says marks "the clear dividing line." Nevertheless, when he left White's office at the end of 1970 to go to Washington to work for Congressman Michael Harrington, he says "there was no gay political activity going on."

Returning to Boston in 1972, Frank ran for the Massachusetts House as a candidate from Boston's Back Bay and Beacon Hill neighborhoods. He won. "I was thirty-two. The fact that I was unmarried was not a big deal. The neighborhoods were sophisticated." Frank resolved that, though he would not come out, he would be "a complete advocate for gay and lesbian rights," even though in those days he often encountered an "ick factor" when he talked about gay rights.

In 1974, Elaine Noble, an openly lesbian activist, ran for a seat in the Massachusetts House and won, the first openly LGBTQ person in the country to be elected to a state-level office. Though Frank was still closeted, Noble's election "delighted" him. Over the next few years, it became increasingly clear that the model for his life that he had in mind—"not much of a private life but a really good public life, which will substitute for it"—was not going to work.

"People have said it's the worst idea I've ever had. Not only does public life not compensate for a repressed love life, but the repression in your public life poisons your private life." Entering Harvard Law School in 1974, he formulated a new model: set politics aside, come out, and become a lawyer, one who, having had some experience in elected office, might be an effective advocate for gay people. By 1978, a year after earning his J.D., he started selectively coming out. Frank assumed he'd only serve for a couple of terms in the Massachusetts House and then settle into legal work. Things didn't quite work out that way.

In 1980, Pope John Paul II ordered priests and nuns to quit any political offices they held. This included Congressman Robert Drinan, a Jesuit, who was serving in the House of Representatives from the Massachusetts Fourth Congressional District. Both Frank and Noble aspired to fill the vacancy. "That was anguishing to me. My first impulse was not to run. She was out; I wasn't." When word got out that Frank was going to cede to Noble, he was invited to a meeting by some of the lesbian political leadership in Massachusetts. "They said, 'What is this crap about you not running? You've got to run. It's not a case of who's out and who's not. It's a case of who will do better for the community. You're the better legislator.'"

Frank ran—he also had the endorsement of Drinan's office—and won. (Noble ended up running for the U.S. Senate, which she lost.)

Two years later, redistricting pitted him against Republican congresswoman Margaret Heckler, a sixteen-year veteran of the House. Frank fought a hard campaign and won again. He has retained his seat ever since.

During Frank's early years in the House, the attitude he encountered from many of his colleagues when he tried to lobby them to support gay rights was, as he wrote in 1992, "the attitude of most straight people toward homosexuality . . . a mixture of active dislike, contempt, and fear." During his first term, he fought against two congressional measures that directly assaulted gay rights: an amendment to bar gay men and lesbians from the Legal Services Program and a resolution to repeal the D.C. sodomy statutes. His efforts failed.

By the mideighties, Frank was planning to publicly come out but held back when his fellow Massachusetts congressman Gerry Studds became embroiled in a scandal after revelations that he had had a sexual relationship with a male congressional page. When Studds was censured, Frank decided, "We had enough to deal with." Finally, in 1986 he told Tip O'Neill, the Speaker of the House, that he was thinking of coming out. "Tip said, 'Oh, Barney, I'm so sorry. I thought you were going to be the first Jewish Speaker,' meaning that as an out gay man I couldn't become Speaker. I could have told him that there had already been two gay Speakers: Joe Martin and Sam Rayburn."

Friends cautioned Frank about the political costs of revealing his homosexuality. "Some of the most liberal people in the world advised me not to come out: 'You're our ally on military spending, housing, civil liberties. If you come out, the only thing you're going to be is the gay rights guy. We don't want to lose you as an ally.' I said to them, 'I can't tell you that's not going to happen, but I'm going crazy. I can't live this way.' Yes, I realized there would be some political benefit to gay people if I came out, but I was also doing it because I couldn't live any other way."

It was already well known by editors at the *Boston Globe* that Frank was gay, but the paper's policy was not to out people without their say-so. "They wanted to write the story, but they didn't want to be accused of being interested in my sexuality. I, too, wanted them to write the story, but here's the problem: I wanted to be able to say, 'Yes, I'm gay but it's no big deal.' I said to the press, 'Look, I'm not going to volunteer it, but if you ask me, I'll tell you.' I didn't want to volunteer it because people would say, 'Why did you volunteer it if it's no big deal?'"

Back and forth went the conversations until the *Globe*, worried that somebody else would scoop the story, finally assigned the interview to Kay Longcope, regarded as the *Globe's* first openly gay reporter. In May 1987, Longcope asked him outright, "Are you gay?" and Frank said, "Yeah, so what?"

Ever since then, Frank has stressed the importance of coming out as a tool for combating ignorance and bigotry. "Had it not been for the mass movement out of the closet," he wrote in the foreword to the third edition of Betty Berzon's anthology *Positively Gay*, "and towards honesty on the part of millions of us, we would have made no political progress at all."

Frank faced the most painful personal crisis of his life when in 1989 Steve Gobie, a hustler he had once hired, revealed his relationship with Frank. Gobie alleged that Frank, in addition to paying him for sex, had taken him on as an aide, written letters to Gobie's probation officials on congressional stationery, and knew about a prostitution service that Gobie was running out of Frank's apartment. Frank denied knowing anything about the prostitution ring.

"He kind of conned me," Frank tells me. "I was frustrated, lonely. When he went back on cocaine and started being a jerk, I fired him. That made him very angry. He said, 'I'll get even with you.' The normal thing for him to do would have been to out me, but by this time I was out, so he made up a whole bunch of stories. Yes, I paid him for sex, but everything else was a lie. It took me a year to prove that."

On July 27, 1990, after a rancorous four-hour debate, the House voted 408 to 18 to reprimand Frank for ethical breaches. Frank apologized to his colleagues. "There was in my life a central element of dishonesty for about forty years, no, thirty-four. And it had to do with my privacy and my private life."

In reflecting on the scandal, Frank tells me, "The fact that I had been out for a while helped. I was tired of making stupid choices and not being strong enough to admit who I was. People said to me, 'It's good you came out, because now you're better at your job. You're not as angry.' I see this in closeted politicians: there is a mean streak, a nasty streak in them, because you need an outlet. It wells up, and it poisons you." Frank says he was surprised by his constituency's total absence of negativism following his coming out and the later reprimand. "I should have come out earlier."

As an openly gay politician, what kinds of responsibilities does Frank feel? "I'm in a position to confront stereotypes. And I make a point of it." As an example, he mentions a recent Democratic caucus over a proposed hate crimes bill. At the meeting, some black clergy expressed concern that, if passed, the bill would make it a crime for any opinions about homosexuality to be delivered from the pulpit. "I said, 'No, the bill only increases the penalty for something that would otherwise be criminal already. If this bill passes tomorrow, it will still be legal for people to call me a fag. I just wouldn't advise it if they're in the banking business.'"

This kind of humor is one of Frank's hallmarks. "I like clever words. My favorite form of entertainment is comedy. I grew up at the height of the Jewish comedians. Words were always fascinating to me. The kind of humor I like has generally been verbal humor. It's a great weapon. It disarms people, it averts boredom. There is nothing worse than being made to look ridiculous."

Doesn't he have lots of enemies just waiting for him to slip up? "Especially after the '89 thing," Frank acknowledges. "I'm careful. Herb Moses, my first lover, understood that and used to tell me, 'You have to walk around with your guard up.' I try to avoid anything where I might be photographed in a compromising way." Frank says that while he may be "constrained about things like that," he does not shy away from acknowledging being gay. "I go places. One day, I was talking to my boyfriend in the antechamber of the House. President Bush came by. He patted me on the shoulder and said, 'Tell him I said hello.' A while later, when the president walked by again, I said to him, 'Hey, I want to tell you. The guy you said hello to was my boyfriend.' The president said, 'Well, tell him how open-minded I am.'"

Frank has enthusiastically claimed his right to be seen as part of a gay couple. Of his former, ten-plus-year relationship with Herb Moses, he once told the *Washington Post*, "Our rule was very simple. We almost never did anything to make a point. But we never not did anything to make somebody else's point. We just decided we're going to live the way we want to live and if that bothered people that was their problem." Moses became the first partner of a gay representative to be given spousal access privileges to the Capitol. Of these and other public appearances, Frank says he knows he's made "an impact."

In 2007, "by the luck of the draw," Frank assumed chairmanship of the House Financial Services Committee, the second largest committee in Congress. On his Web site he states that the chairmanship "offers important opportunities for me to affect public policy in ways that I have long cared about." Such as?

"One is housing. But I want to use that platform to make the broader point that free-market economics is good but not good in itself. It promotes growth but inequality. For years the dominant view was that free enterprise will take care of itself. The biggest decision before us will be, frankly, to help reshape our view of capitalism so that you've got free enterprise *plus* public policy to deal with the shortcomings of the free market."

Frank acknowledges that he is someone who tells each side things that they don't want to hear. "Once you've achieved the understanding that you'll do that, it works in your favor. But it's always hard at first because people think you're just picking on them. People will appreciate honesty, but appreciating honesty isn't their first reaction. The other thing is, you gotta pick your shots, not do it just to piss people off. You have to be clear to people what the problem is. And you have to be accurate. If you keep telling people what they don't want to hear, and it's wrong, you lose credibility."

At the time we are speaking, Frank has been in Congress for twenty-eight years. What does he most love about his job? "The chance to make people's lives better. That's the moral part. And the other part is to actually take a piece of legislation and get it through committee, get it on the floor, get it through the actual maneuvering. I'm good at that. It's an odd talent. Being in Congress is a lot like being in high school. It's OK to be good at it, but you have to be careful. I work hard at getting along with people."

Malik Gillani
and
Jamil Khoury

Indian American Malik Gillani, the executive director of Chicago's Silk Road Theater Project, says of himself and his life partner, artistic director Jamil Khoury, that they represent "the new couple of this century."

"We both embody a global perspective," Khoury explains the morning I meet them at the Silk Road Theater Project offices in the Loop. "We both appreciate the different worlds we come from. We are cognizant of our similarities more than our differences." Khoury, whose father hails from Syria, shares more of the robust, ruddy features of his mother's Polish Slovakian ancestry. "You want to embrace all aspects of yourself, and you want to be able to pick and choose. I like to think that's what we're doing as a couple and as individuals."

Gillani and Khoury had been lovers for five years and going about their lives in the business world when, on September 11, 2001, their world was thrown into a tailspin. "We were pretty certain the attacks were coming from the Arab world," Khoury recalls. "I'm not pegged as Arab, but we were immediately thrown on the defensive."

The defensive soon morphed into the creative when, as Gillani once explained to a reporter, the two of them "did the ultimate American thing and said, 'Let's put on a show.'" At first the aim was to counteract pop-cultural representations of Arabs and Muslims, eschewing both the usual one-dimensional and demonized portrayals. They wanted to put on plays with complex and compassionate story lines "without favoring partisanship or stereotypes."

Soon, however, the company, which mounted its first production in 2002, saw an opportunity for a wider perspective. "I kept running across references to the Silk Road," Khoury tells me. "Here was this really interesting model of cross-culturalism. It included East Asians, South Asians, Middle Easterners, and Mediterranean people. These were voices not being heard on Chicago stages."

The "rule" that SRTP established stipulates that each play they produce be written by a playwright with a Silk Road background and that the protagonist be of a Silk Road background. "As a company we are specifically interested in these voices," Khoury tells me. He is proud of the fact that, as a couple and as a theater company, he and Gillani "assimilate the discourse on diversity in a very real way. That molds how we view each other and the world at large. We feel very much of a tribe that has morphed somehow."

Born in 1965 in Chicago, Khoury was raised in the Syrian Orthodox Church. "Khoury means 'priest' in Arabic," he tells me. "It's an exclusively Christian last name." Gillani, whose parents were from India, was born in Pakistan in 1970, the youngest of six boys. "Most of all, I remember the cousins and attending family events. That's what you do in the East: you don't have friends, you have cousins." In 1977, he and his mother came to the Chicago area to join his father, who had already immigrated. It was in that year that Khoury, twelve years old, was coming to terms with the fact that he was gay.

"It sort of coalesced in my mind," Khoury says, "that sense of difference, that piece of the puzzle. I remember seeing all the boys playing together and the girls together, not feeling a part of either. There was something in the gender system that I was at odds with."

As a boy, Gillani, who is a good head shorter than his partner, experienced a different set of gender messages. "In Pakistan, men touch boys. I was fondled a lot. It didn't disturb me." Within a year after he arrived in the States, he started to develop a crush on guys. "By the time I was finishing elementary school, I already had a reputation for being a flirt. Having five brothers, there was always a pool of guys— their friends—that I could fawn over, flirt with. I didn't have a sexual awareness, but I wanted to be near the guys, touching them and getting away with it. No one said anything."

Meanwhile, Khoury was spending a lot of time in the library of his hometown, Mount Pleasant, reading feminist and gay liberation theory. Gillani interrupts his partner's story to inform me, "He was called the Little Old Man at home."

"Always a desire for information," Khoury explains. "I'd had these questions about gender, and all of a sudden I ran into this wealth of theory and analysis and personal narratives that completely devastated these entrenched notions. Here I was connected to these two worlds, Arab and gay, and no one had a good thing to say about either. I realized that this was going to be tough. I somehow had to challenge those two fronts." Khoury came out in 1983, toward the end of high school.

Gillani already had a boyfriend by the time he was fourteen. "I just kept hitting on men until one returned the favor," he laughs. "But I wasn't out, nor was he. He was older than I. We weren't engaged in sexual activity, just fondling, hugging, flirtation. We were both Ismaili Muslims. He went to the same prayer hall I did. I called him my brother. That's how you work the system."

While Gillani was enjoying his high school flirtation, Khoury was studying in the School of Foreign Service at Georgetown University. Khoury says that "from the get-go" he was part of a liberal, dissenting minority on campus, involved in gay and pro-Palestinian politics. Between his junior and senior years, he took a year off to study Arabic in Damascus. Khoury calls it "one of the most exciting, liberating, fun years of my life."

"In settings like that—Syria was a Soviet-style police state—there is a lot going on under the surface. We used to refer to Damascus as Sin City. It had a libertine underground. I was living with a gay English guy. Our apartment became gay central. In Arab culture, as long as there is not a public declaration, anything goes. There is such a degree of sex segregation that men are very affectionate with each other. My Syrian boyfriend and I could go to Aleppo and get a hotel room together. Men sharing a bed is very normal."

During his final year at Georgetown, Khoury and a fellow Arab activist got to talking about creating a gay and lesbian presence within the Arab community. As a result, he helped found the Gay and Lesbian Arab Society (GLAS), an organization that combats homophobia within the Arab American community and provides support for lesbians and gay men in Arab countries. The next year, he returned to the Middle East, where he worked as a refugee affairs officer in the West Bank.

By then, Gillani had entered St. John's College in Annapolis. Through the college's Great Books program, he read extensively in the Western canon. "I wanted to test my faith, to see whether after graduation I would come out a stronger Muslim." Gillani volunteered for the college's AIDS Support Group, befriending people with AIDS whose families had abandoned them. When he graduated in 1992, he returned to Chicago, where he joined his brothers' information technology company. In his spare time, he made it his mission to educate the Muslim community about HIV/AIDS.

"The Ismaili community is more progressive than other Muslims. I thought that if we really are progressive, then we have to talk about these issues because that's what progressive people talk about."

Meanwhile, back in the States, Khoury was finishing up a master's degree at the University of Chicago Divinity School. He wrote his first play, *Fitna*, an Arabic word that means "chaos" or "disorder." The play tells the stories of three Arab women, each of whom goes against tradition. "The desire to rethink tradition—subvert it, reclaim it—has always been very attractive to me."

The Middle East kept calling to Khoury. He returned, this time to Egypt and Dubai. "For a while, I imagined that my life would be spent in the Arab world. But the political climate of the region was beginning to take its toll on me. What had been fascinating ceased to be. You get tired of this underground. It loses its sexiness. I started getting tired of these communities of Western gay male sex tourists. While these guys were fun to hang out with, there was something disturbing about it all."

When he finally settled back in Chicago, Khoury became an intercultural trainer, working with executives who were being sent overseas. But he had "all these stories from my Middle East years," stories that he began working into more plays. "I knew that these were pieces that wouldn't be the top choice of many theater companies: they weren't mass market."

Gillani and Khoury met in September 1996, "an absolute destiny story," Khoury says in the interview they have videoed for the Chicago Gay History Web site. During the first five years of their relationship, before they started the Silk Road Theater Project, Gillani jokingly says, "We were enjoying life! Everything life had to offer."

They saw a lot of plays. "I remember getting really excited when I saw an Indian actor onstage, someone who looked like me."

A few days after the 9/11 attacks, Khoury and Gillani attended a rally at the Daley Center. "We went with a group of South Asians," Khoury recalls. "The amount of hostility! That chanting—USA!—it felt very fascistic. Not patriotic in a positive way. It was a frightening experience."

Gillani, who is swarthy and easily identifiable as a South Asian, began to experience other troubling reactions. An employee walked out on him. Pictures of Osama bin Laden with a nail through his head appeared at the office. Khoury and Gillani found themselves engaged in conversations with people in the community who felt similarly threatened.

"Our activist impulse required that we shift our lives," Khoury says, "that we start engaging." Gillani adds, "We both felt a responsibility. We needed to create a medium where people would be open to hearing what people like us had been contributing to America." Khoury points out that the historical Silk Road was about more than just trade. It involved an exchange of arts and ideas. As he once told a reporter, "By embracing this range of cultures that were connected by the Silk Road, we realized we could make a very strong statement."

The start-up money came from their own funds and contributions from friends, family, and other donors. The first production, in 2003, was Khoury's own play *Precious Stones*, the story of a Jewish American lesbian and a married Palestinian woman in Chicago who find themselves falling in love. "It was the culmination of my queer activism, my feminist activism, my Palestinian activism, and my need to create intersections. And to show that these three 'causes' can co-exist within the same people. I was particularly inspired by women's activism in the Arab Jewish communities. Women were reaching out to each other in a way that wasn't burdened by the militaristic, masculine discourse that so weighs down all things Arab-Israeli. It felt very true to me that the characters be women and that there be a lesbian attraction."

Despite the controversial nature of such material, Gillani emphasizes the potential for inspiring dialogue. "There are ways of satisfying the tribes so that they want you, so that they don't cast you out. The fact that we contribute to culture is one of the reasons why our respective communities want to have ownership of us, even if they disagree with what we practice in the bedroom." He says that the Silk Road

Theater Project attracts a very diverse audience. About 40 percent is under forty-five; a third is non-Caucasian. "Extremely high for any arts institution. We work hard with the ethnic communities to make them feel welcome. We're speaking culture rather than just English."

Khoury adds, "We don't do celebratory work, the kind of thing that says, 'Oh, isn't it great to be Chinese!' We want to challenge the audience. We've sometimes been pegged as controversial because our plays raise issues that might be seen as uncomfortable."

Indeed they have. According to Khoury, Silk Road's third production, Yussef El Guindi's *Ten Acrobats in an Amazing Leap of Faith*, a play about a Muslim American family wrestling with faith, culture, and sexuality, "set off a huge controversy because of the gay character." A spokesman for the Council on American-Islamic Relations in Chicago pronounced the play's subject matter "distant from the classic struggles of the American-Muslim community." Some Muslim organizations requested a rewrite of the controversial scenes.

At the time we speak, Silk Road has done ten full productions, a number of them with gay content. "We haven't done a 'gay play' yet," says Khoury. "We're careful not to be didactic or polemical, but we're going to give you a lot to think about. At the end of the day, it's all about a strong story."

Would they like to go all out with a big gay play? "Sure," Khoury says, "if we got the right one. Part of our bigger mission is a conversation about homosexuality within Silk Road communities, which is why we are sometimes pegged as a gay theater pushing a gay agenda." Nevertheless, Gillani cautions, "our constituencies are many. We can't get stuck in one. We want to demonstrate a universal theme going across these cultures. You can't exist as a serious institution— and get funding—if the reputation is, They'll do anything."

What's it like being both life partners and business partners? "We disagree on a lot of issues," Gillani admits. "He wants to spend money, and I have to raise money. We don't sit down to a single meal that doesn't center on the theater." His eyes brighten. "We're going on our very first couples retreat."

"A real vacation!" Khoury adds. "No agenda."

"Well, there *is* an agenda," Gillani corrects. "Making time to celebrate who we are and why we're together."

I ask Gillani about a statement he once made to a reporter, that the Silk Road Theater Project is the child that he and Khoury are rearing together.

"It is our child," he acknowledges. "And I still want a real baby!"

"I feel like *this* is the baby," Khoury interjects, "but Malik wants a flesh-and-blood baby." He smiles facetiously. "We can always do the George and Martha thing."

What do they like about living in Chicago? Without hesitation Gillani says, "The diversity. I like the fact that the city has a domestic partner registry, that it helped to create the Center on Halstead, that it recognizes gay people and celebrates them."

Khoury agrees. "I don't think we could replicate what we're doing here in another city. Chicago has been really receptive. It's a global city on the one hand and midwestern on the other. The prairie runs into the city. We're not too far from the farm. That interplay has made Chicago special. It's a deeply American city. It doesn't have a complex vis-à-vis the Old World. It's unapologetically heartland. Once I became more aware of what it means to be gay, the city took on this whole other significance."

Malik Gillani and Jamil Khoury

Hillary Goodridge

The office where Hillary Goodridge works as director of the Unitarian Universalist Funding Program is a small, happily cluttered room. On the afternoon of my visit, sunlight pours in through the windows overlooking Centre Street, the main drag in Jamaica Plain, a neighborhood in Boston known for its liberal politics, diverse socioeconomic mix, and lesbian population. On a bookshelf near Goodridge's desk, a boxing nun puppet rests against a framed poster from the 1949 Laraine Day movie, *I Married a Communist*. Emblazoned across the top, in big bold letters is the caption, "Nameless, Shameless Woman!"

Shameless she may be, but Goodridge is hardly nameless. As lead plaintiff in *Goodridge v. Department of Public Health*, the lawsuit that legalized same-sex marriage in Massachusetts, Goodridge is considered by many as the face of the gay marriage cause. The landmark decision, handed down by the Massachusetts Supreme Judicial Court on November 18, 2003, declared that the state may not "deny the protections, benefits and obligations conferred by civil marriage to two individuals of the same sex who wish to marry." The ruling added another component to what gay historian Neil Miller has called "a landscape unimaginable twenty-five or even ten years ago."

Born Hillary Smith in 1956, Goodridge grew up in Locus Valley, a tony hamlet on the north shore of Long Island. She doesn't shy away from acknowledging that hers was a background of privilege. Her mother came from a wealthy family; her father was a conservative lawyer. "I was in school with Pulitzers and Doubledays. Sigourney Weaver was my babysitter."

She attended private elementary school, where some of her teachers were lefties. "They had us singing protest songs, old Woody Guthrie stuff." Even more than her musical introduction to progressivism was the "devastating effect" that the Vietnam War had on her. "On the news every week they used to scroll the names of the kids—they were *kids*!—who had been killed. In eighth grade my friend and I wore black armbands with the number dead." Asked to remove her armband, Goodridge refused.

She went on to St. Paul's School, a private boarding school in New Hampshire that had only recently begun to admit females. There were forty girls in a school of five hundred. "It was great! The boys weren't grown-up pigs yet. Everybody was a hippie." A self-declared jock, Goodridge played squash, field hockey, and tennis. Although she had boyfriends, she was aware of her attraction to females. Nevertheless, no one talked about homosexuality. "God, no! I don't even remember the words 'gay' or 'lesbian' being said. Were the gay boys doing each other? Yes. Did we know about it? No."

In 1974, Goodridge, following in her father's footsteps, entered Dartmouth, once again one of the first females admitted. She had assumed that the college would be as welcoming as her high school. It was not. "Horrible! They had gone coed so reluctantly. It very much had a tradition of the Northern male. Culture couldn't quite reach up there." Years later, in a piece entitled "Feminist Activism at Dartmouth" published in the *Dartmouth Free Press*, reporter Laura C. Dellatorre wrote: "The women who initially entered Dartmouth were a marginalized minority. Administrators largely ignored the needs of women, and male students regarded them as invaders of their formerly idyllic New England campus. They were labeled 'cohogs,' ignored in classes taught by an almost exclusively male faculty, and made victims of sexual assaults that went largely unnoticed."

By the end of her first year, Goodridge told her father, "This is a waste of your money." She transferred to Smith College in Northampton, Massachusetts. "Loved it! I was in a small dorm. There were sixteen of us. Every one of us was hetero in September. By the time we marched out in June, there were twelve lesbians."

At Smith, Goodridge became a lesbian feminist. "Adrienne Rich had a huge impact on me. Robin Morgan, the Furies collective, New Words Bookstore." When Smith College cut funding for what eventually became the campus's lesbian literary publication, Goodridge took matters into her own hands, organizing dances and other fundraising activities. The college administration deemed her actions out of order. She was not asked back.

Taking some time off, Goodridge moved to Boston, where she shared a house with lesbian novelist Rita Mae Brown, the author of *Rubyfruit Jungle*. When Goodridge's father read an article about Brown in the *New York Times*, he called his daughter up. "He said to me, 'Hillary, I want you to know that we do not approve of her lesbianism.' Well, I'll tell her, Dad."

That spring, Goodridge returned to Dartmouth, choosing to live off campus in a farmhouse with four other women. "Basically, we were fighting the patriarchy. So many things were happening in those years: South Africa, Three Mile Island, access around admissions issues, gay and lesbian stuff." At an interview for admission into a sorority, Goodridge told them she thought the sorority house would be a great place to organize women. "They weren't interested!" She graduated in 1979 with a formal degree in sociology and immeasurable hands-on experience in how to deal with adversity. "As difficult as Dartmouth was, those of us who lived through it came out tough broads."

After college, Goodridge went to work for Simon & Schuster, where her boss encouraged her to take risks. She recalls the "vibrant community" that was the lesbian scene in New York in the early eighties. "I loved it, but then Ronald Reagan got elected, and everything changed." She moved to Boston—a city she says was "definitely more brown rice and tofu" than Manhattan—to work for the Harvard Campaign before moving to the Haymarket People's Fund, a multicultural foundation that supports grassroots efforts to combat injustice.

In 1985, through the efforts of a mutual friend, Goodridge—then still Hillary Smith—met Julie Wendrich at a forum on divesting from South Africa. Of their initial meeting Goodridge recalls, "I liked her, but I was in a relationship and definitely not thinking about settling down." Nevertheless, the two of them became friends and went on to develop a professional relationship, organizing conferences together. When Wendrich announced that she was getting engaged to a man, Goodridge found herself "getting ballistic about it. I was furious. It was like a betrayal to the sisterhood. Obviously, I had feelings for her that I wasn't letting on to."

The engagement plans died, and Wendrich convinced Goodridge, to whom she was now quite attracted, to accompany her to a gay pride parade. Soon they were going off for romantic weekend trips. In 1988, they started living together.

It would be another seven years before they had a child, their daughter, Annie. In the meantime, they were "both busy gals." In addition to their respective jobs, the two organized a Women and Money conference every year. Goodridge also served on the board of Mass Choice, the Massachusetts affiliate of the National Abortion Rights Action League, and on the board of GLAD, the Gay and Lesbian Advocates and Defenders, the organization that would eventually catapult her into worldwide prominence. Ironically, at the time, she found GLAD to be "too lawyer-male."

Goodridge tells me that she "always, always, always knew I wanted kids. It never occurred to me that I wouldn't. Julie didn't want to, but to her huge credit, she opened herself up to that." For a long time, both of them tried to get pregnant—"not at the same time!" she makes clear. Eventually, in December 1994, Wendrich conceived. Annie was born the following September. "We couldn't decide on a name, so we decided to get a new name, Goodridge. It was my grandmother's."

A seven-year relationship, a daughter, a shared name, a Victorian fixer-upper in one of Boston's leafy neighborhoods—the Goodridges seemed married in every way but legally. Still, marriage was definitely not on Hillary Goodridge's mind. "At that point, I felt as if the institution of marriage was a patriarchal construct. I thought, Why would you want to do that?" But when the Defense of Marriage Act was passed by Congress in 1996 and signed by President Clinton, allowing states and the federal government to ignore same-sex relationships as marriages, "even if concluded or recognized by one of the states," Goodridge was furious. "I was at a meeting of foundations in the South. When someone in the Clinton administration rose to speak, several of us got up, turned our backs, and walked out. DOMA was a huge setback, an example of how we can get thrown under the bus, so easily, so quickly."

A year or so later, Goodridge's friend, lesbian writer E.J. Graff, asked her to read drafts of a book she was writing, *What Is Marriage*

For? Goodridge thought, Marriage? Come on! "I thought she was crazy." But in fact, she found the book, which was published in 1999, "stunning." "She changed my mind. I give her all the credit. E.J. and Mary Bonauto."

Bonauto, who was to argue the same-sex marriage case before the Massachusetts Supreme Judicial Court, was a friend of Goodridge's through Jenny Wriggins, Bonauto's partner. Goodridge had known Wriggins "for a million years, since college." One day over brunch, as their children were playing, Bonauto asked the Goodridges if they wanted to be part of the Freedom to Marry lawsuit, which GLAD was planning to file against the state. "Julie and I looked at each other. Julie—she's fearless—said, 'I'll do it.'" They agreed to sign on as one of the seven plaintiff couples. Eventually, they also agreed to be the lead plaintiffs.

"'What does that mean?' I asked Julie. She said, 'It means our names are on it.' 'Fine,' I said." And so *Goodridge v. Department of Public Health* was born. Initially, Goodridge thought it was "just going to be this little thing. I figured the suit would get thrown out, but, to use a sports metaphor, we would have moved the ball a little farther down the field."

GLAD filed suit on April 11, 2001, after the Goodridges had been denied an application for a marriage license at Boston City Hall. "The clerk told us to come back with two grooms. I took notes. We brought all the information back to GLAD." On March 12, 2002, the parties presented their arguments before Suffolk Superior Court Judge Thomas E. Connolly. "We gave the human side of the story. That was clearly our job." In May, the trial court ruled against the seven couples. As planned, GLAD filed an appeal, and the case eventually moved to the state's highest court, which heard arguments on March 4, 2003.

"When you have the expectation that you'll be thrown out of court and that will be the end of it—and then the next thing you know the president is talking about it, and the pope is going crazy—it was hard. We had people in the house all the time. Keeping our jobs was stressful. Maintaining a connection with each other was hard. The biggest stress for Julie and me was how to protect Annie but not have her feel that she didn't have a part. At the same time, I can't stand it when people use children for campaigns. It's gross. We didn't allow her to be interviewed. Mary Breslauer, who did the press work, prepared us very well, but I have huge stage fright. There were two occasions where I threw up before a public-speaking engagement. Who knew that the perfect storm was going to happen? There was no way of knowing. There was no precedent."

Goodridge remembers the day the decision was handed down. "At eight each morning the SJC Web site says which decisions will be released at ten that morning. It was Julie's day to drive Annie to school. I clicked on, and it said, 'Goodridge v. Department of Health.' Julie drove Annie to school, and I threw up."

When she checked at ten, the Web site was jammed. It took some time for her to gain access. "When we learned that we had won, we had to go downtown and have a press conference. It was crazy. Who was going to pick Annie up? We got dressed and went to see her. She was in gym. She came running over. We said, 'We won.' Annie started jumping up and down. Then all of the kids in the class started jumping up and down. But it was clear they had no idea what they were jumping for. The rest is pretty much of a blur."

The wedding took place six months later, on May 17, 2004, the first day legally allowed by the decision. Many reports say that cameras outnumbered the invited guests, among whom was E.J. Graff, whose book had played such an important role in convincing the Goodridges to pursue marriage.

"What tipped me over into sobbing," Graff later wrote in the *Boston Globe*, "was when the Unitarian Universalist President Rev. William Sinkford said, 'By the authority vested in me by the Commonwealth of Massachusetts . . .' At long last, the government was recognizing officially, openly, proudly what was already true between those two, and so many others. I heard nothing after that; I was crying far too hard."

Goodridge says her own most vivid memory is of their daughter "spreading the petals down the aisle. She was just beaming. Finally, she got to have a role. It gave her a place of honor."

Goodridge has high praise for Annie's school, the Park School, an independent day school in Brookline. "Park was amazing around this—around the case, around protecting Annie—they always got it." The school's gay and lesbian parents and several gay and lesbian teachers periodically got together for potluck suppers, which also served to bring the kids of same-sex couples together for play dates. "From the time she was little, Annie heard the words 'lesbian' and 'gay.' We made sure never to make it a bad word. That separated her from a lot of her peer group, many of whom had never heard the word. Julie and I did a lot of parent forums early on. A lot of Homo 101 stuff needed to happen with some of the straight parents."

Since the Massachusetts decision, many states have passed constitutional amendments banning gay marriage. "There's always going to be a backlash," Goodridge notes when I bring this up. "You don't have progress without it. It's such a normal part of the process that I was never among those who freaked out. Eventually, those amendments will be deemed unconstitutional and overturned. They're going to look silly in twenty years."

The lawsuit took a huge toll on the Goodridges' marriage. "I was exhausted afterward. Being a focus of people's scrutiny, we had no time for each other. Annie was the first priority, then the case, and our jobs. What was left? We couldn't refocus when the time came. We gave ourselves to this." On July 20, 2006, Boston's LGBTQ newspaper, *Bay Windows*, reported that the Goodridges were splitting up. A few days later, the *Boston Globe* noted, "They told the world that their relationship was like any other and that's why they should be allowed to marry. Now, friends say, they are showing once again that they are just like any other couple."

"It was horrible," Goodridge tells me. "We wanted to keep it quiet. I still feel ashamed. Was I a failure? We did what we needed to do, and the relationship didn't survive it."

For the time being, Goodridge is living quietly, without fanfare, not far from the house she once shared with her former wife. At the time of our meeting, their daughter is busy with applications to secondary school. "I have a sabbatical coming up at work," she tells me. "I haven't decided what I want to do."

Does she feel like a martyr to the cause? Goodridge doesn't falter. "No. For all of the costs—and they were big—what a privilege to do it, to play even a small part in this. For the rest of my days, I will be grateful to Mary Bonauto and Mary Breslauer and GLAD."

Judith (Jack) Halberstam

I was just at the dry cleaner," Judith Halberstam is saying. "The clerk asked, 'May I help you, sir?' When I told him I was picking up my cleaning, he apologized. The voice is what gives it away. For me, if he didn't go to that 'I'm sorry,' we'd have been good. 'Sir' is good. Way, way better than 'ma'am.' Amazing how these things come to bear on you when you're gender nonconforming."

Professor, writer, and sometime drag king, Halberstam is all about gender nonconformity. With her close-cropped hair, male attire, and butch demeanor, she has deliberately embraced a look—and a life—that disrupts the traditional gender presentation that someone born with a female body is expected to play out. In her scholarly life, too, whether writing about film, music, literature, or performance culture, Halberstam, who is director of the Center for Feminist Research at USC, has called upon queers—and straight people—to overcome what she calls "a failure of the imagination." She says it's all about "gender creativity."

We've met at the house that Halberstam shares with her partner, Macarena Gomez-Barris. Intense Los Angeles sunlight, even this late on a spring afternoon, pours into the living room, spotlighting the coffee table. On it sits a copy of *Oprah* magazine. It's the issue, Halberstam points out, that features an article entitled "Why Women

138

Are Leaving Men for Other Women." She and Gomez-Barris—
"Maca," Halberstam affectionately calls her—are featured there.

Halberstam is in the forefront of thinking about transgender and
lesbian masculinities, a project that she has said involves "rigorous attention to the very different meanings of masculinity." Her ideas are
perhaps best articulated in her 1998 book *Female Masculinity*. There
she argued that because gender is "performative," masculinity need
not be exclusive to the male domain.

"The options available to me," she tells me, "are either to live in
my womanhood, which I'm not going to do, or to try to craft an alternative masculinity. I go as Jack. Some people call me 'he'; others
call me 'she.' I pass about 60 percent of the time. I'm into the ambiguity of it."

From the time she was quite young, growing up during the
1960s and '70s in Nottingham, England, Halberstam was mistaken
for a boy. "Nearly every day. I didn't go around correcting people." In
fact, before she was fourteen, Halberstam "just thought I *was* a boy.
I thought eventually somebody would figure that out. The way a
transsexual would describe their experience—feeling like a boy
trapped in a female body—that's how I was." At the same time, she
was "pretty embarrassed" by this gender ambiguity. "I didn't take
pride in it. I wished I had been of the generation where I could have
owned it, but I didn't know how to tell myself it was OK. I didn't
have the language."

In high school, Halberstam "felt a lot of pressure" from her classmates to present herself in conformity to the traditional norms of her
gender. "English high schools are cruel. There was no gender discourse." Moreover, her stepmother was "concerned that she not be
embarrassed by these children she had inherited. She put pressure on
me, very unsuccessfully."

Halberstam once noted that in Gothic fiction, the Jew appears as
"a monster versatile enough to represent fears about race, nation, and
sexuality, a monster who combines in one body fears of the foreign
and the perverse." As the child of a Jew, what messages did she pick
up about herself and her own potential for monstrosity?

"My experience with anti-Semitism was about the unspoken.
Where I grew up, there was no Jewish community. My dad was so
embittered by his experience in the Holocaust that he did not remain close to his Jewishness. Jewishness was there, but it was a mystery." This "unspokenness," she says, extended to the way her gender

ambiguity was regarded during her childhood. "The fact that I looked like a little boy was remarked upon constantly by other people but not in the family. One of the reasons that I wrote *Female Masculinity* was in order to say there are other narratives one can tell that are different from that narrative of either 'Be quiet' or 'It's embarrassing' or 'You're monstrous.' I have made peace with monstrosity, and that is what that book was about. Which is to say, it's better to be the monster than the monster maker, because the monster maker is the homophobe and the racist."

Halberstam says she was "pretty good at rebelling." She kept her hair "as short as I could" and fell into the punk rock scene. "That fashion gave me an alibi for not being feminine. As soon as I felt I could name my own needs, the world got a lot easier."

In 1975, when she was a young teenager, Halberstam saw a BBC-2 television broadcast of *The Killing of Sister George*, Robert Aldrich's film about lesbians. "I really didn't know what to make of it. There was something in it that I recognized. I thought maybe that was me in George, but, oh, it was all so desperate." It was also about this time that one of Halberstam's gym teachers—"definitely a lesbian"—befriended her. "She probably knew I was queer. She and her partner probably thought I knew, too, but now I realize I didn't know whatever they thought I knew. I knew she was a lesbian, but I didn't have a sense of what that meant. It just seemed like a drinking thing. I didn't see it as anything else."

Halberstam had "a very big crush" on a friend that lasted most of her high school years. "It was unrequited, needless to say. We never talked about it. She cut me off when she figured out what was going on." Though she liked school and had a passion for sports, her high school experience was grim. "I did well enough to get by." Nevertheless, her academic style was beginning to take shape: "I don't learn from organized knowledge. I've never been good at just doing 'a field.' I firmly believe in being an intellectual multitasker."

When her father moved to the United States, Halberstam followed, spending time "tooling around" and, at age twenty, coming out. At this point she was identifying as a lesbian. But the emphasis among her lesbian peers was all on being a woman. "Oh, that was hugely difficult. You think you've found the answer, and you haven't." Eager for something new, she moved to the Bay Area only to be disappointed again.

"San Francisco—the New Agey, leftover stuff from the hippie era and the intense focus on gay men—was so not my scene." She found the dyke-bar culture more to her liking. Eventually, on a whim, she applied to the University of California at Berkeley and got in. "But I could never quite figure out how to be part of this working-class bar scene while being in university." Nor could she figure out how to "get down with the bookstore academic feminists" she was meeting. "I just wanted to get laid." She received her B.A. in English in 1985.

Halberstam went on to do her doctorate at the University of Minnesota. Minneapolis, with its vibrant butch-femme scene, proved to be "a lucky move." She describes meeting "women who were firewomen, who played rugby, who had motorcycles, who had working-class jobs, carpenters, electricians. I just slotted in. It was great. I dated a lot. I suddenly got what I thought my role was. I could be queer, interested in women, *and* masculine. That word 'butch' was a lifesaver. Even though 'butch' was already being vilified by the feminists, I took it up anyway because there was no other term."

During her time in Minneapolis, Halberstam began to see a rise in female-to-male cultures. Talk of sex changes, gender reassignment surgery, and hormone treatment was in the air. "I had to think about it. Did I really want to start messing with my body? I didn't want to be injecting every week. I decided not to. The difference between me and a trans man is not much. I just never pursued the surgery and the hormones."

But she did have the beginning of her own "narrative"—female masculinity. Nevertheless, to write about such an unconventional subject, Halberstam realized she had better get tenure first. After earning her Ph.D. in 1991, she taught for four years at the University of California at San Diego. There she wrote an early piece about female-to-male transsexuals and butches.

"I said I didn't get what the big deal was. Many butches were basically people who just hadn't decided to have the surgery." The piece was criticized by many female-to-male transsexuals who wanted to underscore the difference between themselves and butches, who they insisted were women. "It got on my nerves. I got very pissed off. It had taken me so long to say, 'I am in a female body, but I am a masculine being,' only to have this new identity formation emerge. I got into a lot of skirmishes about this boundary between F-to-Ms and butches."

In 1995, Halberstam left UCSD to do a postdoctoral fellowship at NYU and later served as visiting professor of gay and lesbian studies at Yale. By now she had published her first book, *Skin Shows: Gothic Horror and the Technology of Monsters*, in which she discusses "post-human gender."

"So much of what we mean by human," she tells me by way of explanation, "depends upon the 'legibility' of your maleness or fe-maleness. When someone is illegible, they become monstrous to people. If you're a feminine straight man, you'll get teased just as badly as the gay man. Or if you're a straight woman who's not attrac-tive to men, then you also fall outside the scale of attractiveness that is used against lesbians but also used against you because you look like a lesbian. We still haven't adequately smashed that binary to ad-dress the way prejudice works."

By the midnineties, Halberstam felt ready to articulate her ideas more rigorously. The result, *Female Masculinity*, was a call for "greater taxonomical complexity." As she later explained to Annama-rie Jagose, "If 'lesbian' in this context becomes the term for women who experience themselves as female and desire other women and if 'FTM transsexual' becomes the term for female-born people who ex-perience prolonged male-identification and think of themselves as male, then what happens to those female-born people who think of themselves as masculine but not necessarily male and certainly not female?"

Terms like "lesbian" and "transsexual," which Halberstam refers to as "expert-produced categories," do not interest her as much as "the categories produced and sustained within sexual subcultures." But is the LGBTQ community itself ready to drop "expert-produced categories"?

"Yes and no. On the one hand, people are very attached to that lit-tle rainbow of acronyms. On the other, there is this neoliberal iden-tity discourse that says, 'I don't need a label. I'm just me; I'm unique. I fit in: my neighbors and I get along.' Bullshit! This idea that you can rise above expert-produced categories is a fantasy. The categories grab you; you don't grab them. When I was growing up, I never said, 'I'm a woman.' I could only push it back when I had another category. My point about vernacular categories is that they saved me. Someone gave me another term, 'butch,' and that saved me."

Halberstam says she sees "a weird alliance" between butch les-bians, on the one hand, and postmenopausal divorced women, on the other, both of whom are defined by not being attractive to men. "I often talk about lesbian privilege. Not all lesbians are tarred by homophobia. Two white, well-paid women living together with designer babies: 'hetero-homo' is not going to tell you much. So if you just rely on the category of homophobia, you miss all these other taxonomies of exclusion." It's a good explanation, she tells me, "why some women who seem to be putatively heterosexual"—Halberstam mentions her current girlfriend—"would be interested in someone like me when they've shown no interest in lesbianism. Well, because this isn't exactly lesbianism. What they're interested in is alternative masculinity in whatever form it happens to come in."

In 1999, Halberstam published a nonacademic book, *The Drag King Book*, accompanied by photographs by drag king Del Grace Volcano. Here, too, she wrote about masculinity as a construction, a performance, a "technical special effect"—the "tricks and poses, the speech patterns and attitudes that have been seamlessly assimilated into a performance of realness."

In researching the book, Halberstam encountered resistance from the drag king community. Many drag kings insisted to her that they were "just having fun." They were skeptical of her attempts to say something more theoretical about the kinds of masculinities they were engaged in. "Inevitably someone would say to me, 'Why do you have to keep complicating this? Why not just say that we like to dress up as men?' But a hundred years from now, somebody is going to come along and note this amazing explosion of dyke cultures, including drag kings, and ask, 'What was that about?' All we're going to have to answer that is, 'We were having fun'? Nonsense!"

Halberstam wants to see a change in the discourse around masculinity, including how we teach children.

"My partner has two kids. They're three and five. They call me 'Jack'; they call me 'he'; they call me a 'boy girl.' The little boy says, 'You look like a boy, but you have a girl voice, so you're a boy girl.' We don't correct them, but we don't fool them either. I think if more kids had queer people in their lives, they'd grow with a very different, much more flexible understanding.

"If one was going to be really brave, one would not do this intense gendering in early childhood. I'm in favor of calling babies 'it.' I have seen people look at friends' babies who are wearing gender-inappropriate clothing and get mad. If a girl really is a girl, she'll let you know very quickly. The sad thing is that the little girl and the tomboy meet the same fate when they reach adolescence. The tomboy is punished, but so is the girlie girl. We need to change completely how we raise girls. There is no better indication of that than the fact that a large percentage of girls on campus have eating disorders. A lot of boys, too, might be more open to having a different kind of gendered upbringing. We should expose them to as many genders as possible. It would change a lot of stuff."

Halberstam says that, until recently, female masculinity was a topic that was unthinkable—"disqualified"—as a concept. "I try to think of things that other people have cast off as not a productive site for inquiry. That's where you'll find me digging around. I think we should be chopping up knowledge in different directions, not around identities but around what Foucault called 'subjugated knowledge.' We should not be working in fields like English or history or mathematics."

Halberstam has appeared in a documentary film about the drag king culture, *Venus Boyz*, by Gabriel Baur, and another, *Boy I Am*, about three transitioning female-to-male transgenders in New York City, directed by Samantha Feder and Julie Hollar. At the time we speak, she has contracts for three new books, including one tentatively called *Notes on Failure*.

"I'm trying to say that we need to rethink knowledge itself in order to keep pace with this changing world. I use failure as a rubric to bring together all these subjugated histories. Failure is a nice rubric for me because queers have been seen as 'failed' men and women, 'failed' heterosexuals. But children are quite happy with failure. I'm arguing that if you want to figure out how to engage with transformation, you have to go back to when you were a kid. When you didn't know the 'rules' for the world."

Kim Crawford Harvie

There were candles, flowers, and crowds of well-wishers. There was music by the Boston Gay Men's Chorus. There were promises to love and comfort, to share hopes and dreams. There was an exchange of rings. And then, on May 17, 2004, in the Arlington Street Church in Boston's Back Bay, the Reverend Kim Crawford Harvie, senior minister, raised her hands above the wedding couple, David Wilson and Robert Compton, and . . .

As we sit in her parish office, just below the sanctuary where that historic marriage took place, Crawford Harvie reminisces about the day—the first day that same-sex marriage was legal anywhere in the United States—and specifically about what happened next.

"For weeks I had practiced saying, 'And now by the power vested in me by the Commonwealth of Massachusetts . . .' But I couldn't finish the sentence. I would begin to cry. I would try it in the car, I would try it in the shower, I would try it at the dinner table with the kids going, 'Come on, Mom, you can do it!' It got ridiculous. I would get completely overcome.

"So, the day comes. We've got eighty-six news outlets plugged in. The congregation is completely over the top. People are hanging from the rafters. Here are Rob and Dave before me. And, believe me, I *so* understand that I am absolutely the least important person in the room. I am only a vehicle for this great moment. But I still hadn't been able to convince myself of that to the point where I could stop crying when I got to those words.

"And I'm thinking, Kim, I am going to personally kill you if you don't get through this. You've got to do it. Finally, I was, like, Please God, help me. I really can't do this alone. So I got to the moment, and I put my hand up, and I said, 'And now, by the power vested in me . . .' and the roof came off! The whole place rose and started screaming. It bought me time to bite my bottom lip so I could freaking finish the sentence without completely falling apart. I really felt that God was there."

With her golden smile (and hair to match), Crawford Harvie is a radiant believer in miracles, "unfolding around me all the time," but miracles occasioned by the force of good that she finds in each person. "Good doesn't happen independent of us," the enormously popular preacher (and sometime half-marathoner) tells me. "As Alice Walker says, if we come to church to find God, we're only going to find it in each other. God doesn't exist separate from the way we are with each other."

Her preaching style, she tells me, is all about finding the right story, one that will work on multiple levels "so the youngest or least schooled feel that they have something to grab onto and my most intellectual can go wild." Her favorite word, at least the day we talk, seems to be "spacious," a word she uses to capture the spirit of inclusion that her life and her ministry are all about. A word she avoids using is "hate." "I keep it out of my vocabulary."

Crawford Harvie grew up in Concord, Massachusetts. In 1967, when she was ten, her father left the family. She credits her ability to survive that trauma to the Unitarian Universalist parish in her hometown, which "took a giant mother-may-I step in" and let her know that there were adults who believed in her. She says that the values of Unitarian Universalism and of the transcendentalists, whom she read with her high school English teacher, Marilyn Nicosen, are the values that have informed her thinking and her ministry.

"We'd get to class and Nicky would say, 'Come on, if we walk fast we'll have time to go to Walden Pond.' She would recite as we went. I like to say that I learned to swim in transcendentalism. Emerson's and Thoreau's writings were so influential for me. I was incredibly moved by *Walden*, every word of it. The Emersonian idea of the indwelling God and nature as an open book, a place of solace and renewal. A place not to be close to God but *in* God."

At Concord Carlisle High School, Crawford Harvie "did just about every extracurricular thing you could do." She played field hockey, basketball, and tennis; earned a First Class in Girl Scouting; sang in the chorus; did makeup for the school shows, "probably a chance to hang out with all the emerging gay men." While she had boyfriends, she guesses that she also had crushes on her female classmates and summer camp counselors. "I had really intense relationships with my girlfriends. We wanted to spend all our time together. We slept in the same bed and talked all night. Anything that I was doing with my girlfriends was practice for the real thing. While a lot of my gay male friends were aware of their sexuality from the word go, for many of us lesbians that awareness just hadn't reached Concord, Massachusetts."

At Middlebury College, Crawford Harvie majored in religion, through which she got hooked on Buddhism. During the spring term of her junior year, she went to Japan to study Japanese religion and culture. She ended up at "an amazing monastery in the Japanese Alps," studying and meditating with a Jesuit theologian who practiced Zen Buddhism. "We had a divine time together. I was completely hooked." She notes that in those days traditional Unitarian Universalism did not have a meditative practice. "There wasn't a sense of the discipline of prayer, the discipline of daily practice. That missing piece clicked into place for me through Buddhism."

Back at Middlebury, while still "living in la-la land," clueless about her sexuality, Crawford Harvie began reading feminist writers. "I had amazing feminist teachers who were spoon-feeding this stuff to me—Robin Morgan, Simone de Beauvoir, Adrienne Rich, Andrea Dworkin, and Audre Lorde. I felt a religious obligation to study feminism. I was extremely taken with radical women—still not sexually engaged but totally socially engaged. We would have these brilliant, visionary conversations, talking way into the night. And then I would try to have the same conversations with my boyfriends, and they *so* didn't get it. Straight guys in those days, at least the ones I was fraternizing with, weren't made that way."

One of her most memorable experiences during her college years occurred at a general assembly of the Unitarian Universalist leadership. There she met the director of the church's Office of Gay

Concerns. "He was wearing a pink triangle. I asked him, 'What's the pink triangle?' He said, 'Oh, I'm gay. This is what homosexuals were forced to wear in Nazi Germany.' I was utterly electrified. Here he was, looking like every other guy in a suit. I thought, *What?* This poor man is going through all this just so he can love whom he wants? This is completely incomprehensible to me. I have to give myself to this cause."

At the general assembly, opposition to Anita Bryant's "Save Our Children" movement was in the air, and a resolution calling on all Unitarian Universalists "to use their efforts in stopping such biased persecution and intolerance" was placed before the gathering. Crawford Harvie's pastor and mentor, Dana McLean Greeley—his portrait enjoys a prominent place in her office—got up to speak. She recites for me, almost verbatim, what Greeley said that day: "If we are a faith that believes in the inherent worth and dignity of every person, then how can we not vote to oppose the hatred and vitriol of Anita Bryant and, like our brother the Mahatma, meet her hatred with Soul Force?"

After Greeley spoke, there was silence in the hall except for the sounds of gay men weeping. "I had no idea what was going on. This was a brand new cause for me." When they took the vote, the result was "absolute, 100 percent" in favor of the resolution. "I got a bright orange T-shirt that said, 'Anita Bryant Sucks Oranges.' That was my first gay T-shirt. Overnight I became a spokesperson for the cause." At this point, Crawford Harvie's support for LGBTQ causes was still entirely based on an abstract, albeit lofty, principle, the Unitarian Universalist belief in the worth and dignity of every human being. And even though she was "totally hanging around with queer people," she thought of herself and her friends as "just a bunch of politicos."

"There is a long journey between the mind and the heart. It had served me not to spend a lot of time in my feelings. Things had been tough enough at home. I relied on my brain."

After college, Crawford Harvie spent a year doing political organizing for the consumer advocacy group Massachusetts Fair Share and volunteering with the Clamshell Alliance, which was working to shut down the Seabrook nuclear power plant. She recalls that year as her "adolescence all over again," full of girlfriends and "the exuberance of being free." Though at this point she still had never been to the Arlington Street Church except to drop in on their coffeehouse, she remembers how the congregation rang the steeple bells as the

Boston Pride parade, the first gay pride parade she attended, marched by.

Crawford Harvie went on to do a degree at Harvard Divinity School, where the emphasis on training scholars did not appeal to her. "Coming of age as a lesbian, I wasn't compelled by the old white guys anymore." What did catch her interest were the liberation theologians and the new generation of female theologians, such as Carter Heyward and Beverly Harrison, who were beginning to emerge. In 1984, she was ordained and spent the following year as an intern at First Parish in Brewster, Massachusetts, on Cape Cod.

"That's a gay story. As open and well intentioned as Unitarian Universalists are, in those days the idea of calling a woman, let alone a dyke, was sketchy. Like all of us, I couldn't just be good; I needed to be great, to show people that lesbians are great ministers." She worked hard, "preaching my heart out in that adorable little meetinghouse." Soon the word got out that Crawford Harvie was indeed great. By that spring, she had been invited to become the head minister at the Meeting House in Provincetown, which had been closed for twenty years. The day she assumed her duties, July 1, 1985, the congregation numbered exactly eight souls. "I was so young. What did I know? I was full of spit and vinegar. To be a lesbian and be called to 'Mecca.' It doesn't get better than that. That began my great love story with the Meeting House and Provincetown."

Crawford Harvie says that it is impossible to imagine what her ministry in Provincetown would have been like without the presence of AIDS. "It was the best of times, the worst of times. We were so good to each other. There were ten thousand acts of kindness a week." She recalls the restaurateur who told her he would always provide food at the funeral receptions; another who told her he could be counted on to take care of flowers. "Everyone just did what they could. When we see each other now, those of us who survived that time, we hang on each other and grieve like shipwreck victims."

How did she keep going, a young minister still in her twenties? "The boys who were dying, they were so awake, so alive. Their insights, their passion. I remember one guy, Denis Thibodeau, probably twenty-six years old, who said to me, 'Kim, promise me you won't say the word *hate*. Life is so short. Let's not hate.' I heard what he was saying—let's be more spacious than that."

She recalls another time, an evening when she was driving another young man to the hospital up in Boston. "With the roof of my

Volkswagen wide open so he can see the stars—he's tipped all the way back—and I'm thinking, We're not going to make it. And also beginning to realize that this is completely stupid, a fool's errand, because they can't help him anyway. No one can help. He's lying there, *Appalachian Spring* is playing, it's an absolutely silent, beautiful night. And he turns to me and says, 'Kim, it doesn't get better than this.' Those moments of grace. That's how I kept going."

She tells me that, despite all the sadness and pain of those years, she quickly realized that "you can't just grieve. You've got to celebrate. It's not going to do the ones who are dying any good for us to be moping around. Once we got hold of that idea, we danced at every reception, we sang, we were ridiculous. Suddenly life was so short. That kept me going, too. I'd say to myself, You're not dead yet, girl. Shoulder to the wheel. Let's go."

In 1987, Crawford Harvie received the Maximilian Kolbe Award for Community Service, named after a Franciscan friar who volunteered to die in place of another at Auschwitz. The next year, she was named Provincetown Citizen of the Year.

Soon after she assumed the pastorate of Arlington Street Church in 1989, the congregation began to swell with a large LGBTQ contingent. It's been that way ever since. Nevertheless, Crawford Harvie says that she never specifically wanted a gay church. "Over the years, I've been offered a couple of very sweet pulpits with the thought that I'd plant a gay church. But I'm more interested in the Unitarian Universalist vision of a very diverse world where we all learn to live together. The least homophobic people here are the straight people because they've already done the work on themselves. A lot of queer people here have learned from the straight people how to love themselves."

In addition to parish programs that she started or bolstered—a Zen center, a twelve-step program, Friday night suppers, a drop-in place for street kids—Crawford Harvie has also thrown her energies into cofounding two nonprofit organizations: In the Best Interests of the Children, dedicated to providing assistance to children and families affected by pediatric HIV/AIDS; and The Shared Heart, a traveling exhibition of photographs of LGBTQ teenagers by Adam Mastoon.

Back in the early nineties, Mastoon had shown Crawford Harvie and her friend Mike Ward one of his photographs, a picture of two boys headed off to their senior prom. "Mike just stood there and wept. I saw his reaction and thought, What would it be like for gay kids to have images of themselves and hear from other gay kids?" The result was the traveling exhibition, a stunning collection of large-format photographs with handwritten statements by the kids, and a subsequent book, *The Shared Heart: Portraits and Stories Celebrating Lesbian, Gay, and Bisexual Young People*, published in 1997. The project happened to coincide with the Safe Schools Program for Gay and Lesbian Students, which provided funding by the Commonwealth of Massachusetts to create gay/straight alliances in the state's schools. "A lot of high schools didn't have a clue how to do that. We were the answer. Our first letter was from a teenager from the Deep South. The gist of it was, 'I would have killed myself if I hadn't found this book.' A lot of gay kids found a home in this congregation during those years."

Crawford Harvie met her future wife, Kem Morehead, a mathematics teacher, in 1992. They were married on May 20, 2004, three days after the historic first sex-same marriages in Massachusetts, during an all-day, fifty-wedding marathon at Arlington Street. "Every twenty minutes a wedding would happen," Crawford Harvie recalls. "The average length that people had been together was ten-and-a-half years. One couple was celebrating their sixty-first anniversary that day, with children and grandchildren surrounding them. It was absolutely spectacular."

The couple's three daughters are young adults now, off on their own. Loath to deal with an empty nest, the couple decided to become dorm parents at the school where Morehead teaches, Concord Academy. "Twenty-nine boys, fourteen to eighteen years old," Crawford Harvie tells me, beaming again. During school vacations, Crawford Harvie and Morehead have taken busloads of students on trips to the Grand Canyon, a favorite retreat for them, and more recently to New Orleans, where they did relief work in the wake of Hurricane Katrina. "We just got back from a trip to the Ninth Ward. We put eighty kids on miles of overgrown lots. We cleared from Fats Domino's House right down to the river."

When I ask her what she sees as the next step in the struggle for same-sex marriage, Crawford Harvie has another story. "Very soon after Kem and I were married, my next-door neighbor, a retired state trooper with four kids, a Roman Catholic, yelled over to me, 'Good morning, Kim, how's the wife?' I literally glanced behind me: was he talking to me? He said, 'I think it's great because I love you guys and I never really knew what to call you. And you know what, if I have to be married, you have to be married.' That's not the kind of message he'd heard in church. It's what he heard because we put up an outdoor shower together, and because when he and his wife wanted to go out to dinner, I offered to sit with his mother-in-law. So the next step in this struggle? Just act normal, because this *is* normal. It's amazing how people will treat you if you don't act weird." She laughs. "That's a joke. There's no such thing as normal, but you know what I mean. We all need to integrate ourselves into the culture. My next-door neighbor taught me to say the word 'wife.' Because that's normal. When I say partner or girlfriend, I'm being different from them."

Her secretary calls, reminding Crawford Harvie of her next appointment, but she wants to tell me one more thing.

"You know, we are all ambassadors of queerness. I love gay men. I love how fancy you guys are: you always look so handsome. Those are great ambassadorial skills. When someone says to me, 'You don't look like a lesbian,' I say, 'Oh, honey, this is what a lesbian looks like. Take a good look.'"

Scott Heim
and
Michael Lowenthal

My conversation with novelists Scott Heim and Michael Lowenthal takes place the day after the fortieth anniversary of the Stonewall riots. Sitting around the kitchen table in the house they share in
Roslindale, a working-class neighborhood of one- and two-family
homes in Boston, I ask them how they marked the occasion.

"We were at a fund-raiser for our softball league," Heim tells me.

"I come from a big baseball family," adds Lowenthal, whose third
novel, *Charity Girl*, is set during the 1918 Red Sox season. "My dad's
bar mitzvah speech was all about baseball and the Red Sox. During
summers on the Cape we would drive up to Fenway for games. At
Shabbos dinner on Friday nights, we would make sure the TV was
on before sundown so we could watch the game afterward."

With three novels apiece to their credit, Lowenthal and Heim,
one of Boston's "Power Couples," according to *Spirit* magazine,
spend their days writing—or avoiding writing, as their respective
styles may dictate—and, now that it's summer, tending to their back-
yard vegetable garden.

Heim, the older (by three years) and the first to publish, broke
onto the literary scene in 1995 with *Mysterious Skin*, a hauntingly
weird and beautiful novel about memory and childhood sexual
abuse. "The greatest first novel by a gay writer under thirty since

153

Other Voices, Other Rooms," gushed the reviewer for the New York gay weekly *LGNY*. "Heim is breathtakingly unafraid to take chances," seconded the *San Francisco Chronicle*, "and the fact that he doesn't self-destruct in the process is one of the reasons he can rightly be called a promising author." Lowenthal's debut as a novelist came three years later with *The Same Embrace*, about two identical twin brothers, one gay, the other an Orthodox Jew. It, too, received widespread praise. "An eloquent exploration of the nature of faith, the consequences of judgment and the stubborn endurance of family ties," wrote Linda Barrett Osborne in the *New York Times Book Review.*

On this sunny, early summer afternoon, Heim and Lowenthal are wearing T-shirts that might very well stand for their respective tastes and personalities: Heim's, in chocolate brown, is emblazoned with the name of the indie record label MORR MUSIC. "I worked at a record store when I was a teenager," he tells me. "We would get catalogs. I'd see something that looked interesting and I'd order it." Lowenthal's T-shirt advertises the Strand Book Store in New York. "I didn't buy any of the music my peers were listening to," he confesses. "I almost never went to the movies. I just missed all of that."

"He seriously didn't even know who the Carpenters were!" Heim recollects about one of their first dates. "That could have been the end of it right there."

Heim grew up in Little River, a "minuscule Kansas town." His father, a shop teacher and football coach, was "in some ways very close to the father of Brian in *Mysterious Skin*. He wasn't mean in any way, but he was very emotionally distant. He would assume boys knew the rules of football and how to build a house. I didn't know any of those things. I quit football after the first couple weeks."

Heim says that longing "pretty much defined my entire boyhood. We lived out in the country. I spent an hour and a half on the bus each way to school, reading Steven King, science fiction, unsolved mysteries and murders—anything that was the opposite of hometown Kansas. I wanted to get out." In a poem entitled "The Day I Learned the F Word," from his 1993 chapbook, *Saved from Drowning*, Heim wrote about "the true fascination of the forbidden." When I mention this, he tells me about the "illegal magazines" his mother would bring home from her job in the sheriff's office at a Kansas prison. "I'd read stories in *True Detective* about rapes and murders. To this day, that's the sort of thing that fuels my writing."

Lowenthal says that longing also defined his childhood. "And continues to define my every day. I remember walking around our D.C. neighborhood, wanting to connect with boys. I longed for all sorts of things, including being from a totally different family, from a different kind of place." He looks over at Heim and laughs. "I yearned to grow up in a minuscule town in Kansas."

When he was eleven, just about the time his parents were divorcing, Lowenthal went off to a summer camp that, he says, "completely changed my life in almost entirely good ways." Founded in the thirties by "a strange but visionary Quaker," the camp encouraged the boys and counselors to go without clothing as much as possible. "There I was, hormones coursing through me, surrounded by 150 of the most athletic, charming, beautiful, naked boys and men all the time. Yes, yearning, longing."

Both novelists started writing early. Heim wrote horror stories; Lowenthal "swoony, self-important love poetry." He also served as editor in chief of the school newspaper. "It was about wanting to win approval from people. Doing the school newspaper, you had this built-in audience. You'd write something, and people would respond. I realized the power you could have with that." For Heim, his early writing was about trying to express "the different way I had of looking at the world. I liked the feelings I got when I read something that really moved me, and I thought that would be an interesting thing to try to do to someone else. But until I got to college, I didn't think it was anything I could pursue beyond a hobby."

As a teenager, Lowenthal suffered from what he once called "congenital unhipness." "I was living in the capital of the most powerful nation on earth, and I would rather have been going to political rallies and marching on the Pentagon, or in Vermont, chopping trees and playing my banjo." In contrast, Heim was the "hometown New Wave freak," as he put it in his essay in *Boys Like Us*, an anthology of coming-out stories. "My friends and I were ultrahip. We made sure that we subscribed to magazines so we could know about the latest music."

Lowenthal interjects: "He was ultrahip, and I was nerdy."

"What would you have thought of me?" Heim invites.

"I would have been desperately attracted to you and simultaneously entranced by, jealous of, and contemptuous of your hipness." Lowenthal laughs. "Sort of like now!"

Lowenthal says he was a closeted teenager. "I was having little sexual things with other boys—sometimes at camp, sometimes at home—but I made no connection with the idea that that was an identity. When I was fifteen, I was in this emotional love triangle with a girl and a boy. She was my girlfriend, but I was telling her about my feelings for the boy. She asked me, 'Are you bisexual?' and I thought, Oh, yeah, I guess maybe that's it."

Heim says that he knew he was gay "before I even knew anything about sex. I distinctly remember seeing the whole Anita Bryant shit on TV. During the interview with her, they showed images of the San Francisco gay pride parade—men in leather kissing, drag queens—and she was saying they were going to burn in hell. And I just knew that that was me. I can remember distinctly going to my room and praying, 'Please, God, don't let my life be like that.' Which is heartbreaking now, because I am so happy I'm not straight. But back then, three or four years of my childhood were ruined by Anita Bryant."

Lowenthal takes over: "Looking back, it's so clear and so obvious that I was gay, but going through it, it was such a mystery. When I was a sophomore, I fell madly in love with another kid who was an actor. He was in the high school production of *The Zoo Story*. After that, whenever I was in a bookstore, I would buy up every used copy of the play I could find and hand them out to people. It was only in my late twenties that I went back and read it. It's totally gay. Clearly, I was handing it out like my secret calling card, hoping that somebody would get it, but I wasn't even aware that I hoped someone would get it."

Heim, too, sees mystery and "detective work" at the root of his discovery of his sexuality. "My father coached in a women's summer softball league. I was the batboy, the scorekeeper. I knew three hundred lesbians before I had ever met a gay man. I see pictures of myself back then and realize I was a complete little queen. Now I ask myself, How many of those dykes were laughing behind their hands? I mean, here was their macho coach, and he's got this little queer boy for a son. I should have been identifying as gay, but I wasn't at all."

Heim attended the University of Kansas in Lawrence, where he majored in English and art history. "Freshman year, I discovered Jean Cocteau's *The White Book*—the book with the scene in the bathhouse where a beautiful boy is making love to himself in front of a two-way mirror. I was totally blown away. It was the first time I realized you could read something and get the same effect as you could looking at a naked picture, except a more profound and prolonged version of that. So I just started devouring gay stuff, anything contemporary that I could get my hands on."

During his final three undergraduate years, Heim lived in a dormitory popular with artists and alternative types. "In some ways it was the time of my life. People called it the Homo Hilton. It was full of hippies, Grateful Dead people, witches and Wicca people, punk rockers, deathrockers, gays and lesbians. You were an outcast if you were a normal person." Despite the liberal atmosphere of the campus and his dorm, Heim "didn't have anything close to a boyfriend" during college. "There was this one guy who would come to me—he knew I had these raging, newly gay hormones—and we would go down and have sex in music practice rooms. Hundreds of times. Nobody knew."

By now, Lowenthal had entered Dartmouth, where he, too, pursued a double major, in English/creative writing and comparative religion. He recalls that "at most there were fifteen people in the entire college who would identify as gay." The student body was the most conservative of the Ivy League schools; "homophobic terrorism" was rampant. Lowenthal threw himself into the small but active gay student group, through which he helped to start a gay campus newspaper, "which was very provocative and meant to be." Every year, along with some feminist and African American activists, he mounted an alternative graduation. At one of the homecoming events, the gay group staged a "commando raid," putting pink gels on the spotlights and unfurling a pro-gay banner.

With a grant from the college, Lowenthal spent his senior year, 1989–90, writing a novel. That spring he attended the first OutWrite literary conference, held that year in San Francisco, an event of "so much energy and excitement that it fueled my feeling of, OK, this is where I belong." A few months later, as class valedictorian, he delivered a graduation speech in which he chastised the college for its unwelcoming attitude toward nontraditional students, who had, he said, "too often been viewed as mere add-ons."

Meanwhile, after finishing a master's degree in English literature in 1991, Heim moved to New York to begin an M.F.A. in fiction writing at Columbia University. By then, Lowenthal was living with his then boyfriend, Chris Hogan, in Northampton, Massachusetts, where the two of them set up housekeeping with a lesbian couple, an arrangement they hoped would be "an emblem of and a catalyst for a new wave of lesbian and gay male cooperation in town." He wrote of the subsequent failure of their experiment in a poignant and hilarious essay, "The House O' Happy Queers at 281 State," which appeared in John Preston's 1994 anthology *Sister & Brother*. During his time in Northampton, Lowenthal continued the activism he had begun in college, helping to found ACT UP–Western Massachusetts. He was also publishing pieces, fiction and nonfiction, in anthologies, journals, and newspapers, but the Preston essay, he tells me, was his first big break.

"Gay, gay, gay," Lowenthal says of his early publishing venues. "In some ways I had little sense of having a choice otherwise. Scott had this writing program and someone advising him, telling him he could be a great writer. Nobody advised me to continue with my writing. But I was involved in the gay activist community. That was my world." In 1992, he took an editorial position at the University Press of New England.

When Preston became incapacitated by AIDS, Lowenthal started visiting him in Portland, Maine, "to help care for him and keep his business in order," he later recalled in the introduction to *Winter's Light*, a posthumous anthology of Preston's essays. Preston asked Lowenthal and two other gay writers—Owen Keehnen and Michael Rowe—if he could mentor them. "He told me, 'That will mean you can ask me for anything at any time—advice, introductions to people in New York, help reading a draft.' That was my M.F.A. program. As John got sicker, he started asking me to take over some of his projects." After Preston's death Lowenthal went on to edit several books that the writer had planned.

Heim and Lowenthal met at the 1995 OutWrite conference, which was held in Boston that year. Heim was about to publish *Mysterious Skin*. "We met at opening night cocktails," Lowenthal recalls. Of his boyish-looking future partner, he says, "I thought he was a high school student." Heim continues the story: "I went up, and he swears I said, 'Haven't we met somewhere before?'"

For the next seven years, the two conducted their relationship between Boston, where Lowenthal had moved, and New York. In 1997, Heim published his second novel, *In Awe*, about three outcasts, one of whom, a teenage boy, dreams of writing a zombie novel. The fascination with boys—it would also appear the next year in Lowenthal's *The Same Embrace* and more explicitly in his second novel, *Avoidance*—what's that fascination all about for each of them?

Scott Heim and Michael Lowenthal

158

"Youth is when all the most tumultuous stuff happens to you," Heim suggests.

"I have this photo in my office," Lowenthal tells me. "This ethereally beautiful blond boy at a summer camp. He's about thirteen. I almost cry when I look at it. There's something so . . . it's partly that his youth is about to fade and he can't know that. The second the shutter closes, he'll no longer be a boy, and he'll be that much closer to manhood. Sometimes Scott and I will sit in a café and watch the unselfconsciousness of boys being boys. I'm just riveted."

"It's not about a sexual attraction to boys," Heim adds. "It's not that at all. But that part of me that I wasn't conscious of at the time I was a boy, I wish I could go back and relive it. It's an endless source of fascination."

After the publication of *In Awe*, which did not receive as much critical acclaim as his first novel, Heim's writing career and personal life took a tumble. His editor died, his agent quit the business. He wrestled with multiple drafts of a new novel. Disappointed and depressed, Heim got into drugs. "At first, it was just something I did with friends. Ecstasy. At the clubs. When I discovered other drugs that were more addictive—meth, mostly—they fueled the depression. I was doing it to keep away the bad thoughts." He and Lowenthal separated for a while. "It was a good thing in some ways. I made the realization that if I continued, it would be prison or death or something worse."

At the end of 2002, the couple made an "impulsive decision" to move to Cape Cod for the winter, holing up in Lowenthal's father's house in West Barnstable. "That was the first long stretch of time that I didn't have anything chemical in my system," Heim says. At the end of the winter, he moved to Boston to live with Lowenthal and begin counseling.

And how about Lowenthal? Did he experience anything of the second-novel crisis? He laughs. "I had had much more modest success, so there was nothing to come down from."

Heim interrupts. "I remember you being upset that the second novel wasn't going to be a hardcover. There are so many things in this career that you think are going to be great and wind up knocking you on your ass."

How much did their early careers benefit from the gay writing wave that was sweeping the country in the nineties?

"If you'd have asked me then," Heim says, "my inclination would

159

have been to try to dodge that question. In retrospect, I can only see the good in that. There are so many things that I thought might have been restricting to categorize a book like that. But recently we went to the Saints and Sinners Literary Festival"—a conference for LGBTQ writers and readers in New Orleans—"and it turned out to be a really positive, kind of soul-expanding experience. It made me realize how nurturing it can be not to be pigeonholed but to have a certain niche market. In this day and age, where no one reads, it's better than nothing."

"The gay identification," Lowenthal adds, "meant that I sold a few thousand books instead of zero. It gave me a community, a mentor, and publishing opportunities." At the same time, he wonders if being pegged as a gay writer "restricted the scope of my own ambitions." So was his third novel, *Charity Girl*, which does not include a major gay character, a deliberate decision to sidestep identification as a gay writer? "Thematically it's about the same obsessions I've always had."

The genesis of the novel was sparked by Lowenthal's fluke discovery of a little-known historical incident: that during World War I hundreds of women infected with venereal disease were incarcerated by the government. "I first read about it in Sontag's *AIDS and Its Metaphors*. That association must have been in my mind the whole time. She was saying how stupid quarantining people with AIDS would be by comparing it to this other historical event." But it wasn't until he had finished the novel that Lowenthal realized he had, in fact, come up with "a new way to tell an AIDS story or a gay sexuality story."

Disease also figures prominently in Heim's most recent novel, *We Disappear*, in which the mother of the narrator is dying of cancer. Heim's own mother died of the disease in October 2003. Like the narrator, whose name is also Scott, Heim went back to Kansas to take care of her.

"I'd like to say that I have this huge expanse of wild imagination, but maybe I'm more like Andrew Holleran, who says he can only write about things that happen to him. There's tons of other stuff in the book that didn't happen. But there were details that my editors wanted me to take out because they were dredging through the pain and hell of actual physical death. My mother died on Halloween. Only a few feet away the doorbell kept ringing and kids were screaming. That wouldn't have worked in the book."

Over the years, what has each learned about writing novels?

Lowenthal: "That there are fewer rules that apply. *And* that there are more stringent rules that apply."

Heim: "You can do anything you want in a novel, but it has to work."

"That's *exactly* what I meant," Lowenthal agrees. "I used to be more rule bound—you can't put this in, you can't put that in—but now I try to be more open to whatever the universe is going to give, and yet I've tried to be more hard-lined that it has to fit."

And what have they learned from each other's writing?

Lowenthal chuckles. "From his writing habits I've learned . . ."

Heim finishes the sentence. "Not to be like me! I hate getting up in the morning. I wish I did have better discipline in my work habits. I really admire that about Michael. Even when he doesn't have a thought in his head, he makes himself sit down and work. I can go months and months without writing a word, and then something clicks and I'll spend eight hours a day writing."

"When I read Scott's stuff," Lowenthal says, "I remember that in a novel each sentence should matter and be told beautifully. Scott gets letters from people all over the world who say, 'Reading your book saved my life.' Those letters remind me of the power of writing, that you really can reach people. So I keep telling myself, 'Pay attention, take it seriously, care about it.'"

Jealousy?

"Of course," Heim says. "We talk about it better than we used to. One of us could have a book that sells really well. But the other gets a glowing review in the *New York Times*. He's thinking, Boy, I wish my book had sold better; and I'm thinking, I wish I'd gotten a *New York Times* review."

Lowenthal's mentor, John Preston, once wrote, "One of the first questions that a gay man has to answer revolves around the basic issue: Where do I belong?" At the midpoint in their lives and careers, how would each of them answer that question?

"I don't know if I know where I belong," Heim says. "I'm closer to it than I used to be. As frustrated as I still get, and depressed as I still get, there are days when I realize, I'm alive, I have a house, I've been with the same person that I still love for fourteen years. We don't have to get up and go to a job every day that we hate. We have a lot of great friends. For a long time it was those things that I took for granted. I'm finally coming to a place in my life—maybe that's part of growing up—where I realize it's those things that really matter."

"You go through life thinking there's supposed to be some big payoff," Lowenthal says, "and then you realize it's been happening all along."

"Yeah," Heim agrees. "I never, ever thought that one of the biggest joys in my life would be walking out to the garden to see how the tomato plants are doing."

Jennifer Higdon

The afternoon I meet Jennifer Higdon in the spacious apartment she shares with her partner of almost thirty years, she remarks on how quiet it is outside. It's a broiling summer day in Philadelphia's Center City. "I think everyone went to the shore," she says. That may be true, but it's no beach day for Higdon. She has already given one interview today and, once our conversation is over, she'll return to the violin concerto she is writing for Hilary Hahn.

"When I thought of writing for Hilary Hahn, I asked her what pieces she liked, what she felt comfortable with. She likes a lot of things. I listened to the Schoenberg concerto—she's just recorded it—because I wanted to see what the instrument can do at its extremes. I thought, All right, let's do an American version of these sound worlds for Hilary."

Those who know Higdon's music might be surprised that she would have lavished so much attention on Schoenberg's concerto because the sonic worlds of these two composers are completely different. Higdon's music has been described—not always flatteringly—as "audience friendly," a far cry from the dissonant astringency of the early-twentieth-century inventor of the twelve-tone system. Indeed, with 250 performances of her music a year and numerous prizes and honors, Higdon probably enjoys greater accolades than her Viennese counterpart ever did in his lifetime.

Higdon arrived on the musical scene at a felicitous moment, when the tyranny of the one academy-sanctioned style, with its near dogmatic insistence on atonal music, most of which she finds "boring," no longer prevailed. In Higdon's compositions critics have found echoes of many of the great twentieth-century tonal composers—Aaron Copland, William Schuman, Samuel Barber, Stravinsky, Bernstein, Messiaen, Steve Reich—without, as Tim Page put it in the *Washington Post*, "really sounding like any of them."

"It's the weirdest combination of people!" Higdon acknowledges. "It's desperation to try to find a way to explain it. My pieces change dramatically from piece to piece." Each new composition from this astonishingly prolific composer—one year, she wrote four concertos—has been met with increasing critical acclaim and wide audience approval. At the time we are meeting, Higdon has commissions for the next five years. She turns down requests for new pieces at the rate of two or three a month. "I can't get them into my schedule."

As we make ourselves comfortable in the living room, Higdon introduces me to her partner, Cheryl Lawson. Lawson then disappears into a large front room that serves as Higdon's composing studio—"She's printing out orchestral parts to a piece we have to send out," Higdon explains—and we settle down to talk.

Born in Brooklyn in 1962, Higdon spent the first ten years of her life in Atlanta, where her father was a commercial artist. Before she was in high school, the family had moved again, this time to East Tennessee. It was there that Higdon, who still speaks with the vestiges of a Tennessee accent, began hearing Appalachian and bluegrass music, sonorities she later rediscovered when she wrote her piece for string quartet, *Southern Harmony*.

Higdon's formal musical training came late. She grew up listening to the Beatles, Bob Marley, Fleetwood Mac, the Rolling Stones. Other than the local NPR station, she heard almost no classical music. "Classical music is not a serious endeavor in East Tennessee." She took flute lessons one summer but was otherwise self-taught. In high school, she played in the concert band, where she met Lawson. "Cheryl says she noticed me the first day she came into the band. She could tell you what I was wearing. I was so into the music I was clueless, but Cheryl knew right off the bat. There was a group of us that hung out together. Now that I think about it, quite a few of our band mates were gay. But no one ever talked about it."

The friendship blossomed into a romantic relationship during the final two months of Higdon's senior year, just before she went off to Bowling Green State University. Lawson was still in high school, and the two kept up a long-distance relationship—450 miles, Higdon says—until Lawson joined her. "It's a miracle when you think about it, because a lot of relationships don't withstand that, but teenage relationships! It was well worth the wait."

At Bowling Green, Higdon declared flute performance as her major. "When I look back, I think, my God, what made me think I could major in music." She took all the standard classes—theory and harmony, ear training—though for her "it was all really new. I was way behind everyone, trying to catch up." As a flute player in the university orchestra, she came to love the twentieth-century repertoire. "Because I came to classical music very differently than most people, the newer stuff had more appeal for me than the older."

After she graduated in 1986, Higdon went off to the Curtis Institute of Music in Philadelphia for a two-year artist's diploma. (Lawson, who was two years behind her at Bowling Green, transferred to Temple.) "I used Curtis to switch over to composition. I hadn't really been composing long enough to develop a portfolio, but somehow I got in. I learned more at Curtis than anyplace. It was intense. I was put into the most musical atmosphere I could have ever landed in. It gave my brain a chance to switch from being a performer to a composer." Of her early compositions—a viola sonata, an oboe concerto, songs, pieces for flute, a few orchestral works—Higdon says that there were "some things I kept and much that I threw away!"

After Curtis, she took a year off and then entered the University of Pennsylvania, where in 1994 she earned a doctorate in composition. "I was in trouble a lot at Penn. I was already writing what I wanted to write and not what they were telling me I should write. If you wrote melody, you got harassed for it. There is no way I could have written atonal music. I sure as heck didn't feel that language was natural to me."

By the midnineties, Higdon was producing a solid body of work—"laboring all along, working on it, working on it"—turning out mostly chamber pieces on commission. In 1996, *USA Today* chose her twelve-minute orchestral piece, *Shine*, as the "Best New Classical Piece" of the year.

"At that point I was just getting going. I had only one or two pieces that I would claim. The others I had withdrawn. They were just hideous." Within a few years, however, her "chicken scratchings," as Higdon calls those early apprentice works, had evolved into mature pieces, one of which, an orchestral composition called *blue cathedral*, she wrote on commission for the seventy-fifth anniversary of the Curtis Institute. "As I was writing this piece," Higdon wrote in the liner notes for the later Telarc recording, one that made the Classical Billboard charts, "I found myself imagining a journey through a glass cathedral in the sky. Because the walls would be transparent, I saw the image of clouds and blueness permeating from the outside of the church."

The piece, a memorial to her brother, who had died of cancer, attracted considerable attention from the critics and public alike. "An otherworldly atmosphere of floating sound," wrote one critic. Another praised the "transparent orchestration, melodiousness and concision." Deemed "among the most daring and inventive new compositions to surface in years," *blue cathedral* has emerged as Higdon's most frequently performed composition and, according to the American Symphony Orchestra League, the most performed contemporary work in America.

Even more than *blue cathedral*, Higdon says that it was the 2002 premier of her Concerto for Orchestra that catapulted her career. Commissioned by the Philadelphia Orchestra, it premiered during the national conference of the League of American Orchestras. She recalls the evening as the one that "altered my life forever."

"Three thousand orchestra managers. They'd come to Philadelphia to see the new hall and to hear Wolfgang Sawallisch and the orchestra play Strauss's *Ein Heldenleben*. I know they looked at the program and thought, Who's this Jennifer Higdon? I was completely unknown. Three thousand orchestra managers—the most jaded crowd you can have! My entire life was coming down to those thirty-five minutes. I thought, either I'm going to be working at McDonald's tomorrow, or it's all going to take off."

Higdon's piece comprised the entire first half of the concert. When the orchestra finished playing, she was standing backstage, where she had been for the entire piece. "I was so nervous. There was so much adrenaline in my system, I was deaf. The piece finished and Sawallisch came off the stage with this look on his face. He was really shocked. It was time for me to take a bow. I walked out and they were all standing and yelling, a prolonged standing ovation. I had this moment like, Oh, my gosh! What happened? It was surreal. I was not expecting the reaction. I read somewhere recently that luck is 'preparation meeting opportunity.' When the door opened, and I had a chance to do something, I did the very best I could."

In the summer of 2003, Higdon became the first woman composer featured at the Tanglewood Contemporary Music Festival. Honored as she must have been, did she also experience that moment as a burden? Did she feel she was being asked to represent all female composers? "No, I considered it just a thrill. I never think of these amazing opportunities as a burden. I don't ever think about the fact that I'm a woman. All I'm interested in is the music. Is it well written? Is it going to be interesting for the people who have to sit in the audience?"

Higdon says that she loves the "huge collection of colors, the big box of crayons" that writing for an orchestra allows her. She is a remarkable orchestrator, one who employs what David Patrick Stearns in the *Philadelphia Inquirer* has called a "dazzling blizzard of sounds." To what does she attribute her keen ear for orchestration?

"Fear!" she laughs. "Fear of boring people. Which makes my brain leap forward trying to find unusual colors. When I would look around at concerts, people were snoozing. That's a pretty hideous way to spend an evening. I can remember playing flute in Ravel's *Daphnis and Chloé*. Being inside that sound was something I'll never forget. I think about that a lot every time I write a big tutti section for orchestra."

Higdon's approach to composition has been described by her champion, conductor Robert Spano, as "one of following her keen intuition." When she sets out to compose a new piece, what guides her? Is it mood, rhythm, texture, ensemble, form, color, theme?

"All of it, except form. That's the one thing I don't think about. I don't ever think about form. Ever, ever, ever. A lot of my male colleagues do. That's the first step for them. Oddly enough, even my pieces that get done a lot—I couldn't tell you what the form is at all. My method of writing is instinctive, trying to find those sounds that are interesting to combine. When I do talks at universities, the professors are horrified when I say that I just follow my ear."

Would she agree with her former teacher—and fellow gay composer—Ned Rorem, who once said that all artists are children? "That's true. I think some of the best art comes out of tapping into that. You do all this training, but then you let go of that so that you can do what the seven-year-old does."

And what's it like to be a female in a world that has been historically dominated by males? Is being identified as a "female composer" a ghettoizing or demeaning label?

"Well, I don't think it actually is. At one time it probably was, but a lot of my predecessors—Joan Tower, Libby Larsen, Ellen Zwilich—they kicked the door open." I share with Higdon what a lesbian composer friend of mine once told me, that "outness" in the classical music world is very different for lesbians than it is for gay men. Because lesbians are often "less obvious" than gay men, doesn't she have to answer for being a female composer more often than for being a lesbian composer?

"That may be true. There have been a couple of big articles about me in the *Inquirer* that talked about Cheryl. The first time that happened, I thought, Well, this ought to be interesting. We'll see if we get a reaction from the public. But it surprised me. I had all these little old ladies coming up to me, saying, 'Honey, we were so glad to hear you were a lesbian. My granddaughter's a lesbian.' Whoa, that was not what I was expecting at all. They were matter-of-fact about it."

In 1998, Higdon was included on a CRI album entitled *Lesbian American Composers*, a companion to their two-volume *Gay American Composers*. "I thought it was a lot of fun. But all of the women on the disc were upset by the cover." A soft-lit sepia photograph of two naked women embracing reposefully on a plush sofa, the cover, according to Higdon, "looks cheesy and doesn't reflect the music or the women on the disc."

Higdon is skeptical about the suggestion that a "lesbian identity" might come through in her music. "I don't know if anyone can actually tell that. I'm always too busy thinking about whether this music is interesting to listen to." She says that the "queer signature" in music was always a big discussion at Penn. "The professors were like, 'Yeah,' but the composers said, 'This is bullshit.' Queer music? If you did a blind test, I don't think you would be able to tell."

Fair enough, but so many of the adjectives that critics have applied to her music—fiery, swaggering, swashbuckling, spiky, assertive, muscular—are adjectives that are traditionally applied to men. To what extent does her sexuality free her up to explore sonorities and emotions that might, in the past, have been discouraged in women? "That's just the Ravel effect," she says, laughing again. "It's more attributable to the thrill of sound. There is something amazing about having an orchestra that plays full out."

Jennifer Higdon

But does she ever wonder if she has won over more critics because of that full-out, "masculine" sound? "I have no idea. It's such a complex answer. If the musicians are convinced, they will play the heck out of it. I have a lot of soft music, but people pay attention to the louder stuff."

By her own estimate, Higdon puts twelve to fourteen hours a day into the business of making music. Four to six hours are for composing. "The ideas come around fast. My brain is constantly working on pieces. I don't hit many walls. I sit down and say, I gotta write. I'm very persistent. I won't let myself get distracted. There is nothing like getting that brochure in the mail that says your premiere is coming up."

How about an opera? "It's coming. I'm working with a professional librettist, Gene Scheer, and we are doing a commission from the San Francisco Opera. It is scheduled for 2013." Higdon tells me how struck she was by the Max Färberböck film *Aimée and Jaguar*, which was based on the true story of two women, one a Jew, one not, who fell in love during the Nazi regime. "You have to find a story that resonates. We worked hard to get the rights to *Aimée and Jaguar*, but no luck. Because of timing, we've had to move on and are close to securing the rights for another story."

A few years ago, Lawson quit her job as a meeting planner in order to devote full time to taking care of the business end of Higdon's life. "Cheryl and I think so much alike. Because we met so early, we kind of grew up together. We're not coming from separate backgrounds. It works really well. She's a real trooper; she comes to all my concerts. I call her my muse. She provides such a safe place for my emotion and my heart. That's the hardest thing in art: to allow yourself to stay emotionally exposed. Cheryl makes me feel safe enough that I can communicate better with the people who play my music."

Of her piece *running the edgE*, Higdon once wrote that it reflects "the possibilities of going beyond the expected." To what extent does that intention—of "going beyond the possibilities"—inform all her music?

"All the time. I'm always searching for moving beyond. It makes the art more interesting. Otherwise, I'd be bored and I'd probably write boring music. We don't want to do that! There's enough of that around. For a long time, reporters would whisper the word 'accessible' about my music. And I'd say, Do you mean 'communicative'? I'm of the mind that you can write quality music that speaks. The whole point is just to have it speak."

Frank Kameny

"A homosexual is a person whose heterosexual function is crippled, like the legs of a polio victim." "The acts of these people are banned under the laws of God, the laws of nature, and are in violation of the laws of man." "Homosexuality is . . . a masquerade of life."

Such was the prevailing "wisdom" during the years when Frank Kameny was waging a courageous campaign against the federal government and the American Psychiatric Association on behalf of the right of gays and lesbians to live their lives without interference, criminalization, or the stigma of pathology. A major pioneer in the early gay rights movement, Kameny, according to David K. Johnson in *Before Stonewall,* "helped move gays and lesbians out of the shadows of 1950s apologetic, self-help groups and into the sunlight of the civil rights movement."

On a mild June evening, I meet Kameny at his home in a quiet residential section of Washington, D.C. The house has recently been designated a D.C. Historic Landmark, "not because of its gabled roof or side-hall plan," wrote the *Washington Post* in an article reporting the event, "but because, for thirteen fiery years, it was the epicenter of the gay rights movement in the nation's capital." Kameny has lived here since 1962. It's the house where he coined the motto "Gay Is Good," which, he once said, "epitomizes my entire half-century gay rights and equality effort; which provides the conceptual, foundational basis for that effort; and for which, above all else, I wish to be remembered."

Kameny tells me we have until ten o'clock, when the news comes on. He wants to watch the coverage of the city's gay pride parade. "I may well be on it." Indeed, that afternoon I watched from the sidewalk on P Street as Kameny, one of Capital Pride's 2009 "Super Heroes," passed by in an open car, waving to the crowd.

"A few years ago, this would have just been a very busy ten days," he tells me of all the appearances, ceremonies, and interviews he has participated in during this, the fortieth anniversary of the Stonewall riots. "Now it's all I can do to keep up."

In fact, he's looking remarkably buoyant. The day's hoopla has not in the least vitiated his considerable stamina, intelligence, memory, or verbal dexterity. The man who chose "not to adjust myself to society but with considerable success to adjust society to me" is ready to tell his story one more time.

Kameny was born on May 21, 1925, in New York. "At three o'clock in the afternoon, so I am told. I don't recall." The quip illustrates two aspects of his personality that will surface many times during the evening: his wry sense of humor and his acute memory for dates. "Anything with numbers," he confirms. "Dates, quantities, addresses—if it involves numbers, yes."

A precocious youngster, Kameny avidly devoured books. By age six, he knew he wanted to be an astronomer. "I was never terribly adept socially. I went to school every day, came home, did my homework, and went to bed." He finished high school two years ahead of his peers and entered Queens College a few months after his sixteenth birthday. "September 1941. Somewhere in all of the articles on me, that got downgraded by one year. The fact is I was sixteen."

In the middle of World War II, Kameny interrupted his college career to enlist in the army, three days before his eighteenth birthday. At his induction, when asked if he had "homosexual tendencies," he said no. Decades later, in an interview, he acknowledged, "I've resented for sixty-three years that I had to lie in order to serve."

"The point," he tells me, "is that while the 'military gay ban' became statutory law in 1993, the *policy* goes way, way back. On March 10, 1778, George Washington court-martialed Frederick Gotthold Enslin for being gay and four days later, on March 14, drummed him—literally, that's not a figure of speech—*drummed* him out of the service. That has been policy ever since. Hopefully, we will get rid of it, two and a half centuries overdue, in the next few months or a year."

Of gay life during his stint in the military, Kameny says, "There was a certain amount of it, but I hadn't come out. I had one or two little episodes the whole time I was in. Nothing meaningful. Had I been much more knowledgeable, there could have been quite a bit, as far as I can perceive." He makes it a point to remind me that "back then the whole concept of being homosexual didn't really exist. What you got is, 'This is a stage everybody goes through.'"

When he returned from the war, Kameny finished his degree in physics at Queens College, graduating in January 1948. That winter he entered Harvard as a graduate student in astronomy. He notes that the Kinsey Report, which was to inform his later thinking about homosexuality, came out within weeks of his entering graduate school.

During his graduate studies, Kameny spent a year at the Steward Observatory of the University of Arizona at Tucson. It was there that he carried on what he calls "a golden summer" with a young man. "He was seventeen and seduced a very willing me." Kameny marks that affair (he was twenty-nine) as his coming out. "We fell out of touch until a few years ago. He lives in Holland now with his partner of many years. They invited me to their marriage. I didn't go, but it reinstituted communication, and we exchanged commemorative e-mails on the fiftieth anniversary of our meeting."

After a year doing astronomy in Northern Ireland, Kameny returned to Harvard in 1955 to finish his doctorate, "dividing my time 50–50," he told Kay Tobin and Randy Wicker, the coauthors of *The Gay Crusaders*, "between my thesis and cruising the gay bar scene in Boston and Cambridge."

"That and Cambridge Common and the riverfront," he tells me now. "Those were the outdoor areas where people cruised. I had to go to Boston for the bars. The Napoleon Club had just opened. Another place was the Punchbowl. Both those names ring not only a bell but an extremely loud bell. Yes, indeed."

After earning his doctorate in 1956, Kameny taught at Georgetown for a year and then moved on to a civil service job as an astronomer with the Army Map Service. Evenings and weekends, he immersed himself in Washington's gay life. "It was a lively gay social scene. There was a small number of bars, which I would go to with considerable frequency." Kameny was good at his job, but in December 1957, after being informed that the government had information that he was a homosexual, he was straightaway dismissed. Such a turn of events might have sent many an individual into a state of depression, shame, self-hatred, and worse. Not Kameny.

"People keep asking me why I didn't fold or commit suicide. As with most things I do, I have a deep-seated feeling that I am right, the opposition is wrong, and that is that. I've never been ashamed of anything. The firing was unjust, improper, and fundamentally unconstitutional. It had to be fought."

And so Kameny appealed. "All the way up to the president, and to the House and Senate civil service committees." When he got nowhere, he sought the help of a lawyer, who took the case and prosecuted it through the federal courts. Again, Kameny did not prevail, at which point his legal counsel bowed out. Undaunted, even when he was reduced to "living on twenty cents of food a day, twenty-five when I could put a pat of butter on my potatoes," Kameny resolved to "follow things through to the end." Acting as his own counsel, he appealed to the Supreme Court. "To the best of my knowledge it was the first gay rights legal brief filed anywhere." In March 1961, the country's highest court refused to take up Kameny's case.

The decision effectively ended Kameny's personal battle but not his overall crusade. "By that time, I had gotten in touch with the tiny gay movement of the day. I decided that something needed to be done. There were obvious wrongs here." In November 1961, he and Jack Nichols, another early gay rights activist, formed the Mattachine Society of Washington. (Out of the original Mattachine, founded in Los Angeles in 1950 by Harry Hay, other chapters had emerged, but Kameny is at some pains to let me know that Mattachine Washington "was not a chapter of anything but a totally independent organization.")

"The homophile organizations that existed gave enormous credence to the so-called experts and authorities of the day. They weren't really militant. That wasn't me or my style. It was my opinion that we gays alone are the authorities on ourselves and our homosexuality, and others should listen to us. Once we got going in Washington, we proceeded to push forward."

Kameny tips his hat to Donald Webster Cory, whose 1951 book, *The Homosexual in America*, helped formulate his own thinking about homosexuals as a persecuted minority group. "He was very much a hero of the movement, such as it was. But eventually he bought into the theory that homosexuality was an illness. As the sixties moved on, he and I had very intense differences of opinion. But the fundamental concept of gays as a minority was set out by him. I proceeded to develop it and run with it."

Within a short time of its founding, Mattachine Washington began to challenge the American Psychiatric Association's classification of homosexuality as a mental disorder. Addressing an audience at New York Mattachine in July 1964, Kameny said that "the entire homophile movement . . . is going to stand or fall upon the question of whether or not homosexuality is a sickness."

At first, even some within Mattachine Washington were reluctant to embrace the antipathology position. But Kameny was adamant. He argued that "those who considered it an illness had the obligation to present the evidence." Kameny's position prevailed, and in March 1965, Mattachine Washington issued a statement, which Kameny recites for me from memory: "In the absence of valid scientific evidence to the contrary, homosexuality is not considered a sickness, disturbance or pathology in any sense but is merely a preference . . . not different from heterosexuality."

"And fully on par with it!" he adds. "That was the opening of the battle. It shifted the burden of proof. Those who considered it an illness had the obligation to present the evidence. In the ensuing decade, they never did."

At the time that Kameny was waging this campaign, he was also helping to organize demonstrations against other forms of gay discrimination. "In the sixties, picketing was the mode of dissent par excellence. In those days you didn't need a permit to picket in front of the White House. The policeman on duty would simply assign you a location. If you had a complaint, that was the thing to do."

The first demonstration in front of the White House took place on April 17, 1965. "We did it with no advance publicity, intentionally, so that some bureaucrat would not find a way to prevent us from picketing. We simply assembled at the southwest corner of Lafayette Park." There were ten in that original group, seven men and three women.

"As we marched," Jack Nichols later recalled, "I looked about at our well-dressed little band. Kameny had insisted that we seven men must wear suits and ties, and the women, dresses and heels.

New Yorkers later complained that we Washingtonians looked like a convention of undertakers, but given the temper of the times, Kameny's insistence was apropos. 'If you're asking for equal employment rights,' he intoned, 'look employable!'"

The demonstration went off so smoothly that Mattachine Washington decided to picket again a month later. "And this time we did publicize." They picketed the Civil Service Commission in June, the Pentagon in July, the State Department in August—"they were publicly rigid about being antigay"—and again in front of the White House in October. The largest of these demonstrations managed to assemble "about forty-five to fifty-five picketers." Kameny recalls that they met with "no meaningful harassment." The most offensive encounter occurred when one of the female picketers "was told that she should get herself a good man."

Kameny contends that these early demonstrations—and the annual Fourth of July pickets in front of Independence Hall in Philadelphia, which Mattachine Washington joined—paved the way for the Stonewall uprising in 1969. "By virtue of our coming out of the closet collectively, it created the mindset for protesting, so that when the events of the moment created the eruption on Christopher Street, people were primed."

Under Kameny's leadership, Mattachine Washington was becoming the trendsetter among the few homophile organizations in existence in those days. "The things that were being done were being done by us here," he told a reporter for the *Washington Blade* in June 2009. In a paralegal capacity, he began to handle a large number of civil service, military, and security cases, winning some significant victories. "We should have won them all." In fact, Kameny claims to have become the country's "authority on security clearances for gay people." He also started calling for a repeal of the military's policy of excluding gays from service. His confrontational style became known as "ferocious."

In 1971, Kameny ran as a nonvoting delegate to the House of Representatives, the first openly gay candidate for the U.S. Congress. "Given my activities, I seemed the obvious person to do it." When collecting the necessary five thousand signatures on the nominating petitions proved disappointing, Kameny's campaign staff sought the help of "the gay organization that was in the forefront of *everything* in those days," the New York Gay Activists Alliance. "One or two busloads of GAA people came down. We met them and escorted them to private homes that night. In the morning, we assigned them to spots around the city to gather signatures."

That Sunday night, Mattachine Washington sponsored a dance for the GAA volunteers. While the festivities were in progress, Kameny's campaign director came in. "He had a huge roll of petitions under each arm. Sixty-six hundred signatures! We were certified by the Board of Elections."

Running as an independent, Kameny took the opportunity to make his views known. "I had to become an instant expert on everything—from trash collection to taxes. But in parallel I ran it as a gay rights campaign." From a pile of papers in the living room, he hands me one of the original bright orange campaign posters they used that year. (Indeed, memorabilia from his half century of activism clutters every room I can see.) At the election, Kameny came in fourth out of the six candidates. Undaunted, he immediately turned his attentions to the American Psychiatric Association.

The APA had invited Kameny, by now "the most notable homosexual activist in Washington," according to Ronald Bayer, to organize and moderate a panel of "nonpatient homosexuals" at its annual meeting, which in 1971 was to be held in the capital. The invitation was an attempt to placate gay activists, who had staged a guerilla invasion of the association's 1970 meeting in San Francisco. Kameny accepted and got to work. With the help of the newly formed Gay Activists Alliance of Washington, Mattachine, and "the fading, but not faded, GLF," he planned a disruption of the Convocation of Fellows, a plenary session of the entire convention. "I have always referred to it as the Ordination of the New Psychiatrists. Sitting in the back was a row of elderly psychiatrists wearing gold medals on ribbons." His pale gray eyes brighten. "Wait. That's relevant."

Kameny's presence on the panel gave him a legitimate entrée to the convocation. Other protestors quietly infiltrated the meeting room in advance and "wedged open the fire doors." In the middle of an address by guest speaker Ramsey Clark, the former attorney general, they burst in. "Whereupon the elderly psychiatrists proceeded to beat them over the heads with their gold medals and chased most of them out, including the person we had designated to seize the microphone and denounce them."

Kameny saw that "either something gets done or this whole thing was going to fade into utter nothingness." When he grabbed the mike, someone pulled the plug. "But I have a very loud voice and don't need microphones. I continued to denounce them while they shook their fists at me and called me a Nazi." At the panel session three days later, Kameny continued to scold the psychiatrists. "We're rejecting you as our owners," he told them. With his scientifically trained mind, Kameny was able "to bring coherence to the critique of psychiatry that had surfaced in the preceding years," writes Ronald Bayer in his riveting account of these years, *Homosexuality and American Psychiatry.*

By now, the APA was paying attention. At the 1972 meeting in Dallas, Kameny was included in another panel discussion, at which a gay psychiatrist, John E. Fryer, wearing a mask, also participated. Kameny also authored a brochure, distributed at the convention, that called upon the APA to repudiate its theory of homosexuality as a sickness. He takes great delight in telling me that during the dance that followed the association's banquet, he and a gay man from one of the Dallas organizations danced together "while the psychiatrists danced around us." The tide was turning. A sentiment was growing within the profession that homosexuals might be psychologically healthy after all.

Of the 1973 meeting, which took place in Honolulu, Kameny remembers three things: first, "a gay bar there, where the gay psychiatrists went. They were scared to death, but we assured them that we wouldn't reveal them." Second, a speech by Ron Gold, one of the founders of the National Gay and Lesbian Task Force, entitled "Stop It! You're Making Me Sick!" And third, the vote that year to remove homosexuality from the list of mental disorders in the APA's *Diagnostic and Statistical Manual,* "which meant we were cured en masse."

Two years later, in another victory in the early gay rights movement, the Civil Service Commission dropped its policy of discrimination against gay men and lesbians. "After an eighteen-year battle, I heard something that I have always cherished—something one does not often hear in life: 'The government has decided to change its policies to suit you!'"

Kameny rehearses for me the subsequent steps the government took in strengthening the new policy: the Civil Service Reform Act under Jimmy Carter; Bill Clinton's Executive Order 13087, which explicitly forbids discrimination on the basis of homosexuality; and finally, President Obama's appointment of John Berry, an openly gay man, as director of the Office of Personnel Management. "He invited me to be present at his swearing-in ceremony and mentioned me in his remarks. A storybook ending. I had been fired because I was gay. Fifty-two years later the head of the Civil Service Commission is an openly gay man. I still haven't ceased being amazed by it."

Kameny has not rested on his laurels. He has served on the district's Human Rights Commission, was a member of the board of the National Gay Task Force, and mounted challenges to the D.C. sodomy law, which was eventually overturned in 1993.

"That took me thirty years, one month, four days, and approximately eleven hours." He still works on military cases and proudly tells me that he recently sent "a very long memorandum" to the congressional office that is drafting the latest version of the bill to repeal "Don't Ask, Don't Tell." He's also working with the D.C. City Council on the same-sex marriage issue. (The bill passed in December 2009.)

In 2006, the Library of Congress acquired Kameny's papers. "Seventy-seven thousand sheets of paper. Boxes and boxes. I'm a pack rat. I have all the signs from those pickets, including the very sticks they were carried with. They've gone over to the Smithsonian. They're in a collection—I've been there and seen it—a small wooden folding desk upon which Jefferson wrote the Declaration of Independence, a pair of ornate metal inkwells with which Lincoln wrote the Emancipation Proclamation, a variety of items from Martin Luther King, *and* my signs. All in one collection!" He chuckles. He might well chuckle, too, at receiving in 2006, along with Barbara Gittings, the first John E. Fryer, M.D., Award from the American Psychiatric Association, given in honor of the brave masked psychiatrist who joined Kameny on the panel at the 1972 APA Convention.

Nowadays, Kameny spends his days much more quietly than he used to, though he still monitors the Far Right and occasionally fires off nasty letters to them. "If I had stayed on at the Army Map Service, we would have moved over to NASA. I would like to think that in due course I would have volunteered to become an astronaut. I might have walked on the moon."

It's not stretching the metaphor, I tell him, to suggest that he has walked on the moon of gay liberation. At that he chuckles again. "Fair enough!"

Frank Kameny

Randall Kenan

Randall Kenan and I originally met in 1993 in Provincetown, Massachusetts, where I interviewed the native North Carolinian for my Saturday morning WOMR radio show, *Something Inside So Strong*, an hour-long conversation every other week with a gay or lesbian writer. At the time, Kenan had published a novel and a highly acclaimed book of short stories. He was living in New York and teaching writing courses at Sarah Lawrence and Columbia. "Do you plan on returning to the South to live?" I asked him at the time, to which he responded with his appealing country-boy joviality, "As to whether I'll take up the sink and the bed and move back, I can't say yet."

Fifteen years later, I catch up with him again, this time in Chapel Hill, where, with four more books to his name, Kenan has risen to an assistant professorship of English at the university. The recipient of a Guggenheim Fellowship, a Rome Prize from the American Academy of Arts and Letters, and many other awards, Kenan seems to embody what he himself once called the "new New Negro"—one who is "singularly, dynamically, importantly a success." Those new books include a biography of James Baldwin and three other books of nonfiction, including *Walking on Water: Black American Lives at the Turn of the Twenty-first Century* (1999), which was nominated for the Southern Book Award, and *The Fire This Time* (2007), a memoir that is, in part, an homage to Baldwin.

So why did he return to North Carolina, I ask him now on this beautiful spring morning, one of Kenan's "Lionel Richie Sundays," as he calls his end-of-the-week relaxation days.

"Look around, my brother!" His infectious, deep-voiced jollity returns. "Mid-April in these parts is breathtaking. Once a lot of impediments were taken away, the attractiveness of the Sunbelt is undeniable."

Kenan, who was born in 1963, knew a very different South when he was growing up. In *The Fire This Time*, he recalls his early youth as a "dirt-poor, illegitimate black country boy, growing up amid the snake- and deer-infested swamps of Duplin County, North Carolina." "My rural background," he tells me now, "has informed so much of my life: those country values, those country people, the sense of landscape, the sense of legacy. Even when I was in New York, I was a country boy in the big city. Even when I'm among black folk, I'm a black country person. I'm a country queer. But people are leaving; it's a dying way of life. Small-town farmers are really an endangered species. It's a part of me that's becoming a ghost, so I cling to it more tenaciously."

Many people had an enormous influence on what Kenan calls his "mischievous mind," none more so than his great-aunt. "I learned a lot from her. It was just the two of us for quite some time. I stayed with her one weekend and never came back. She was the mistress of how I negotiated that realm."

In *Walking on Water*, Kenan wrote that though he experienced racism in North Carolina, he knew "nothing as hellish as what James Baldwin had encountered." The comparison made you feel "in some way not black enough, somehow—ridiculously—inauthentic." He explains to me now: "A lot of people of my generation were looking at prior generations as being much more certain about their identity. The political aspect of their identity was much more to the fore." Would he draw a parallel with young gay people today? Did the previous generation of gay people—the ones who knew outright discrimination and fought against it—feel "more certain about their identity" than this newest generation of gay people, the inheritors of gay liberation?

"When I came of age and was conscious of what was going on, there was a heavy political component to being gay, and that ramped up with the AIDS epidemic: ACT UP, Queer Nation. You felt you had to be a part of some civil disobedience. Now even AIDS as a political issue is off the front burner for a lot of these kids, sometimes with dire consequences. In many ways I envy them because of their enormous freedom. But at the same time I'm wondering how they formulate an identity."

As a youngster, Kenan read a lofty pantheon of dead white male writers: Dumas, Dickens, Hugo, Jules Verne, Robert Louis Stevenson. He chuckles. "I didn't hold that against them! Wasn't like I had a Eurocentric necrophilia thing going on. Everybody was reading them at the time. But the black press was very much pro–letting us know that Dumas was an octoroon. I never really thought of him as a white guy. I mean, look at that curly hair. He's a brother! Reading those books was just sheer joy. To be locked up in a cell, dreaming how you would escape, reinventing yourself. Great, great fun!"

Kenan has often written about the importance of church, in his case the Baptist Church, in a young black person's upbringing. In *Walking on Water*, he writes, "For better or for worse, regardless of how I or anybody else felt about that church-haunted, Christ-haunted, sin-haunted background, that same background empowered us, and made us more humane than we realized."

He tells me now, "The church was the center of community, the center of economic power, spiritual power, social power. That's a lot of power to be concentrated between four walls. A church community was as strong as its pastor, which is a strength and a weakness." Did he experience any homophobia from the pulpits of those congregations? "Oh child, please! They had a nontolerance policy back in the day. There was also a double standard, because there was always somebody who, as they'd say euphemistically, 'had a little sugar in his blood, a little sugar in his pants.' If he went along, he could get along. If she didn't tell or throw it in anybody's face, they were going to cover her in Christian love and pray for her soul. Let me retread. Those should all be masculine pronouns. Lesbianism was beyond the pale. It was all about effeminacy. The idea of a masculine man being a queer didn't enter one's mind."

How did he square those two experiences of church: being embraced by a community of love and at the same time hearing vitriolic comments about gay people? "It's difficult to square. If you internalize it (because 'it's a sin; says right here in the Bible, it's a sin!'), you're in for a bumpy road, full of self-hate. That fundamental Christian way of looking at things and the reality of being a same-sex-loving individual, they don't go together very easily."

By the time he went to college, the University of North Carolina, Kenan was "pushing at both doors at the same time": he was a religious seeker and a young man who knew he loved other men. "Of all things, Alice Walker's *The Color Purple* gave me all sorts of permission to look at religion. I came out with a little more expansive vision of spirituality. When I was here as an undergraduate, my three closest friends all went on to become theologians. I was out to them. Homosexuality was as fascinating to them on an intellectual level as it was to me."

At the time, the university was predominantly white. Kenan feared that so much contact with white folk "would in some way put my Negro 'soul' in danger." He explains: "Coming out of that first desegregated generation, the children of affirmative action, we didn't really know what was going to happen to us. Venturing out on this new path without the restrictions of the previous generation led to a lot of anxiety." He joined the black student movement choir—"I liked the people; I thought it was fun"—and wound up having a black circle of friends.

Kenan started out as a physics major, but through the encouragement of a professor he "caught the bug" and turned to literature. He spent a summer at Oxford studying drama criticism, the "literature of Oxford," and Shakespeare. After graduation in 1985, he went to New York City, the "prototypical country boy aloose in the big city," as he writes in the prologue to *Walking on Water*.

"It was sheer and utter enchantment," he tells me. "It was Dorothy in the Emerald City. It was Samuel Johnson in London. Yeah, yeah," he adds with a guttural chuckle, "I was thoroughly fulfilled and happy. Poor as a church mouse. Did not care. Going out every night. I have no idea how I lived. I was making damn near nothin'. I got into trouble financially often, but it didn't stop me one whit. I think to be young and foolish is a great—" He can't finish the sentence without chortling. "A great antidote to any of life's realities!"

Starting out as an "office boy in waiting," Kenan ended up working at Knopf, where he eventually became an assistant editor. In 1989, he published his first novel, *A Visitation of Spirits*, about a precocious sixteen-year-old black boy who hopes to become a famous physicist but whose attraction to men has "frightened him beyond reason" and eventually leads to his suicide. His second book, a collection of short stories, *Let the Dead Bury Their Dead*, published in 1992, received considerable mainstream attention, including a nomination for the *Los Angeles Times* Book Award, a finalist designation for the National Book Critics Circle Award, and a "notable book" listing in the *New York Times*.

By the next year, Kenan had set out on a six-year American odyssey, traveling the country, researching and interviewing for the book that would become *Walking on Water*, an attempt, as he put it in the preface, "to chronicle, chart, eviscerate, enumerate, analyze and explain the nature of blackness."

"This idea formulated fairly early. It came out of being a kid of the eighties, not feeling the strong moorings that earlier generations did. I knew all these other black men who were asking the same question. We'd sit up late at night, bending our elbows, speculating. I was always a fan of travel literature. I was going to figure out how to do it myself.

"I tried to go to places where you don't hear a lot of black folk. I wanted to take an idiosyncratic way of looking at how black people are woven into the fabric of American society. My black readers found this really exciting. That's what captured their imaginations. White folk came at it from a slightly different view. They were interested in the same old places: North versus South. This monodimensional preoccupation with the 'Negro problem.' A lot of white Americans don't take much time to learn about black folk. They're satisfied with the received thing—what they get off the boob tube, the *New York Times*."

In the book, Kenan wrote of being struck "by the vast amount of African American history that either lay gathering dust in hundreds of libraries or had gone unrecorded." Who, I ask, is impoverished by the loss of this knowledge? "All Americans. But more than anybody, young black folk. I don't know how they learn any history at all. Especially the ones who don't have active parents. I keep thinking, But here are the proteins, the vitamins you need! A lot of people in disadvantaged areas still have those mental shackles on. These narratives I uncovered—a black marshal in Oklahoma in 1890, black businessmen—have been out of their ken. And I'm not just talking about upliftery. There are lessons in these stories that are important. The respect of the larger community, the larger nation would be more easily accessed if people had a full picture of their history."

Kenan's position, articulated again and again in *Walking on Water*, is that "race is only one element of being black." Ultimately, he concluded that to be black "is to be composed of three essential ingredients: political, cultural, and emotional." Would he say that the same three ingredients are the essential components of what it means to be gay?

"If you can put *desire* in there somewhere. I just read a draft of a friend's story, a straight guy, about a lesbian Episcopal priest. He was coming at it from a purely theological perspective. I said to him, 'Brother, this is all fine, but the thing that makes her a lesbian is her desire for another woman. That's not in there.' It had never occurred to him. Desire is an essential part of gay identity. That's the prime mover. Everything else builds on that."

What that "everything else" is Kenan is unable to say. "The idea of a gay culture is built on the thinnest of tissues. Sure, there is a specific *camp* culture. It's very urban. It was very important to an earlier generation. But where is gay culture now? There is a new group of same-sex-loving men who don't even use the term 'gay.' For them, gay connotes something entirely different from what they do sexually with somebody else. Gay to them has all this baggage: camp culture, a political consciousness that they aren't necessarily down with. They don't want to think about AIDS. The whole DL culture that has become so popular. Where it's going, I don't know."

Toward the end of *Walking on Water*, Kenan writes about the "peer pressure" to be black enough. Does he think being gay has freed him to pursue a black identity that is authentic to himself? "I've come to realize that that was a blessing and a curse. I'd probably be preaching somewhere on a Sunday morning had I not been gay. Being gay forced me to look at things theologically, sociologically, and artistically in ways that I wouldn't have otherwise. That was my path."

The journey to understand blackness—and gayness—continued for Kenan in his next book, *The Fire This Time*, his homage to James Baldwin, which he published in 2007. "When I first started, I was threatened by the very idea of Baldwin, the monolith of Baldwin, which was very intimidating. He's it. Either you live up to him, or you ain't crap. I met him when I was an undergraduate here. Around the time the *Price of the Ticket* came out, I started reading him, not just studying him but *reading* him. My appreciation of him soared."

Baldwin famously wrote about the power of the blues to speak powerfully of the black experience in America. Kenan, too, has turned his attention to a black musical form, hip-hop, but for him there is "something quite poisonous" in it.

"It's complicated. You can look at it in a very complex way, which says there are all types of hip-hop artists with all sorts of messages, or you can look at it very simplistically and dismiss it as 'just rap music.' It angers me when I think that this is informing a whole generation of white boys about what it means to be black—the black, aggressive, hypersexualized thug. We've had these images for so long. The fact that in the twenty-first century this is considered OK, it's just galling!"

Kenan is also critical of what he calls "disturbing trends" in the Hollywood studio movies that portray blacks. In the main, he says, these films have little to do with "real folk." Does he think gay people are getting any better deal in the way they are portrayed in the movies and popular culture? "I feel like such a harpy on these issues! Sure, we've come a long way, baby. But at the same time, it's so aggravating that you see the perpetuation of the same types of roles. We all know that Hollywood deals in stereotypes. And television is even worse."

Kenan has noted how writers who identify as gay and "ethnic"— gay and Asian, gay and Italian, gay and African American—have an opportunity to "revivify two canons at the same time."

"When they get me, they get three for one: I'm black, I'm queer, and I'm a Southerner. A lot of people don't want to think about how many groups they straddle, but I think it's true of more people than they realize. That twoness, or threeness, is not a burden any longer for me. It's a strength. I'm teaching a beginning fiction class now, and I want to butt my head against the wall when we get into character. They want to make everything a stereotype. I tell them, 'That's not how it goes. *This* is how that person would act. Human beings do strange stuff!'"

As we wrap up, I remind him that in *The Fire This Time* he quoted James Baldwin: "One is responsible to life." What is his personal connection with that quotation?

"I think it's important to search and to delve and to understand— all those wonderful things that Socrates and Benjamin Franklin and Martin Luther King, Jr., exhorted us to do. To take responsibility, first for ourselves and then for others. For me, as a secular humanist who is also respectful of religion, the basic ideals are the ideals of the Enlightenment: to balance some sense of rationality with some sense of spirituality. To be good to one another, or, as that wonderful movie from the eighties said, 'Be excellent to one another.' You can't get much better than that."

Sharon Kleinbaum

In 1981, Sharon Kleinbaum served six months at Alderson Federal Reformatory for Women for attempting to wrap the Pentagon in yarn. Twenty years—and many arrests—later, she was honored with the Jewish Fund for Justice's "Woman of Valor" Award. As senior rabbi of Congregation Beth Simchat Torah, the largest gay and lesbian synagogue in the world, Kleinbaum is no stranger to trouble. Over the years, the hippielike style of her politics may have waned, but her fervor, commitment, and chutzpah decidedly have not. In 2006, while in Jerusalem to lend support to the rancorous struggle of Israeli gays and lesbians to hold a pride parade in that city, she marched down to the city council chambers, plunked herself into the mayor's seat, and announced, "Tell the mayor of Jerusalem that a lesbian rabbi sat in his chair!"

I meet Kleinbaum in her cramped, windowless office on Bethune Street in New York's West Village. It's a serious scholar's den, piled with books, correspondence, and manuscripts. Whatever free space remains is decorated with photographs, mementos from loving congregants, and a yarmulke-wearing Elmo hand puppet. ("Shl'Elmo," she calls him.) On one wall, a young child's drawing of two raven-haired women dreamily facing each other while valentines burst from their heads is inscribed with this message: "HeLLO i AM WRIHGTING THIS LETTER TO SUPPORT GAY PRIDE! i THINK THAT iT'S WRONG WHAT THE HAReDIM ARE DOING AND i HOPE THEY MAKE PEACE. GO GAY LOVE." It's from a very young member of her congregation.

Named one of the country's "Top 50" Jewish leaders by the *Forward* and *Jewish Week*, Kleinbaum hardly seemed like a candidate for the ministry when she was growing up in Rutherford, New Jersey, a working-class town with a heavily Italian American population. Her father, born into a Yiddish-speaking socialist family in the Bronx, had never been to a synagogue until he married. He met Kleinbaum's mother through the Jewish social work world. They married in 1950. Kleinbaum, the youngest of four, was born in 1959. In an essay she contributed to *Lesbian Rabbis: The First Generation*, Kleinbaum wrote that as a child she never experienced congregational life as "vibrant, passionate, or world changing."

"Not at all," she tells me. "I hated it. We belonged to the local conservative synagogue. It was characteristic of so many synagogues in the sixties. There was nothing genuine happening there. The message we got over and over again was 'Because of the Holocaust, you have to be Jewish. Because of the state of Israel, you have to be Jewish.' Those are very important factors, but it wasn't very meaningful to say that this was the whole reason for being Jewish."

As a youngster, Kleinbaum took up progressive causes. She spent Saturday mornings helping one of her brothers distribute grape boycott flyers at the local A & P. When she was nine, she was "walking around canvassing for Eugene McCarthy." During her eighth-grade year, she became active in the McGovern presidential campaign. At a school debate before the national election, she announced that Nixon's foreign policies were "bankrupt and that he should be impeached for war crimes." The following January, she participated in the March on Washington to protest Nixon's inauguration. Kleinbaum says that such "obnoxious" behavior was punished by the school's barring her from membership in the Honor Society.

As a result, her parents pulled her out of public school and sent her to an Orthodox Jewish private school, Frisch Yeshiva High School in northern New Jersey. Of her time there, Kleinbaum says, "The overall thrill of being treated intellectually like an adult blew me away. It was challenging, provocative, stimulating. The adults cared how they lived their lives. They were grappling with questions of identity and practice, of how you diminish the gap between what you believe and how you act in the world."

During high school, Kleinbaum was "conscious that I was very different." She had little interest in dating boys. Instead, she threw her energies into the Orthodox youth movement, where she became a "superstar," rising to become the first female president of the New York Inter-Yeshiva League. When she was a senior, one of her friends told her that one of their eighth-grade teachers had just come out as a lesbian. "I was seventeen years old. It was the first time I had heard the word 'lesbian,' and stuff started clicking. I remember feeling a sense of panic. On some level I knew that was me." By the end of high school, Kleinbaum had left Orthodox Judaism. "I couldn't accept the stuff about women—forget the lesbian part—and I couldn't accept the attitudes toward non-Jews. I couldn't reconcile those with my broader vision of social justice."

She attended Barnard, where, freshman year, she had her "first real girlfriend." She also engaged in radical politics, especially the movement to get the university to drop its investments in companies doing business with South Africa and the antinuclear movement. She was arrested and jailed several times. By then, she had started calling herself a lesbian, though not publicly, because "I had the idea that if I was visible as a lesbian it would hurt my credentials as a radical."

Kleinbaum, who studied Yiddish in college to fulfill a foreign language requirement, came to appreciate Yiddish culture as "very gender nonconforming." She explains: "In Yiddish literature and Eastern European culture, women are supposed to be physically strong, zaftig, and men were supposed to be a little nebbishy, but very smart and clever and witty and urbane in the way that we think of gay men today. When you think of a Yiddish story, the humor is very gay. It's sarcastic; it's turning things on its head. And the women are tough. They're not pushovers or giggly blonds in the background."

Kleinbaum also began studying Judaism again "with some of the greatest Jewish thinkers, which was very exciting." Many years later, she wrote that her years at Barnard "opened to me the possibility that I could be Jewish and still be me. That was news to me that you could be a liberal Jew and still be politically progressive."

In the summer of 1981, having graduated, Kleinbaum, who had gone to work for the War Resisters League, went to Europe to participate in a peace walk from Copenhagen to Paris. When she returned, she happened to meet Aaron Lansky, founder of the National Yiddish Book Center. That meeting essentially changed her life. Lansky, who in his memoir, *Outwitting History*, recalls the twenty-two-year-old Kleinbaum as "smart, feisty, and acutely political," offered her a job. For the next three years, she served as his assistant director, throwing her energy and talent into "a real cultural rescue operation" that involved salvaging thousands of Yiddish language books. Lansky eventually encouraged her to consider rabbinical school.

Kleinbaum entered Reconstructionist Rabbinical College in Philadelphia in 1985, "not to become a rabbi but to study the texts of our tradition." The previous year, the school had begun accepting gay students. "They didn't know what that policy would mean. So I entered completely closeted. That's what the world was like then." Though the gay rabbinical students identified each other "pretty quickly," and though she had a girlfriend, Kleinbaum remained "culturally not out to the straight world."

Then in 1986, she attended a secret conference for lesbian and gay Jewish professionals. Kleinbaum pulls a scrapbook from one of the shelves behind her desk to show me her notes from that meeting. The conference was called Aron Ha-Kodesh, Hebrew for "the Holy Closet," a double entendre that refers both to the place where the Torah is kept and the clandestine conclave of gays and lesbians who had gathered for the historic meeting.

The conference was transformative for her. "To be with this small group—we were about thirty people—to be together and do the Jewish stuff *and* have the gay stuff out there! We weren't pushing that part of us out of the room." Until then she had assumed that to be a rabbi she was going to have to live with an unbridgeable division between her religious life and her sexual identity. The conference opened her eyes. "When I experienced a breakdown of that bifurcation, I really got how sick that was."

Kleinbaum returned to the rabbinical college and, with her characteristic roll-up-the-sleeves approach, started a committee called What Now? The school's liberal admissions policy was a step in the right direction, but there was more work to be done. "If you're going to let gay people in, but if the culture doesn't change at all, if there are no jobs for gay people, if there is still a heterosexual bias in our theology and the way we teach, that's not going to work."

By now gay and lesbian synagogues had sprung up in places like Los Angeles (Beth Chayim Chadashim in 1972) and New York

(CBST in 1973). "It is hard to convey how radical that was," Kleinbaum says. These first congregations were mostly small social groups led by laypeople. It was a place for gay people, mostly men, to get together. "The men had a sense of entitlement to Judaism that women were more conflicted about. Thank God for those gay men. You need a sense of entitlement to say, 'I'm not losing this.' They were the ones who started the gay Jewish synagogue movement."

In 1987, while still a theological student, Kleinbaum was asked to fill in as rabbi for another such gay and lesbian congregation, Atlanta's Bet Haverim, founded only two years earlier. There she "began to develop an appreciation for the radical transformative possibilities of a gay/lesbian synagogue."

"Atlanta had lots of Jews. I got the sense that I might have something to offer. I loved the work I was doing. As a gay rabbi, I got how it felt to be in a gay environment. I understood what the issues were facing gay people because it was me; I wasn't trying to pretend. I had some wisdom to share. We understood each other."

During the final three years of her studies, Kleinbaum continued her relationship with the Atlanta congregation. By her final year in seminary, she was going there every six weeks. "I got that congregational life could be vibrant, full of mature people asking adult questions." Senior year, she came out publicly at Reconstructionist Rabbinical College, the only person at the time to do so. While the announcement did not cause a stir at the school, she found it difficult to land a job.

As the time approached for Kleinbaum to be ordained, she assumed that she would return to political activism. Instead, in 1990, the Atlanta congregation offered her a permanent half-time position. She hoped to combine that with another half-time position at Emory University. Although she emerged as one of the university's two finalists, and even when the other finalist dropped out, Emory did not hire her. She suspects homophobia was behind the decision. Unable to find a congregation that would take her on full-time, Kleinbaum got a job as director of congregational relations at the Religious Action Center of Reform Judaism in Washington, D.C., where she worked for two years until 1992, when she was called to take up duties as the first official rabbi of Congregation Beth Simchat Torah.

Her first years at CBST were tough ones. "We were having funerals all the time. It was all AIDS related. There was always somebody dying, somebody going into the hospital, somebody mourning. The primary social event was memorial services. I was very moved to be of service. We were all so mad at the larger political nightmare that was going on. It was a way to channel that anger: I was actually doing something. Most of the funerals I did were for people my age or younger. It cemented my skepticism toward the larger Jewish world and the larger religious world, how slow people were to respond, how cautious, how frightened the institutions of the Jewish world were. And how long it took them to take a stand and do proactive things. I felt more and more like this was my home."

Under Kleinbaum's leadership, the congregation has been "on the cutting edge" of gay and lesbian Jewish religious life. Since 1994, the synagogue has taken an active part in educating rabbinical students about gay and lesbian issues, acting like a training hospital, a place where they can get firsthand experience in ministering to the needs of LGBTQ Jews. "We work very hard to help mainstream synagogues accept openly gay people."

Kleinbaum has also spearheaded projects for greater liturgical creativity. She has been instrumental in insuring that the synagogue's music program would be "as sophisticated as any in New York." And she is "intensely proud" to have led a committee that wrote a new siddur, the congregation's prayer book. The readings include passages from Walt Whitman, Adrienne Rich, Muriel Rukeyser, Steven Sondheim, Tony Kushner, William Finn "not just because they're beautiful writers; they're *gay*! They have something to say to our souls." Ten years in the making, the siddur, which was published in 2007, includes a section on AIDS, a Pride Shabbat, prayers for the Transgender Day of Remembrance. "We're not afraid to say that sexuality and spirituality are deeply interwoven."

Kleinbaum, whose indefatigable energy invests everything she does, says her next mission is to lead the congregation toward greater participation in social, economic, and racial justice. "We should take our position as gay people and Jews and really foster a commitment to worldwide social justice."

And then there are the kids. Kleinbaum, who raised two daughters during her earlier years at CBST, says that nowadays the congregation is experiencing the baby boom that is hitting all segments of the gay and lesbian community. "I'm now teaching the parenting classes, which, when I came to CBST, was as unfathomable as the fact that there would be kids here at all. It's fantastic. We have gay men, straight families, lesbians, single parents, kids adopted from Africa,

China, South America, artificial insemination, surrogacy. Some the old-fashioned way, even." She laughs. "They're the minority.

"It's just so fantastic. On Rosh Hashanah, we have a blessing for the children. Last year we had ninety-five kids come up on the bimah. You could see congregants, even if they didn't have children of their own, just weeping to imagine a gay community in which there would be children. So many people in the congregation lost custody, or had to give up having kids, or had to make a decision to be gay or have kids."

Membership is booming. As of 2008, the congregation counted 850 dues-paying members plus children. Shabbat services are held at an Episcopal church in Chelsea. On the High Holy Days, they see upward of 3,500 people at the Jacob Javits Center.

The struggle for LGBTQ people to be embraced by mainstream Judaism is hardly over. Kleinbaum has been the target of vitriol, especially from the Orthodox community. One rabbi has pronounced her the "greatest moral terrorist alive today." Another told her directly that she was "worse than Hitler because Hitler just killed Jewish bodies; I'm killing the Jewish soul." During a demonstration against her support of a gay pride march in Jerusalem, ten thousand Hasidim stood on Second Avenue and shouted at her the Yiddish word for "whore."

"It strengthens my resolve not to let them ultimately decide the discourse or the language. This is why I absolutely reject the idea that Orthodox Judaism or evangelical right-wing Christianity gets to have a monopoly on religion. I absolutely believe that anybody who uses religion to advocate antigay rhetoric is blaspheming God's name. I respect their right to have different interpretations, but they don't have the right to codify their interpretation into a law that discriminates against me."

Kleinbaum passionately affirms what she calls "the wisdom of gay people." She says, "It would be a shame if our centers of culture disappear and everybody simply assimilates into a larger culture. I think it's wonderful that there are synagogues and other Jewish institutions that accept individual gay people, but the concerns we have will never be the top of their political or social agenda."

Kleinbaum's partner of eighteen years, Margaret Moers Wenig, is also a rabbi and teaches at Hebrew Union College. Kleinbaum says that their shared rabbinical careers have contributed to "total cross-fertilization" when it comes to ideas, sermons, projects. "She edits everything I write. She's a brilliant editor." Asked about raising their daughters, she says, "We did that very well together. We loved it." Adults now, the young women, Liba and Molly, have moved out of the family home in Brooklyn. "That's why we got puppies," she jokes.

Next steps? "I don't know. I have a lot of dreams for CBST, a lot of places I think we could go." Space is a major issue. Even though the synagogue's present location sits squarely in the middle of "gay central," Kleinbaum has convened a committee to hunt for more adequate quarters. "We'd like to be in gay central but with a little more space." And then she whispers, "I'd also like a window."

Andrew Lam

It was strange to have had a privileged life as a child while the world around you was sinking into horror," Andrew Lam tells me. "Strange to escape the bulk of it when the rest of your people went through re-education camps, died on the high seas, were raped by pirates. While I tried my best to remove myself from that, I couldn't run far enough."

We are talking in a small conference room in the cluttered, bustling offices of San Francisco's Pacific News Service, where Lam works as a writer and editor. As a Vietnamese immigrant, Lam is a powerful witness to what he calls "the obligation of memories." For him, telling stories—about being a refugee, about survivor's guilt, about forging a new American self—is a duty, one Lam has carried out with subtle and measured eloquence in both his nonfiction and fiction.

Lam began freelancing for Pacific News Service when he was still in graduate school, working on a master's degree in creative writing. By 1996, he had cofounded the PNS-sponsored New California Media, a consortium of more than four hundred ethnic news organizations, which later grew into New America Media. Today, NAM represents two thousand news outlets and is accessed by almost a quarter of the adult population of the United States.

As an immigrant and a homosexual (or bisexual)—I never quite get him to pinpoint where he locates his sexuality—Lam brings to his writing an acute sense of what it is like to be different. "For the refugee child in America," he writes in *Perfume Dreams*, his book of reflections on the Vietnamese diaspora, "the world splits perversely into two irreconcilable parts: Inside and Outside." This contention between dualities—between the private and the public, the Confucian and the modern, or, as he puts it in "Close to the Bones," one of his longest short stories, between "old shame and new exhilaration"—is a major theme in almost all his work. Now in his forties, Lam, who still retains the boyish good looks of his youth, is most comfortable identifying himself, as he once did in an essay entitled "Re-imagining the Self . . . Re-imagining America," as a "San Franciscan and a citizen of a global society."

Lam's childhood, which he calls "sheltered" and "pampered," hardly suggests this later global perspective. His father, a high-ranking general in the Vietnamese army, was the paterfamilias of a rigid, "Confucian-style clan." Lam recalls having to "fit within that sense of harmony and hierarchy and cookie-molded behavior. I never challenged it. I never knew there was another option." There was a country villa, limousines, chauffeurs, and servants. Lam attended the prestigious Lycée Yersin in Dalat, where he learned French, a language that still creeps into his conversations. The self-declared bookworm was soon reading Tintin adventure comics and simplified versions of the French classics.

"Perhaps it's bit *précieux* for one to say that this childhood was everything and live in that sense of nostalgia. But my childhood world did have its own insularity and, therefore, its beauty. To grow up in a wartime country like Vietnam with a father who had access to such things as a helicopter was just out-of-this-world crazy." Lam recalls chopper rides to the beach and releases from school in order to attend parachuting competitions. All that changed in 1975, when, two days before the country fell to the Viet Cong, Lam and his family escaped Saigon in a C-130 cargo plane. He was eleven.

"I don't think I knew that I was leaving for good. There had never been a Vietnamese diaspora before. The idea that you would leave the homeland en masse was unheard of. There were so many people jam-packed into the plane. I watched people on the ground screaming and crying. I was mesmerized by the surreality of it all."

Hours later, they landed on Guam. "To go from someone who lived in a walled garden and couldn't tie his own shoes to living in a refugee camp with army tents and shared latrines was abhorrent. Part of me shut down. I went numb to protect my senses. I had a deep desire to run away as fast as possible from the memory."

Despite his willed numbness and the destruction of all the family photographs—incriminating evidence that his mother had ordered him to burn in the days before they fled—Lam writes beautifully about the resilience of memory, its refusal to be relegated to oblivion.

"There is a special period in human life when the power of imagination and of living in a magical childhood world still has a hold on you. When you are abruptly taken away from that, memory becomes consolidated into a value. The walled garden, the helicopter rides, the smell of jasmine rice ripening at dusk—all those things remained so vivid in memories, even as I made the transition from a Vietnamese French-speaking boy to a totally Americanized teenager. For years I didn't evoke those memories, but they played themselves out nightly in my dreams. If I could just hook my dreaming brain to YouTube, I'd be famous by now."

Within a month, the Lams had settled in San Francisco, living in a crowded two-bedroom apartment. "Everything about the United States was not how I had imagined it. When I was a child living in Vietnam, America was full of magical things, crazy, powerful, wonderful things: a Baskin and Robbins thirty-scoop ice cream cone! To imagine America through the lens of ice cream was a wonderment. I pretended that the Vietnamese child had disappeared and that I was someone completely new."

Lam took to his new homeland, so much so that his mother complained that he had become a "cowboy." He made friends easily. "Samoan friends, black friends, Filipino friends. At home, the old system was still trying to work itself out, but we spoke back. We spoke English, we disagreed with our parents, we challenged their values. There were lots of fights."

By high school, Lam was experimenting with sex. "Girls and boys. In some way, I still have attraction to both. I wasn't allowed to date. In my family's Confucian ethic, talking about sex was shameful. It was a threat to stability and the status quo."

Lam moved on after high school—"fled," he says in *Perfume Dreams*—to the University of California at Berkeley, where he majored in biochemistry because his parents wanted him to be a doctor. After graduating in 1987, he worked in a research lab for two years, preparing for the MCAT, but also took extension courses in creative writing. It was his creative writing teacher who encouraged him to consider a different path. He abandoned his medical school plans and entered the master's program in creative writing at San Francisco State University.

"I thought my mom was going to kill me. That's not what she had been boasting to the community about."

At San Francisco State, one of his assignments was to write an autobiography. Impressed by what he had written, a classmate who was a freelance writer at Pacific News Service took Lam's piece to her boss, Sandy Close, who was looking for "alternative voices." When Close called him to ask if he wanted to write for PNS, Lam initially said no. "I don't even read the newspaper," he told her. Close persisted, persuading him to write a little piece about his memories of Christmas in Dalat. "The next thing I knew, I got a check in the mail. I couldn't believe it." He also received in 1993 the Society of Professional Journalists Outstanding Young Journalist Award.

It was while he was on assignment in Hong Kong, doing a story on the forced repatriation of Vietnamese boat people, that Lam began to reconnect with his own refugee past. "Here I was from a family who had survived intact. I had already transitioned into this Americanized kid. But every time I went back into the 'inside world' of memories, I found a narrative of loss and grief. Eventually the grief started pouring itself out into my writing. Part of it, I would venture to say, is survival guilt. It became such that in order to move on I had to move backward to address those things."

Lam identifies two writers in particular—James Baldwin and Richard Rodriguez—as having had a big influence on his writing. I point out that both are nonwhite and gay. A coincidence?

"I never thought of them as gay writers. They're gay and they write. I find their voices so different from the drones of the established voices. They say honest things but beautiful things. I thought to myself, If this person from that background can say something and matter, then I, coming from this disenfranchised history, can say something and matter."

While some of Lam's articles have looked into gay issues (he once interviewed a male prostitute in Thailand), he says he does not specifically seek out gay stories. But as a person who has "been to gay bars all over the world," would he like to venture any general observations about gay life abroad?

"It's much more fluid. Here one is often pressured to declare one's sexuality as a way to make an alliance or a political statement. In other parts of the world, there is a subtle language in which you understand without saying. They don't see identity in the political sense, whereas in the United States it is all about rights, legality, representation. I'm not putting a value on this comparison, but personally I feel more comfortable with the fluidity than the identity."

Lam has never formally outed himself in any of his nonfiction. Does he think it might be important to do so at some time down the road?

"One of the aspects of my Confucian past that still has a grip on me is that it's considered embarrassing to talk about sexuality in the pages of the news. I find it weird that straight people never have to talk about their sexuality, so why does someone who happens to like their own sex have to talk about that part of their sexuality? Of course, when it has to be done for a serious issue, I'd like to reserve that as an option. But to think that it is a requirement for being gay in America, I find that equally stifling."

Lam's fiction—he's in the process of putting together a book of short stories—does include gay characters. Has it been easier for him to address gay themes in fiction?

He laughs. "Well, my agent says that if one reads between the lines, my nonfiction is gay too! I don't necessarily start out a short story thinking of a theme. I start out with a character or a situation. If the character happens to be gay, then it happens, but I never consciously make a character gay."

In reference to his refugee past, Lam once wrote, "If you don't tell people what happened to you, nobody will know, and you will remain invisible in the American imagination." Are those same feelings specifically behind his interest in letting gay and bisexual characters emerge in his stories?

"It's part of the future project. There are parts of my romantic life I need to address in fiction or memoir. But one of the reasons holding me back has to do with the disclosure of the other person involved. At some point, I have to overcome that limited sense of what I can say and what I can't. I've come to realize that it's my own narrative. I just need to be respectful. This is actually the first time I'm talking publicly about my sexuality."

What does fiction allow Lam to say that journalism doesn't?

"Fiction has a way of capturing a human character or, as Flannery O'Connor says, the 'mystery of personality' in a way that no nonfiction I've seen has managed to capture. There is a marvelous way that fiction can shoot in so many different directions at one time that even the best literary essay cannot."

In one of his short stories, "At the Love Leather," a Vietnamese American thinks to herself, "This whole subculture, its obsession with sex and youth and physical attributes and—more curiously—the penis, was all very perverse to her." Was Lam expressing his own feelings there?

He laughs again. "I'm not necessarily turned off by sex, but there is a naïveté to thinking of sex as the endpoint of culture. It is a turn-off when sex and body and physical beauty become the dominant ground in any culture. It leaves less for the imagination."

Does that go for pinpointing one's identity, too? In declaring oneself as "something"—gay or bisexual or refugee or Vietnamese American—does one cut oneself off from the fullness of his own experience?

"What I've come to realize is that identity is an issue that is never ending simply because, as a human being, I keep growing. I take on new layers, shedding old layers. Identity is never fixed in stone but something constructed, earned, garnered. That's what Buddhism teaches us, that there is no true self."

Joan Larkin

Gay poet Edward Field once wrote, "With its dedication to ambiguity, Modern Poetry fit right in with the need of gay poets to be closeted." On the day I meet Joan Larkin, she has brought that quotation with her and reads it to me, intent upon establishing her solidarity with Field, whose criticism of obscurity, ambiguity, and the modernist highbrow tone she avidly shares.

"A lot of the drive I've had in writing poetry has been toward clarity. I've always been, in my writing especially, very self-exposing." Larkin's clear, astringent, unpityingly honest poems are "unflinching, direct observations of women's lives," according to Cynthia Werthamer in her entry on Larkin in *Contemporary Lesbian Writers of the United States*. "For her," writes critic David Ulin, "poetry is a form of witness; she offers no false hopes, no resolutions, except to reflect, as honestly and directly as she can manage, the complicated, at times uncontrollable, messiness of being alive."

At the time of our visit, Larkin has just received the Audre Lorde Award for Lesbian Poetry for her most recent book, *My Body: New and Selected Poems*. "It feels great!" she tells me. "I thought maybe I was jumping the gun, maybe I should have more books out before I put this together. But because of my age and because I had enough work almost for another book, it was time."

Growing up in the Boston area, Larkin became "a poem-writing child." Before she graduated from Brookline High School in 1956, she had already won a poetry competition in the *Atlantic Monthly* and a public speaking contest, for which she memorized a sonnet sequence by Edna St. Vincent Millay. "As with a lot of adolescent poets, she was an influence." Larkin's first awareness of lesbian feelings occurred at Girl Scout camp when she was fifteen. A counselor accused her and one of the kitchen assistants of looking at each other "like a pair of lovers."

"I didn't know what the word 'lovers' meant. That was the innocence of those times. But I got the message: I had these feelings, they felt really beautiful and sacred to me, but they were punishable. That's why it took me so long to come out. It was the fifties: you were punished for those feelings." Larkin says that secretiveness and shame were a part of her family's constellation—"about the body, about sex, about being Jews, about being less-than economically. I grew up on hand-me-downs and scholarships. We didn't talk about a lot of things."

In a piece he wrote in the *Los Angeles Times*, Ulin noted that Larkin was of "a generation of women who often subjugated their truer selves to social expectation." Larkin cringes at the memories. "Oh, God! Circle pins and poodle skirts and hair in curlers at night. I was obsessed with looking right, wanting to have the right clothes. Wanting to fit in. Sex was this very glamorous, forbidden thing."

She began drinking as a teenager—"high-school kids faking boredom," she writes in a poem called "Storyville." In the jazz clubs in Boston, "drinking metallic orange juice and gin," she would try "to get this / drink down fast and order another." It was a practice that spiraled down into an addiction.

Larkin did her undergraduate degree at Swarthmore College, a place she calls "somewhat liberating." She majored in English and worked on the college literary magazine. "Modernism was the thing. I had the idea from my education that poetry was a hermetic language. Poetry was safely secret in that way." Larkin had secrets. She got pregnant at Swarthmore and had to go away to get an illegal abortion. When she returned, she was allowed three fifteen-minute visits with the school psychologist. "One of my reactions to the trauma of the abortion was to become promiscuous. Oh, and a drunk, by the way, but I thought that was normal." She tells me that her memories of her days at Swarthmore are "mixed with booze and sex. Waking up in various strange beds." Programmed to think of alcohol as glamour, she formed a "gin club," went to class drunk, and ended up losing her place in the honors program. At the same time, she kept feeling attractions to women, attractions that left her "just burning," though she shied away from any outright romances.

After graduating in 1960, Larkin moved to New Haven, where she did a few semesters at the Yale School of Drama and picked up a little money posing for art classes. There she met her first husband, a painting student. They got married "out of a longing for convention and safety," she guesses. The marriage kept conflict and anxiety at bay for a while; it would be a few more years before she questioned the straight identity she wished for.

The couple moved to Tucson, where she did graduate work at the University of Arizona. She recalls those years as offering a "close-up exposure to a broad spectrum of contemporary poetics and poets, including Beats, Black Mountain poets, and more traditional poets. There were important visual artists teaching and working there, too. I was lucky to begin living an artist's life among people who were passionate about poetry, painting, and music and who took my practice of poetry seriously. I hadn't found a voice yet, but I learned a lot of what I know about poetry." Her first poem was published during those years.

While earning her master's degree, Larkin took up pot and psychedelics. "The marriage wasn't working, and I had decided to leave. I shared a ride to New York with a young woman—she was more straight than not—for whom I started to feel intense desire, feelings not acknowledged by word or gesture on my part. I had no clue what she was feeling about anything. I think we were stoned a lot. It was only after being in New York for several months that one night we fell into bed together. We never did this again and never talked about it! I was terrified. I didn't want to face my own feelings."

In New York, Larkin "found a Bohemia that I was in love with." She lived in a cold-water flat on the Lower East Side and worked as a secretary for a midtown gallery. She took a poetry workshop and began writing the poems that would eventually make it into her first book. Pregnant, she got married again, to another painter named Jim Larkin. Her daughter Kate was born in 1967.

"Jim and I were miserable together. He was a more active alcoholic than I was. He told me in no uncertain terms, 'You're a lesbian.' I didn't leave him to live a lesbian life, though that happened soon after." They parted for good when Kate was sixteen months old. About five years later they divorced.

By the early seventies, Larkin had convened a writers group, Seven Women Poets, which included other young lesbian poets such as Irena Klepfisz and Jan Clausen. All of them believed, as she later wrote of Muriel Rukeyser, that "the core of a woman's writing must be her own vision and experience."

"The line everyone was quoting in the 1970s was Rukeyser's 'What would happen if one woman were to tell the truth about her life? / The world would split open.' It was an endorsement of the path I was on." Judy Grahn was another influence. "She gave me the sense of the importance of each individual lesbian life. Her Women's Press Collective was an inspiration for us to get our work out without help from mainstream publishers."

About this time, Larkin joined a lesbian therapy group. "It was touchy-feely days with a roomful of articulate lesbian feminists. I required of myself that I have a lesbian lover. It was, 'Let's get on with this task!' I was with a very butch woman named Inez. Those were the days of open relationships. And I was still drinking. The bar you went to was the Duchess. I picked up women and brought them home."

What did it feel like to be part of that whole lesbian feminist wave?

"You just can't imagine. Being in New York! It was just the most exciting thing in the whole world. There was a women's coffeehouse. I dragged my daughter to readings, concerts. I was listening to people like Audre Lorde on WBAI." Larkin eventually started her own interview program, *The Poet's Craft*, on WBAI, which she calls "our left-of-NPR station."

These were the years when Larkin, with rare exceptions, "didn't talk to men unless I absolutely had to." She laughs when I remind her of this. "You know, one of the slogans in those days was 'Abort All Male Fetuses!' If a man asked you a question, you were supposed to withdraw because we weren't going to give our energy to men. That was another area of conformity for me. I didn't feel comfortable with it, but I talked the party line."

In 1975, "swept up on this wave of feminist publishing and writing," Larkin and coeditor Elly Bulkin brought out *Amazon Poetry*, an anthology of poems by lesbians. Eleven publishing houses turned down the anthology before the two decided to publish it themselves through a small press they founded called Out & Out Books. "We were ambitious. We mimeographed—*mimeographed*! Those were the days. We got a thousand submissions. I remember my daughter and Elly's daughter coming up to us one day and saying, 'Lesbian, lesbian, lesbian! That's all you two talk about.'"

Amazon Poetry included poets—May Swenson, Adrienne Rich— who had never published in a lesbian context before. Larkin says she can't remember exactly why she and Bulkin decided to avoid the word "lesbian" in the title of that anthology. "There was something closety about it." There was no such ambiguity in the title of their next anthology, *Lesbian Poetry* (Persephone Press), published six years later. "Which was deeply irritating to May Swenson," Larkin remembers. "Swenson had her generation's preference for remaining politely closeted in print. 'Why can't you call it *Amazon Poetry II*?' she asked us."

Larkin's first book of poems, *Housework*, also appeared in 1975. When I note that the book is a kind of manifesto of what it means to be a woman, a single mother, and an alcoholic, Larkin says, "Except that I wasn't identifying myself as an alcoholic." Then how does she account for all the poems about drinking?

"Probably in some ways I was romanticizing the drinking. Look, I came home from Brooklyn College one night. I'm pouring from the jug of Almaden. And my daughter said, 'I think you're an alcoholic.' I told her, 'Don't be silly. All sophisticated people have wine with their meals.' I've had to make amends for that statement!"

Though the poems in *Housework* "were coming out of a necessity to talk to myself about my experience," Larkin says that she was "pretty unconscious of what I was putting out. Other people probably knew more about what I was saying in that book than I did. There was a lot going on in those poems barely below the level of my conscious awareness." No matter how obvious the signs, she was in denial. "I remember one day when I had the shakes, I didn't know what I had. My closet was filled with bags of unopened envelopes and unpaid parking tickets. I couldn't be bothered to move the car. I used to bring wine to my poetry workshop." Finally, in 1980, she "made a decision . . . to live."

Larkin says she got sober "in an almost accidental way. I had read an article in the *Village Voice* about allergies. I decided to go on this purity kick. I gave up sugar and white flour and pot. And alcohol, incidentally, ended up on that list. Within a day, I was in withdrawal. I didn't know what it was. I was climbing the walls. A friend took me to a twelve-step meeting. I had no doubt that this was the place I should be. Even so, it took me three months to really get it that I had drunk enough to qualify. My denial was immense." Larkin says that while the women's movement gave her the permission to come out as a lesbian, "it didn't save my life to come out as a lesbian. It saved my life to acknowledge my alcoholism and other addictions." Now, over twenty-nine years sober, Larkin has—as she puts it in "Clifton," a poem from her second collection, *A Long Sound*—"habits strict as the former ones, / meetings, books, service."

In 1988, Larkin coedited with Carl Morse her third anthology, *Gay and Lesbian Poetry in Our Time*. "The most important collection of gay and lesbian poetry yet published," wrote the critic in the *Bay Area Reporter*. The book is remarkable for the number of its offerings: ninety-four poets, including such lions and lionesses as Auden, Rukeyser, Swenson, and Langston Hughes. "Our hope was to gather in one place as much good gay and lesbian poetry as we could, and in equal numbers, showing what these communities shared in common. This was a first." The book won a Lambda Literary Award.

Larkin's third collection of poems, *Cold River* (1997), includes a number of poems that focus on AIDS. "All around me people were dying. All the guys I knew in the meeting rooms in New York. It was the days of the death sentence. The artists I cared about, the friends I was closest to, the people who had helped me save my life, my role models, my beloveds—they were all dead or dying. That book came out of my need to express my grief and create a remembrance."

Poet Alicia Ostriker calls Larkin and Adrienne Rich the "scrub-women of truth." In an appreciative review in the *Women's Review of Books*, Ostriker writes, "Is it because [Larkin] was so well trained in trouble—abortion, early marriage and divorce, alcoholism—that she handles human pain so well? Larkin's list-poem 'Inventory' . . . may be the best single poem I have ever read about AIDS."

That same year, Larkin and gay writer Jaime Manrique put together a small book of love poetry by Sor Juana de la Cruz, the seventeenth-century Mexican nun. In the afterword to that volume she notes that Sor Juana's "mastery of poetic forms offers structures for the unpardonable." What aspects of the nun's "unpardonable" behavior resonated with Larkin?

"I don't know whether Sor Juana had physical relationships with women, but there are love poems addressed to women in there. I'm guessing that there was intense, passionate, emotional involvement with women in that community. I probably identified with my idea of what Sor Juana's life was, which was a combination of freedom and repression—freedom coming through music, language, and permission to participate in artistic performance. Her life had such a tragic outcome. She was forced to sign a retraction in blood. And forced to give up books and musical instruments. In my mind, she died of a broken heart. For me, there is always the idea that 'they' can take it away from you."

Was there anything she found resonant in Sor Juana's particular political situation, writing in the shadow of the Inquisition? "When the Board of Higher Education didn't grant me a promotion to associate professor, the department chair told me she was sure it was because of homophobia. These are not exactly inquisitions—nobody is going to burn me at the stake—but when your résumé has 'lesbian, lesbian, lesbian' all over it, it's more likely to be tossed in the we're-not-interested pile."

In 1999, Larkin edited *A Woman Like That: Lesbian and Bisexual Writers Tell Their Coming Out Stories*. "I didn't anticipate the rich complexity of experience these memoirs would encompass," she wrote in the book's introduction, "nor did I suspect the powerful impact they would have on me personally. I recognized feelings I thought no longer lived inside me. Reading this book, I encountered my vulnerability, anger, and optimism, my core of emotional strength."

Having written so much about the body, now that she has reached her seventies, what is her relationship to her own body? "I accept it more than I once did. Humor, self-acceptance, and gratitude for survival. I've recently started meditating. The first experience I had of focusing on my breathing was just to feel overwhelmed with gratitude for being alive every single day. I'm lucky to have a body. I can still put on my sneakers and walk a few miles on the streets of New York."

What is she proudest of in her life? "I'm proud that my daughter has turned out to be the beautiful soul that she is. I'm proud to have been able to live that life that I was given a second chance of. And to come back into a life of writing and teaching and giving some help to other human beings rather than being one of those unfortunate people who goes around complaining bitterly about everything at every minute. I'm proud of the writing. I'm grateful that I got to grow up."

Stephin Merritt

Composer, arranger, lyricist, singer, instrumentalist, and the quirky brains behind the smart-rock band the Magnetic Fields, Stephin Merritt has been called a genius, "the Steven Sondheim of indie rock." His prolific output (over two hundred songs) amounts to an eclectic traversal of genres and styles, from mainstream American songbook to jazz to traditional rock to Glassian minimalism to John Cage. Merritt himself once described his music as "nonmacho, somewhat quiet, quite polite, and rather bisexual." Straddling a tightrope between satire and sincerity, his songs frequently goof on the style they imitate but always with a whisper of respect. His instrumentation—often the "thin sounds" of ukuleles, banjos, toy pianos, pennywhistles—is unconventional, playful, smart, and always interesting.

As a lyricist, Merritt brings a prodigious literary talent to the words of his songs, which frequently make allusions to books and authors he loves. (He's a voracious reader. In the course of our conversation he mentions reading Gertrude Stein, James Joyce, Oliver Sacks, the *New York Review of Books,* and Alex Ross's history of music in the twentieth century, *The Rest Is Noise.*) Critics find his lyrics both "viciously funny" and "painfully intellectual." He's been called "the best lyricist since Cole Porter."

Merritt the singer generally opts for a deadpan, almost emotion-less delivery. His baritone register is capable of a lush and mellow res-onance, which he only rarely allows to come forth. Most of the time, he affects a hollow, amateurish sound—"the least possible sexy voice," he once told Terry Gross. The overall effect is charmingly goofy, like listening to a nerdy environmental studies major (which he once was) cajoled into singing at his fraternity's Talent Night.

The range of Merritt's interests and creativity is remarkable. In addition to his albums with the Magnetic Fields, he has also written theater pieces, a few soundtracks (including the music to James Bolton's 2000 film *Eban and Charley*), and even a quirky, and very entertaining, introduction to *The Paris Review Book of People with Problems*.

On the afternoon we meet—in an empty classroom at the Har-vard Extension School, where he was once a student—Merritt has just driven for several hours through a pouring rain from Northamp-ton, where the Magnetic Fields performed the night before. Tomor-row the band will play a Valentine's Day concert at the Somerville Theater. But for now, he's in no mood for hearts and red roses. The traffic and the downpour have put him in a cranky mood.

To smooth things out, I tell him that I've had a very enjoyable couple of weeks getting to know his music. As a huge classical music fan, I stopped listening to pop music after high school. After that, it was nothing but classical. "What year was that?" he asks, and when I tell him—1966—Merritt launches into me.

"You stopped listening to popular music just before *Sergeant Pep-per*! You picked *exactly* the wrong year in the entire twentieth cen-tury to stop listening to pop music. Whoa! Do you also believe in the division between higher and lower art in cinema or theater? In a post-Warholian world, it's particularly strange for a gay person to have this high art/low art division. I make the sort of music one would make not believing in a division between high art and low art. I like bubble gum and experimental music, and I like them for some of the same reasons."

Sufficiently chastened, I move us along.

Born in that momentous year of 1966, Merritt has been listening to music and writing songs "since I could walk." When he was seven, he started taking lessons on various instruments—piano, guitar, per-cussion. "Organ for a while. Big pipe organ. I would have loved to have been an accomplished organist, but that will never happen. I can't even read the newspaper and play two notes in a row with my feet."

Merritt was raised by his mother, a convert from Roman Catholicism to Tibetan Buddhism. "We didn't have a whole lot of books, but we had the complete Shakespeare. I read that early. And we listened to music that had interesting lyrics. I thought *Magical Mystery Tour* was a normal record, and musicians dressed as animals who sang 'I Am the Walrus' was what everybody did."

By junior high school, he was studying composition, theory, and arranging with a professor of music at Berklee College in Boston. He dismisses a lot of what he learned as "a series of rules to get to the fifth and back," but that didn't discourage him from trying to write music. By the time he was fourteen, he had a four-track tape on which he was recording "very, very bad songs."

At the progressive Cambridge School of Weston, which he attended for high school, Merritt was "a long-haired hippie weirdo" who everyone assumed was gay. The school encouraged—"commanded," Merritt says—the students to be creative. "If you weren't creative, they kicked you out. I took a playwriting class every year for four years. I took all of the dance classes. It was a good environment for me." And he kept listening to music. "I went from the sort of prog rock typified by Yes to the sort of post-prog rock typified by Brian Eno. I guess I started out with hard rock, and by the end I was listening to experimental music."

For a while after high school, Merritt attended film school in New York and then returned to Boston to enroll at the Harvard Extension School, where he studied visual arts and environmental studies. He worked as a contributing editor at *Time Out New York* and also wrote "a little bit" for *Gay Times* and *IN News Weekly*, a Boston gay paper. He even did an astrology column. "Each week, as Madam Sheba, I would subvert the idea of an astrology column."

I ask him if subversion is the aesthetic behind his music as well. "I don't think of it as subversion. It's not like I'm planning to overthrow the political order. I think of it as play, I guess. From a position of high art or power or macho, it might sound like I'm a trickster figure. From a position of perverse and low and unpowerful, it might just sound sort of sassy. I just think of it as being playful. I'm not trying to ruin anyone's day."

Merritt resists being pigeonholed. Even the label "indie rock" is one he rejects, claiming that there is no one particular kind of music that he writes. In fact, the "multivocality" of his music—the word is musicologist Mark J. Butler's—may be Merritt's way of "playing with identity," his challenge to "stable categories of sexual definition." Merritt tells me that he doesn't even necessarily set out to put openly gay content into his lyrics. "I snigger at openly gay lyrical content much of the time. It's corny. Liberating for people who are a week or two from coming out, but otherwise it's corny."

Would he at least say that his aesthetic is "gay"? "I don't avoid or try for a gay aesthetic. I certainly use completely mainstream gay historical references—Warhol, Stein, Wilde, Cocteau—as much as anyone does. Gay songwriters are not in a position to write as gay songwriters for a general audience. No one wants to hear the details of our sex lives anyway. So either we write for an extremely small ghetto of people who would like to hear the actual details of our actual lives, or we cultivate an interest in artifice and deflection, as gay people and pre-gay people have always done. We haven't really changed our situation. Aesthetically, we're still the funny uncles and aunts.

"I don't think it's especially clever of us to work this way. It's an economic necessity. It happens to be a *fun* economic necessity. I enjoy tweaking it with songs such as 'Zombie Boy,' where I go out of my way to inject transvestitism and necrophilia into the discussion of homosexual sex, but that's just making fun of the situation. The play that I'm doing is not any more or less socially mandated than the similar play in Negro spirituals where all the political discussion is deflected to both religious and mythical language.

"I don't feel that I'm being inventive by doing that. And I'm not saying that I'm much more socially aware than anyone else in the world, but I am more socially aware of what my situation is and what I do for a living. If I wanted to express my actual feelings, this is not the forum I would do it in. I have learned that it is so much more fun not to be direct. Since I will never have the opportunity to be direct, I don't want to be."

Merritt's 1999 three-disc box set, *69 Love Songs*, was another foray into indirection—"a denial of inspiration and confession and autobiography and sincerity"—the very qualities one usually expects in a love song. Merritt has called the project "a stunt," one that should be awful but isn't. "It's too big to be silly," he once wrote. "If it were forty love songs, that would be silly. Sixty-nine is grandiose." Yet the album earned him a wider audience than ever before. It was, in fact, Merritt's breakthrough project.

He tells me that in *69 Love Songs* he was applying Warholian repetition to the idea of the love song. "As with Warhol's 'A Hundred Marilyns,' the quantity would shape the meaning. I feel sorry for anyone who buys one volume of *69*. They miss the point. I was parodying the definition of album, overdefining what 'album' is, at the end of the Album Era. It's a song cycle, a ludicrously long song cycle. Where the cycle part is more important than the song."

The album finished second in the *Village Voice* critics' poll, one of the best-reviewed albums of the year. Called "the twenty-first-century edition of the great American songbook," it earned Merritt comparisons with Cole Porter and Steven Sondheim, comparisons he rejects. Thomas Bartlett in *Salon* magazine opined that Merritt "may be the best writer of love songs around today."

Merritt ascribes the enormous popularity of *69 Love Songs*—whether facetiously or not, it's hard to tell—to the title and the logo. The number "69" in bold, black letters occupies the entire face of the CD jacket, the two numerals performing *soixante-neuf* with each other. "If I had just written out the words 'sixty-nine love songs,' I don't think it would have been a popular album. The visual representation of '69' both illustrates the sexual aspect and cartoonizes the concept, illustrating and defusing it at the same time."

And what about his own love life? "I learned a long time ago never to discuss my actual sex life in interviews because it changes by the time it's published. If I ever have a boyfriend for fifty years, maybe I will mention that. People who take things too seriously don't find me a very good partner. Which is a lot of people. Music has not worked at all for me romantically. No one has ever approached me romantically based on my being a rock star or whatever I am. People don't seem to find it particularly sexy that I'm a singer."

At the time we spoke, Merritt and the Magnetic Fields had just released *Distortion*. A strident, noisy, ear-grating experience, the album's punishing sounds—what reviewer Joseph Curtis Henderson called "cacophonous, clanging and clattering with tinny Jesus and Mary Chain–style overdriven guitars"—underscore Merritt's dark, wounded take on love.

"The album has its own built-in philosophical problems," he tells me, "problems that were interesting enough that I was happy to do a whole album about it. The title refers to the production style. We're using all these electrified instruments that are not usually considered in need of electrification, as though they were electric guitars. We've done that with *all* of the instruments except the bass drums and vocals. What is it about the guitar that makes it popular to distort rather than, say, the piano or the accordion, which sounds great distorted? Or the cello. It's only a philosophical problem to me."

Merritt has also written at least four theater pieces, including two Chinese opera adaptations for which he wrote the music. Once again, he cautions me about trying to label them. "Neither tradition—opera or musical—is really like them. It's best not to use these labels, and then it doesn't get confusing. If I say 'Chinese opera adaptations,' maybe it doesn't imply that they're operas; if I call them 'musicals,' then you expect something very different from what you end up hearing."

To illustrate his point, he mentions "an exchange of hostilities" between Steven Sondheim and Ned Rorem about whether *Sweeney Todd* was an opera.

"Under what conditions would one need to know? If it is performable by the New York City Opera, and *they* don't need to know, then who needs to know? Seeing that Sondheim is far and away the best lyricist ever in musical theater, I don't know what English-language opera you would compare *Sweeney Todd* to. What's better than *Sweeney Todd*? It succeeds in being silly, grotesque, comic-book poetry. Is it high art, is it low art? Who cares?

"I sometimes think my entire output boils down to the hippie slogan 'Don't label me.' Am I a radical Chomskyite? A postdeconstructionist? Or am I just a snotty little trickster figure? My mother thinks that my religious views are shallow and that I don't understand the seriousness of the world. She thinks it's quite a shame that I don't believe in the profundity of Tibetan psychology and the wisdom of the East."

In his *Paris Review* piece Merritt wrote, "With never enough clothing, we have to express our bootless rage not through the second skin of fashion (it's too cold) but through the third skin of our décor." What's his own apartment like?

"A tiny apartment in the East Village. If you take a music room and a library and put them together in a very awkward way, that's my house. A piano and ten bookshelves. My mother thinks I should get rid of my books once I've read them. But there's hardly anything I read that I don't want to refer to again. And CDs and DVDs. And lots of instruments. The most conspicuous instrument right now is the harp, a Celtic folk harp—four feet tall. I'm taking lessons."

Merritt tells me he has recently moved his recording studio to Los Angeles. "The fact that Manhattan is too expensive for any artists to live in—does that mean the end of Western civilization? Sort of. Yeah."

But then the lightness is back: "I'm trying to accomplish a particular objective, much of which is having fun and having an interesting say without being ostracized, thrown into prison, or offending anybody. I don't see myself as a modernist at the top of some historical mountain. That has the potential to be a distraction."

As for the label "genius," Merritt says he doesn't recognize the validity of it. "Not as applied to me. No. In fact, I would prefer to be admired for the amount of work I put into my music than thought really smart and capable of exploding precious little musical jokes. It's fun, and I would be doing it anyway, even if I weren't being paid for it."

Stephin Merritt

213

Greg Millett

Back in the late eighties and early nineties Greg Millett was an angry young ACT UP activist. He had never heard of the Centers for Disease Control until one of his fellow protestors told him that the Atlanta-based public health agency was just "part of the establishment that wasn't doing enough to find a cure to stop the raging epidemic." Years later, as a behavioral scientist for that very organization, Millett saw firsthand "the other side of the story."

"There are an awful lot of incredible people at the CDC who are very dedicated," he tells me the evening we meet for coffee in Grant Park, the southeast Atlanta neighborhood where he lives with his partner. Millett, an African American with a winning smile and a fondness for cultivating orchids (he's a member of the Atlanta Orchid Society), speaks like a convert, but one who readily acknowledges the role that gadfly organizations like ACT UP have performed. "The us-versus-them construction is really artificial. There are a lot of people at CDC who are part of the lesbian and gay community. There are people there who are positive or have partners who are positive. I don't think that *that* story is told enough."

Millett began working for the CDC in 1998, when he took a break from his Ph.D. in epidemiology and health behavior at the University of Alabama, to accept a two-year internship at the foundation. Before that stint was up, the CDC had published a survey that found HIV rates to be alarmingly high among young gay men and, in particular, African American men. "We couldn't figure out why. It caused a huge media sensation. The whole public health community paused. All of a sudden there was this intense focus on what's happening with black gay men and why they might be so disproportionately affected by HIV." When a position became available to do an epidemiological project to try to answer those questions, Millett applied for the job and was hired.

On the surface, a career in public health and AIDS would seem like a natural path for Millett. His father, an immigrant from Panama of Cuban Jamaican extraction, was a microbiologist at St. Vincent's Hospital in New York's Greenwich Village, the "ground zero," Millett says, of the epidemic. "I remember my father talking about it quite a bit when I was a kid. In those days, the early eighties, it was called GRID, Gay Related Immune Disease."

In fact, science was not Millett's first love. He was far more interested in other things, including, he recalls, braiding the hair on his sister's doll. When his father found out, "all hell broke loose." He remembers his father muttering to his mother, who was also from Panama, "Why is he so different?"

"In Caribbean culture, girls and boys have strict roles. When you transgress, it can get pretty ugly."

Millett says that from the time he was in the first grade he knew he was different. He remembers, as early as preadolescence, crying himself to sleep at night. "I was attracted to boys, but I didn't think there was any framework in my world for men to be attracted to men. Even though I grew up in New York City, and even though my father worked in Greenwich Village, and I would pass many gay bars on the way to visiting him, I felt that I was destined to be completely lonely and celibate. I felt trapped."

Millett continued to "torture the heck" out of himself over his sexual orientation until he read James Baldwin's *Giovanni's Room*. "I was scared to death to get the book out of the library. I read it furtively under the bedsheets. I remember crying while reading. There was so much that felt natural. It spoke to me." He tears up now, recalling that episode back in his early teens. "That discovery—this is what I'm about!—I felt so happy to know that there were other people who feel the same way as I."

As a result, Millett figured that when it was time to go to college,

"I had to go far enough from home that I could explore this." That school turned out to be Dartmouth, which he entered in 1986. But the Ivy League school in the wilds of New Hampshire was not the haven he thought it would be. Instead, he found "a difficult, scary place."

"Dartmouth was incredibly conservative. There were five thousand students, and maybe thirty of us had progressive politics. We spent our four years there counseling each other. I remember asking myself, Why are we here? What did we do to ourselves?" Millett and his friends were troubled by the student body's prevailing attitudes toward women, minorities, and gay people. "We'd go down to Harvard to the Queer Student Union parties. There would be hundreds of men and women there. Everyone was out. Same at Yale. And then I'd go back to Dartmouth, and it was so oppressive. It was not a good place to be gay or lesbian or, God forbid, transgender."

Despite the oppressive atmosphere, or maybe because of it, Millett says that all of his various identities started to gel at Dartmouth. Through the recommendation of a campus librarian, he started reading Audre Lorde. "As much as I loved Baldwin, she was the first person who spoke to how these multiple identities—Caribbean, queer, progressive—fit together. I thought to myself, She understands *exactly* where I'm coming from." He also started going to "a lot of feminist conferences and just loving it. It was another part of my awakening."

Sophomore year, Millett moved into the African American Society, where he met other black people who had multiple identities. "It was incredible to be a part of that community." By the end of his sophomore year, he was being courted by several fraternities. Over lunch one day, a frat guy made an off-the-cuff homophobic remark. Millett was outraged. He wrote an op-ed piece for the *Daily Dartmouth*, the student newspaper, in which he came out.

"I expressed my disappointment to have found so much bigotry and small-mindedness on campus." All the fraternities that were recruiting him withdrew their invitations. He remembers losing some friends. Other friends looked at him in disbelief, saying, "But you just don't look gay." Even many of his black friends at the African American Society began to hold him at arm's length.

"I took the role of being a thorn in their side. I had a partner by then, a blond-haired, blue-eyed guy who would stay at my dorm overnight. We would go to all the Society dances. For the most part, he'd be the only white person there. People thought I was just grabbing for attention. Ironically, they had been saying that they didn't fit into their own black communities back home because they didn't conform to some narrow parameter of what black is supposed to be. And here they were doing the same thing to me."

Millett remembers a meeting of the African American Society where the subject of a campus gay bashing came up. "One of the members said, 'This has nothing to do with us.' I just exploded. I rattled off lists of names of famous black gay people from the Harlem Renaissance through the civil rights movement, people whom they revered. 'All of these people are your brothers and sisters,' I told them. 'This struggle is also your struggle!' I stood up and let them have it. How could they just dismiss anything dealing with homosexuality?"

After graduating in 1990 with a double major in sociology and history, Millett spent three years in New York working as a paralegal while he deliberated his career path. By then, he was also volunteering at the Gay Men's Health Crisis, teaching HIV prevention workshops for black and Latino men, and going regularly to ACT UP meetings. "In one particular year, I knew twenty people who had died. Some close, some not. My father was in his early forties then. I remember one day he tried to solicit some sympathy from me because a friend of his had recently died of a heart attack. I just turned on him and said, 'I've had twenty friends die this year, and I'm only twenty-three. I have no sympathy for you.' He was in the middle of the vortex, at St. Vincent's Hospital, with people losing loved ones every day, and he didn't seem to recognize that a holocaust was happening."

In 1993, Millett decided that he would pursue a career in public health. He entered the University of North Carolina at Chapel Hill to do a master's degree. From the beginning of his studies, he readily took to the scientific method. "The elegance of putting together an epidemiological study really appealed to me. I felt armed to deal with problematic statistics and shoddy science. There was something comforting and interesting and empowering about that, to have all of this stuff demystified." Two years later, he enrolled in the Ph.D. program at Alabama. "The rest is history," he says.

Much of Millett's work at the CDC has focused on black men and AIDS. At the time he and I speak, the HIV rate among black men who have sex with men (MSM) has reached a staggering 46 percent as compared to 21 percent among white MSM. "From the midnineties until now, we've known that the rates were high for black gay men. Folks kept saying, 'What's going on in this community? What are these guys *doing?*' Essentially, it was some sort of victim blaming."

One of his first published studies, in the *American Journal of Public Health* (June 2006), was a critical review of the literature on black men who have sex with men and HIV transmission. Millett's conclusion was that the high rates of HIV infection for black MSM were "not attributable to a higher frequency of risky sexual behavior, non-gay identity, or sexual nondisclosure, or to reported use of alcohol or illicit substances." While the evidence was insufficient to evaluate the remaining hypotheses, his study tore a hole in the prevailing notion that the traditionally suspected culprits for high HIV rates among blacks—substance abuse and being on the "down low"—were major factors in the higher incidence of HIV infection.

"What I'm happy about from my research is that when you compare risk behaviors, you find that black gay men engage in comparable, if not less, risk than white gay men. You find less substance use overall, fewer partners, less likelihood to engage in unprotected anal intercourse. It turns out that for blacks, engaging in high-risk behavior, low-risk behavior, no-risk behavior—it doesn't matter—you're more likely to become infected with HIV compared with whites. So it's not about what you're doing; it's about other factors around you. That's incredibly important, because in the past we were looking at the epidemic as a one-size-fits-all situation, as if what's happening in white gay communities can be translated to black gay communities and Latino gay communities. In fact, even though the epidemic is increasing in all these communities, the risk factors are not the same."

So what are the factors that are contributing to the escalation in rates of infection among black MSM?

"We need to realize that it takes two people to have unprotected sex. We don't focus enough on the context in which all of this is happening, on what other types of forces beyond the individual are at work. Like social support: we know that not having a supportive family or supportive friends is associated with unsafe sex. Not having friends who you believe are also engaging in safe sex is associated with unsafe sex. Childhood sexual abuse is associated with unsafe sex. There are all these other factors—poverty, income, access to health care, proper housing, mental health, substance use—that feed into health issues. It is finally starting to dawn on public health officials how complex this issue is and how we need to work in concert to tackle the problem."

Complacency, Millett says, is the biggest challenge that the HIV prevention community faces these days. "We have gotten to a place in the epidemic where people in the United States don't see it as a crisis. Earlier, we had a generation of men who were dying in front of us, rapidly. I used to see folks with KS [Kaposi's sarcoma] all over the streets of New York, people wasting away. We no longer have those physical manifestations of being positive. That sense of urgency seems to have disappeared. That's regrettable. As the numbers that the CDC just released show, we MSM are still the only transmission group where the epidemic is increasing, going through the roof.

"Again, not speaking for CDC but personally, I feel that more has to be done. When you compare the number of effective behavioral interventions that are available for gay men overall—you don't even have to look at black gay men—it's so few compared with what we see for heterosexuals or for IV-drug users. And when you compare that to the infection rates in the country, there's an obvious imbalance there that has to be rectified."

Millett points out that a vaccine still seems years away. "Just this year we got word of another vaccine trial that failed. That really sent shock waves through the HIV community. I'm not a clinician, but it seems we still don't understand the virus well enough yet to do effective vaccine research."

So if black MSM are not engaging in higher rates of risk behavior than their white counterparts but are still converting disproportionately, what can be done? "We black men need to be even more vigilant in taking care of ourselves. The overall standard of testing once a year is not appropriate for black MSM. We need black gay men to test more often because rates of undiagnosed infection are so high in our community. When you have a rate of possibly one in two black MSM who are positive in urban areas and two-thirds of them don't know they're HIV-positive, that's a major wake-up call. One slip up for us has entirely different consequences than for MSM in other communities."

Millett's most recent work has been to look at the correlation between circumcision and HIV transmission. In October 2008, he published a report in the *Journal of the American Medical Association* that concluded that "there was no evidence that being circumcised was protective against HIV infection among black MSM or Latino MSM." Why was this study necessary?

"There were a lot of questions out there about whether circumcision was effective among MSM. We concluded that there is a need for more research. We really need more data desperately on the issue. As a researcher, I was discouraged with the results, but—again, speaking personally—as an African American man, I wasn't necessarily discouraged, because, given the history of people of color and penises in the United States, I was afraid of what would happen if we found a significant protective effect. How would that be perceived in black gay communities? Would the perception be, Oh, so people want to circumcise us now!

Millett, who left the CDC in 2009 on an extended detail as Senior Policy Advisor for the National HIV/AIDS Strategy in the Obama administration, admits that discouragement has "absolutely" been part of his experience as a public health researcher. "But I remember my experiences at Dartmouth. Even though I felt I was biding my time there, I know darn well that just by being vocal I made a difference. I have to draw upon that to remind myself that we are not going to have major breakthroughs all the time in the field, the way we had with antiretroviral therapy. But the little things I'm doing are making a difference in creating a research agenda that might be effective for black gay men. There are so few researchers doing this work, focusing on black gay men, and even fewer black gay men doing the work. I couldn't possibly see myself doing anything else."

P. J. Raval

Recently, I started saying 'queer,' not 'gay.' I identify myself as a person in the queer community." Filmmaker and cinematographer P. J. Raval is telling me how he changed after he made his award-winning documentary *Trinidad*, about the lives of three transgender women in the "sex-change capital of the United States," Trinidad, Colorado.

"Until *Trinidad*, I really didn't know anything about the transgender community. Here I was in the LGBTQ community, and I never quite understood the T part. Growing up, my gender identity was never in question. My *sexual* identity was in question. Now I understand how they're all connected. As a queer individual, I don't feel I'm like most of the population of self-identified gay men. The buff Abercrombie-looking guy—that's not me. I'm not going out and having surgery, but I'm making films about transgender people, and I'm out there calling myself queer."

We're sitting in the living room of Raval's apartment. The soothing sounds of water gurgling in his fish tank intermingle with quiet, New Age music on the stereo. He serves me a mug of herbal tea. The night before, Raval threw a party, but this morning the house is already tidy and clean again. Asian tranquility in Austin, Texas.

"As I was working on *Trinidad*, the Austin Gay and Lesbian Film Festival mounted a showcase of all my films up until that point.

When I watched them, I realized that a lot of my work has to do with roles—the role of a boyfriend, the role of a partner, the role of a son, of a father—and what happens when people challenge those roles and reject them. I felt that that was what had been happening my entire life: watching people put me into categories. They'd say, 'You're a scientist,' and I'd say, 'But I'm also an artist'; and they'd say, 'Well, you're a photographer,' and I'd say, 'No, I'm also a filmmaker'; and they'd say, 'Well, you're a narrative filmmaker,' and I'd say, 'No, I also make documentaries!' Or they'd say, 'You're gay,' and I'd say, 'No, I'm queer!' Labels: I'm interested in what happens when people go beyond them and challenge them. That's what I loved about Trinidad. It was a group of people who were challenging the roles."

Raval is in his midthirties, but he's already racked up a host of impressive honors for his work in film, including awards in directing, screenplay writing, and cinematography. He's made narrative films, experimental films, documentaries, music videos. *Filmmaker* magazine recently named him one of the "25 New Faces of Independent Film" and noted his penchant for "cinematographic genre jumping." As gay people—as *queer* people—are we somehow more open to "genre jumping"?

"I would like to think that being a minority figure in society opens doors in terms of accepting other things, looking at things differently, being comfortable with being different. If that's the case, then, yeah, being queer lends itself to genre jumping. It keeps things fresh for me. I don't like to be completely pinned down, tied down."

The son of Filipino immigrants who came to the United States to "have their own adventure and find their own path," Raval grew up in Clovis, California, a small conservative town where "no one even knew where the Philippines were." Shy, quiet, and introverted, Raval says he was the type of child who was perfectly content to "wander into a corner with a toy, take it apart, and come up with some crazy story in the process."

Very early on, he realized that he had feelings for boys. He remembers a time during the first grade when he spent the night at his best friend's house, "staying up really late at night, kissing each other, acting like this is what moms and dads do. I always knew there was something a little different about me. I could hang with the boys, but I couldn't fully be one. I ended up surrounding myself with friends who were like-minded. There was this weird unspoken thing between a lot of us. But nowhere in there did I have someone to understand me. No one was out in my high school. I didn't know anyone who was gay."

His first day at the University of California at San Diego Raval signed up for an art class and realized that something had been missing in his life. He ended up staying at UCSD for five years—"a real opportunity to reinvent myself"—double majoring in media art and biology and minoring in psychology and studio art.

"Art really opened me up; it coincided with my coming out. I was figuring out ways to express myself." At first, Raval took up painting and sculpting, but he slowly found his way toward photography. When he ran out of photography classes, he enrolled in his first film class. "The photography work I was doing was narrative; I loved the idea of working in this other medium, film, that was even more narrative."

Nevertheless, by the time he graduated, Raval still did not see himself as a filmmaker. His first jobs out of college were "weird jobs" in multimedia. After two years, he says he found the courage to reject his family's traditional path—medicine or science—and try his hand at a career in the arts. "I decided that if I'm going to work this hard, I wanted it to be something that I really cared about. I will sacrifice any paycheck gladly, any comfort, any sensible profession to do what I really love. That, too, coincided with coming out: you have to live on your own terms."

On a whim, Raval "randomly applied" to the film program at the University of Texas at Austin. "I loved the idea of moving to Texas. How crazy is that! My application statement was about wanting to explore my sexual identity and my Asian American identity in film. It was an experimental essay." The university awarded him the Jacob K. Javitts Fellowship.

Raval initially hated Austin. "It wasn't California. It was even tougher being a gay Filipino in Texas. There aren't a lot of queer Asian Americans running around Austin. But all these things allowed me to excel. I feed off these things. I feel more empowered." Empowered enough to start exploring gay themes in his films. The first film he made in graduate school, *100% Cotton*, was about "two guys breaking up in a laundromat." It won Best Narrative Short at the Chicago Gay and Lesbian Film Festival. Raval's next film, *Holding Patterns*, looked at how two strangers at an airport manage to make connections.

One night on a holiday trip back home from graduate school, Raval and his father sat up late talking. "I told him, 'Dad, I realize

I've hated you for so long, and I don't want this hate, I don't want this in my life.' I had never once told my father I was queer. He knew, but I had never said that face-to-face. I said, 'I want you to know that I am proud of this. This is who I am. I'm never going to be that son with the beautiful wife, never going to be the doctor. I'm going to be your son who does these crazy art projects.'"

When he returned to Austin, Raval knew he had the material for his thesis film. In that film, *Lead Role: Father*, which he wrote and directed in 2003, a Chinese American film director reluctantly auditions his father for the lead role in his new project. The lines soon blur between the son's fictional account of his father and the real father he has failed to connect with for many years.

"It's not really about the father in any way. It's about the son and the world he's created and his inability to see beyond that. My father worked all his life to provide for his family. And in the process, he didn't know me. As time went on, we were complete strangers to each other. I realized I didn't know who he was. I just had this 'role' in my head about who he was. I started realizing how similar we were. The similarities scared me."

His voice falters and he chokes up. "I had a lot of problems with the way I was relating to my father because I had a lot of problems with the way I was relating to myself. I hadn't learned to love myself. Part of making that film was about me saying that it's not my father holding me back, it's myself. I had essentially become my father because I was the person holding myself back. I had to learn to love myself."

By the time he received his M.F.A., Raval was already working professionally, in high demand as a cinematographer. In 2005, he shot *Room* for director Kyle Henry. The film was shown at Sundance and Cannes and earned Raval a Haskell Wexler Award for Cinematography. Another of his cinematographic projects, *Wake* (2005), directed by Keun-pyo Park, won him the ASC Charles B. Lang Heritage Award.

Until *Trinidad*, Raval's most notable effort in cinematography was *Trouble the Waters* (2008), a documentary directed by Carl Deal and Tia Lessin about a couple's struggle to survive in the aftermath of Hurricane Katrina. The film incorporates amateur, on-the-spot video footage by Kimberly Rivers Roberts, the young black woman featured in the film. "Kim's footage is amazing. It's so raw, so powerful. As a cinematographer, I asked myself, How do I make this film raw and powerful and not take away what she started? In other documentaries I'd done up to then, we'd done more traditional interviews. I'd had time to light the set, set up the composition. This film wasn't about that. I tried to find a way to visually keep that raw, this-is-happening-right-now energy."

Did his being gay in any way inform the way he went about filming *Trouble the Waters*?

"As a cinematographer, my job is to gain the trust of the subjects. Maybe part of that is my feeling that everyone has an interesting story to tell, making them feel comfortable, that it's OK to have a different story to tell. Maybe when I'm doing documentary work, I am just naturally not judging. I'd like to believe that my minority status opens doors in terms of accepting other things, looking at things differently, being comfortable with being different."

Raval began working on *Trinidad* in 2004 after hearing about the place at a dinner party. "When Jay Hodges and I got there, we were walking around, checking things out. This truck stops. A woman rolls down the window and calls out to us, 'You're not from here, are you?' I thought, Oh, shit, here comes the gay bashing. She said, 'Well, welcome to Trinidad. Have a good time!' and she drove off."

Raval speaks rapturously of the three trans women featured in the documentary—Marci Bowers, the doctor who performs gender-reassignment surgery at the local hospital; Sabrina Marcus, a former NASA scientist who takes charge of fixing up Morning Glow House, a transition facility for transsexuals; and Laura Ellis, a preop transsexual who arrives in Trinidad ready to undergo the surgery.

"We knew from the start that Marci had to be part of this film. What she was doing was so amazing. As we met Marci, Sabrina and Laura moved into town. Suddenly here were these two new women with incredible stories, too. I loved how all three of them were so different, living in the community and functioning in the community very differently."

In the film, Raval gets up close and dirty with each of them. Marci, who considers herself a woman, not a trans woman, is a portrait of someone who is, in Raval's words, "all about excelling." Her utter confidence and professional expertise define her role in the film. She takes pride in having developed new techniques that have turned the process of reconstructing genitalia into surgical artistry. And Raval includes graphic footage to prove it: penises miraculously transformed into vaginas.

"At first we weren't going to include that. We thought it would be too sensational." The first version of the film did not contain that footage, but Raval says it became obvious that this was a serious omission that had to be rectified. "We were talking about surgery, about modifying the body. There needed to be some acknowledgment of what these people were undergoing." So in the new version, he added Marci's medical slides of her surgical reconstructions, placing them early in the film to address right off what he assumed would be his audience's curiosity about "what's going on down there."

Marci also allowed Raval to film an operation in progress. "I don't think I could have actually sat there and watched it—using the scrotal skin sack to build the interior vaginal cavity—but sitting behind the camera, I was fine."

Raval says he identifies most with Sabrina, and his camera lovingly and sensitively captures the many charming aspects of her life: her sweetness, her wisdom, the parental love she has for her children and that her children have for her, her spirituality (she's a practicing Catholic), the indefatigable energy she brings to the transformation of Morning Glow House.

For Laura, who walks into town with sad but hopeful eyes and a heavy layer of pancake makeup that can't hide her five o'clock shadow, the operation doesn't solve anything. She ends up leaving Trinidad, an outsider still. It's Sabrina who pinpoints the issue: "You have to fix your mind first before you fix your body." Still, Raval manages to capture Laura's courage, dignity, and resilience in the face of all her disappointment.

Raval says he finds it "incredibly empowering" to be a queer filmmaker. "Artists and queer people live beyond what is already known, established, sanctioned, familiar. I have license to explore. I feel that I'm excused from having to be a certain way." He chuckles. "Obviously, I have restriction issues, but it's nice to try new things out. That's why I jump around. When I get tired of documentaries, I jump back to narrative films. It's all about experience. There is no set road in terms of what your experience should be. That's what I'm hungry for. That's how I learn, how I move forward."

Gene Robinson

On the sunny, snow-melting January day that I meet him, Gene Robinson cannot contain himself, he's so excited by a piece of mail he has just received. It's a copy of the foreword to his soon-to-be-published book of essays, *In the Eye of the Storm: Swept to the Center by God*. I have hardly sat down in his office at the Diocesan House in Concord, New Hampshire, when Robinson, the first openly gay bishop in the American Episcopal Church, starts telling me the story of how Desmond Tutu came to provide the statement.

"We met in September 2007. It was a thrilling, humbling experience. Often people are at a loss for words when they meet me. That's how I felt meeting Tutu." The two spent time together, after which Tutu offered to provide Robinson with some words to open his book. Weeks, then months, went by without the promised statement. "As late as a week ago, I was watching Tutu on TV. He was trying to quell the violence in Kenya. And, of course, I was thinking, Why isn't he home writing my foreword!" But at last Tutu's piece has come, and Robinson pronounces it "astounding."

"What he does—and I don't think Tutu has ever done this in print before—is to apologize to all gay and lesbian people for the harm done them by the Anglican Church. He reiterates the idiocy of condemning people for something they can't change."

227

Since his election as bishop, Robinson has fallen into the eye of a fierce ecclesiastical and theological storm. Conservative parishes and dioceses have threatened to leave the Anglican Communion, the worldwide body of churches with ties to the Church of England, of which the American Episcopal Church is one branch. He has been subjected to a smear campaign and been barred from the Lambeth Conference, the once-every-ten-years convocation of Anglican bishops. Archbishop Benjamin Nzimbi of the Anglican Church of Kenya, reflecting the sentiments of many conservative Christians, said of Robinson, "The devil has clearly entered the church."

Robinson, who has been called "the most controversial Christian in the world," grew up in rural Kentucky in an area where "virtually everyone was a tobacco farmer." His parents were sharecroppers. The most important aspect of his childhood, he tells me, was the "grounding in Scripture" he received from the Disciples of Christ, his parents' denomination. "I proudly had thirteen years of perfect attendance: an hour of Sunday school followed by an hour of church."

During his adolescence, Robinson began having homosexual feelings, which he tried to suppress. By the time he left for college he had begun to feel how "unnecessarily and unflatteringly narrow and judgmental" his congregation was. He was ready for something new. And he found it at Sewanee: the University of the South, a private liberal arts college in Tennessee owned by the Episcopal Church. Although he chose Sewanee "for purely academic reasons," the required chapel services led him to "fall in love with two things": the Episcopal liturgy and the church's two thousand year history with its emphasis on apostolic succession. He was confirmed in the Episcopal Church on Easter Day of his senior year, 1969. The following September, he enrolled at the General Theological Seminary in New York. When the homosexual feelings persisted, he sought help in therapy.

After his second year at General, Robinson took a leave of absence to do an internship as chaplain at the University of Vermont. It was there that he met his future wife, Isabella Martin, known as Boo. By the next summer, despite continuing fears that his homosexuality was not under control, he and Boo married. The following year, he completed his degree at General. Six months later he was ordained into the Episcopal priesthood. After serving for two years in a parish in New Jersey, Robinson, with the help of his wife, started Sign of the Dove, a horse farm and conference center in rural New Hampshire, where they led retreats for religious groups, committees, and parishes. The couple's daughters were born in 1977 and 1981.

I ask Robinson about his coming to terms with his homosexuality. "We have come so far in this movement. It's hard for young LGBT people to imagine a world without *Will and Grace*, without Ellen, without Greg Louganis and Martina Navratilova. Or to remember back to what a hero Harvey Milk was. The way that process of coming to terms happened for me is that I began to reclaim Scripture and to discover that those stories were my stories: God's voice came through despite what my church and the culture were telling me. I was the prodigal son, welcomed home by the father, not because being gay was bad but because of how I felt about myself.

"You know, Moses and the Exodus is the greatest coming-out story of all time. Like Moses, I knew what it was like to hear the call to freedom, to be afraid to leave, to get the courage to leave, to find myself just on the other side of the Red Sea, as on the other side of coming out, and discovering not the promised land but the desert, wandering in the desert, feeling the temptation to turn back. That is our story! I kept recognizing myself as a gay man all through Scripture and learning, as all people on the margins have the opportunity to learn, that there is good news there."

Robinson credits John Fortunato's book *Embracing the Exile: Healing Journeys of Gay Christians* (1982) with changing his life. In reading Fortunato's book, he knew he had to leave his marriage. In 1986, he and his wife separated and subsequently divorced. Shortly afterward New Hampshire bishop Douglas Theuner hired Robinson to be on his staff, the first openly gay person on any bishop's staff in the country.

During his years as canon to the ordinary—Episcopal Church parlance for the bishop's chief of staff—Robinson did work in youth ministry, clergy wellness, conflict resolution, and mediation. He also coauthored AIDS education materials, advocated for antiracism training, and spoke out for socially responsible financial investing. In short, he tells me, he learned "as much as you can learn by being close to the bishop's chair without actually being in it." Twice his name was put forward to be a bishop, but he lost both elections.

So why does he think he was elected bishop of New Hampshire in 2003?

"The world assumes that the Diocese of New Hampshire was trying to make some big political statement. You know, I had been out in this diocese as a gay man for more than twenty years. They had known me married, single, partnered. I was out in every congregation. It just wasn't a big whoop. They knew how I worked. What they underestimated, as did I, was the size of the storm that ensued. And while that storm has been pretty enormous, it's also important to understand that it was a storm that had been brewing long before my consecration."

Robinson contends that the leaders of the conservative movement "have been unhappy since the ordination of women and have been wanting to foment some kind of split." His ordination gave them an event to focus on. "I think it's about the end of patriarchy. First of all, this is a far bigger issue for men than it is for women. The thing that is so scandalous seems to be a man who allows himself to be 'treated like a woman.' Nothing could be worse. We are born with privilege by virtue of being male, and to allow ourselves to be 'treated like a female' is flying in the face of that privilege. For a very long time, straight, white, Western-educated, heterosexual men have made all the decisions for most of the world. And then in the sixties we started letting people of color in, and women in, and *Oh, my, now it's gay and lesbian people!* For traditionalists, that just seems too much to bear."

Robinson's election precipitated a rash of protests, hate mail, and even death threats. He was put under twenty-four-hour protection from the FBI. At his consecration, which took place in a hockey rink at the University of New Hampshire on November 2, 2003, he had to wear a bullet-proof vest. There were police patrols outside; plans were in order for evacuating him in the event of a bomb threat. Angry protestors brandished signs that read, "Homosexual: Abomination to God" and "God burned Sodom and Gomorrah." Afterward, Rowan Williams, the archbishop of Canterbury, issued a statement: "The divisions that are arising are a matter of deep regret; . . . it will not be possible for Gene Robinson's ministry as a bishop to be accepted in every province in the communion."

I ask Robinson about schism within the Anglican Communion. At this point, is it inevitable? "For the first couple of years after I was consecrated, I thought we were all trying for reconciliation. But recently the leaders of the American conservative movement have said flat-out that they are not interested in reconciliation. If schism happens, it will be because they chose it."

Over the years, the central message of Robinson's ministry can be summed up in one of his oft-quoted phrases: "God loves us beyond our wildest imaginings." What, I ask, is the matter with just being self-affirming? Why does one need a God to affirm one's being?

"Nothing wrong with self-affirmation at all. But self-affirmation can be self-serving. I always need the check of the community to keep my ego reined in. I use a spiritual director to help me make sure that the voice I hear in my head is God's voice and not my own ego doing a magnificent impression of God's voice. There is no reason why I should be as happy as I am. I ought to be bitter, angry. And the reason I'm not is something that goes beyond rationality. What I get in my relationship with God is unspeakable empowerment."

Since his consecration, Robinson has never had any doubts about the path he's taken. "Never. Now, am I sorry that this has been very painful for people? Absolutely. But I never, ever got any notion that I should not do this. To this day, I get e-mails and letters from people around the world telling me what this means to them."

Robinson has been with his partner, Mark Andrew, since the two met while on vacation in St. Croix in November 1987. "I don't think I could have done this without him. Despite the fact that this has been Mark's idea of a nightmare—he doesn't like being in the spotlight— he's been my anchor, my best friend. We used to share everything around the house. Now that I'm gone so much, he's just picked up all that stuff. But we're still having fun along the way. I mean, four years ago, we wouldn't have been invited backstage to meet Elton John."

When I ask him which of the many awards that he has received pleases him most, he relates another story. "I have this blessedly wonderful relationship with the women at the New Hampshire State Women's Prison. It started three days after my election when I got a note from a woman who said, 'I'm neither gay nor Christian, but there is something in your election that makes me believe that there might be a community out there who could love me despite what I've done.' I went to visit her. She was eighteen years old. When she was fifteen, she killed her mother. That visit started a relationship with these women. I spend every Christmas Eve with them. It's a horrible night to be in prison. The women don't necessarily know where their children are; they're not putting toys under a tree. We sing carols and we have a Eucharist. And I preach. A couple of years ago, they presented me with a set of vestments that they had made. They're blue vestments—Mary blue—for Advent. They told me they wanted to do Advent vestments because they consider themselves a community in waiting. I promised them that whenever I wore them I would tell stories about them because they just feel so forgotten."

Robinson has recently led a five-day retreat for gay Catholic priests. When I ask him about it, he bursts out laughing. "It was amazing! First of all, seventy-five gay Roman Catholic priests gathered around a piano singing 'How Do You Solve a Problem Like Maria?' I thought I was going to have a coronary! It was so great—unspeakably fun. Second, it was indescribably sad. They were meeting clandestinely. They're just scared to death. The hierarchy is still making the connection between homosexuality and pedophilia, a totally debunked theory. I have said publicly that that's an act of violence against gay men."

Robinson turned down a speaking engagement in Jerusalem in order to accept the invitation to be with the priests. "What I felt called to say to them was: 'It's all well and good for you to find support in a closed setting, but if it stops there, then this is just a gay fraternity. Your next step is to figure out how to help your institution change. And because of this close link between misogyny and homophobia, and because of the whole patriarchal thing, I'm not sure the Roman Catholic Church is not to going to get anywhere on the gay issue until it gets someplace on the women's issue.'"

In February 2006, Robinson voluntarily sought treatment for alcoholism. With his characteristic exuberance, he says that when he finally acknowledged his problem, he said to God, "You know, I've learned enough for one lifetime, so enough already with the teaching me!" Nevertheless, he insists that the twenty-eight-day program he attended was "just one of the most wonderful things that's happened to me. You're plunged into the middle of a community that's talking about the very thing that you have avoided talking about forever. No radio, no TV, no music, no books other than books related to spirituality or alcohol. No escapes!"

Almost three years later, on January 18, 2009, at the Lincoln Memorial, Robinson delivered the preinaugural invocation, "A Prayer for the Nation and Our Next President, Barack Obama." In part, that prayer asked the "God of our many understandings"—a phrase he learned in his twelve-step recovery program—to "bless this nation with anger—anger at discrimination at home and abroad, against refugees and immigrants, women, people of color, gay, lesbian, bisexual, and transgender people." The prayer was not included on HBO's coverage, and there are accusations that the president's transition team had deliberately cut it. With characteristic goodwill, Robinson later told the *Advocate* that "the controversy about why [the prayer] had been eliminated probably gave it more attention than it would have gotten if it had been included in the broadcast."

Robinson has been seen by some as having a prophetic role in his church. "What I've decided," he tells me, "is that, if this accident of history puts me in the limelight, then I want to be as good a steward of that opportunity as I can be. When I do a radio interview, I try to remember to bring every answer back to God. I write down on a piece of paper, 'It's about God, stupid,' and put it right in front of me."

Richard Rodriguez

I don't sit still on the page," Richard Rodriguez tells me. We are sitting at a café in the Lower Pacific Heights section of San Francisco. The author of a trilogy of powerful memoirs that focus on class, ethnicity, and race, Rodriguez is explaining to me why he bristles at the notion of being considered a niche writer. He pauses just long enough to take a sip of coffee.

For instance, he continues, on a recent trip to Egypt, surrounded by beautiful men, he found himself thinking instead about the Arabic occupation of Spain. "And then I'm wondering whether there are aspects of my being that are Arabic. *That's* what I'm thinking on a day in Cairo. I don't think about whether I'm the Latino here."

Nor, he asserts, is he interested in writing about being gay. "I'd much rather write about camels or monks in the desert. Did you see my piece about Jerusalem in *Harper's*? I'm interested in the feminization of desert religions. When I think about male beauty—I don't mean Calvin Klein or naked men in their underwear—I think about how it is unmistakably a violation of the male orthodoxy."

During our conversation, the range of topics Rodriguez brings up will include Olympic swimmer Michael Phelps, the Catholic Church, his impatience with today's gay movement, the latest novel by André Aciman, affirmative action, the personal affronts and slights he has suffered, Medici Florence. And, of course, his books.

We talk for almost three hours, which is ironic since, a few months earlier, in response to my request for an hour and a half of his time, Rodriguez had replied, "I don't think we'll need ninety minutes, since I am not a 'gay' writer. I am a morose Hispanic-shelved 'Latino' in most bookstores, far from the muscled and naked fiesta that takes place on the Gay and Lesbian shelves in another part of the store."

And yet—he takes another sip of coffee—"I like being gay in the world. I like the complication of it. I like that I'm walking down a street in Cairo and some kid who has a T-shirt that says 'Hollywood' in spangles pinches my ass. I like the *difficulty* of that. I like the tension in sexually repressed societies. I like the way touch occurs in conversation, or proximity of face, or intimacy of voice. When I go back to Europe after the Middle East, everything is blatant: *'I'm gay!'* It's not sensual. It's not erotic. It's nothing. It's just a political billboard."

Rodriguez flashed onto the literary scene with the 1982 publication of *Hunger of Memory*, the story of his intellectual odyssey from Mexican American scholarship boy to Yale-courted scholar of Renaissance literature. Educated away from the culture of his parents, he gained a "public identity," assimilation into the larger world, which, he maintained, was to be valued and nurtured, even as he suffered "a diminished sense of *private* individuality."

In the book, Rodriguez recounted how, keenly convinced of the injustice of affirmative action, he withdrew his name from consideration for prestigious university professorships. It was a courageous insistence on freedom—"the freedom," he writes, "so crucial to adulthood, to become a person very different in public from the person I am at home."

Since that 1975 exodus from the academy, Rodriguez has gone on to the life of a freelance writer, lecturer, and teacher. His views on affirmative action and bilingual education have made him, as he has written, "notorious among certain leaders of America's Ethnic Left." He's been called a "brown Uncle Tom."

He hasn't fared much better with the gay establishment. In "Late Victorians," an essay in his second book, *Days of Obligation*, Rodriguez meditated on San Francisco's gay community and the death from AIDS of his friend César. He wrote about his own skepticism toward the gay pursuit of an earthly paradise. It was, in many respects, his coming-out essay. In response, he tells me, he received "a lot of letters saying how dare I write such an essay, that it was a regression to the guilt-ridden fifties. I knew at that point that I would never be a 'gay writer.'"

Rodriguez was born in 1944 in San Francisco to parents who were immigrants from Mexico. They settled in Sacramento, a few blocks from the "Fabulous Forties," a neighborhood of grand homes in the manner of Beverly Hills. His father enjoyed steady work—factory and janitorial jobs—and eventually became a dental technician. Pride ran in the family.

"We were not diminished by our poverty. We always had a sense of our worth. But nonetheless, I wanted entrance into the opposite society, the learned and the well spoken. I felt I had nothing to offer. I decided not only that I was embarrassed by my parents but that I wanted to know rich people." Invited into their homes, Rodriguez studied his Anglo classmates "like specimens—the china, the silver, the linen, how they decorated the living room, their Sinatra records. I knew that conversation was very important to those people. If you could talk, if you could say amusing, interesting things, you'd be invited back."

He decided that he "had to fill the glass with learning in order to exist. Every book became one more step in my being." By the time he was twelve, he was reading the great English novels, a habit that "fevered" his imagination. "I was not repressed in that sense. I thought about eroticism. I imagined lovemaking as much as the Brontës did. The frustration, the secrecy, the wall—it did not trap me. It made me wild. I didn't have a boyfriend or girlfriend, but I was already leagues ahead in terms of my erotic imagination."

Rodriguez speaks glowingly of the Irish nuns who were his teachers. "They were not sentimental about education. They knew the path to inclusion: learn English, don't be Irish, participate in the American experience, build St. Patrick's Cathedral. And show the bastards. Paint the green line down Fifth Avenue and make them stand at attention."

In turn, his teachers were "dazzled" by his precocity. "I knew poetry by heart. I had accumulated a great deal." He was also "thinking about sex all the time." At the professional wrestling matches he attended as a boy, he was "awed by the wrestlers' sweaty bodies, the thickness of their muscularity. I would slap their backs. The slap of leather on flesh!"

He reminisces about a classmate, "clearly a gay boy," who was already dancing in summer stock shows. "How wonderful to leap through the air, to have that confidence. Although I could say interesting things about *West Side Story*—the hopeless romanticism of the updated *Romeo and Juliet*—I wasn't active in the same way." Rodriguez began to imagine a life in which he "would know everything about sexuality," though he himself would never be a sexual creature. "I would be talking to girls, reciting Shakespearean sonnets, not making out. I would never know passion because there were too many words."

The Church, too, sparked what, in *Hunger of Memory*, Rodriguez calls "a very private sexual excitement," an experience he describes for me in more detail. "It was everywhere in the Church—the smell of flowers on the altar. Or serving as an altar boy at weddings, I would appraise these handsome young men. Or at funerals. There I am in my cassock and my Keds, carrying a casket, feeling the weight of a body. This is pretty heady stuff for a child who never dated, never kissed. That proximity with death was so erotic."

In *Days of Obligation*, Rodriguez asks whether certain "darling affinities" are innate to homosexuality or compensatory. I ask if he thinks his early affinity for books and education was a way to compensate for his sense of sexual difference. "No. The gayness came later. Going to theatrical productions, the only person my age in the audience, I realized that I wanted a *cosmopolitan* future. I wanted to go to Europe, live in a great city. Clearly I would not be able to do that in Sacramento."

The cosmopolitanism of the public library—a place where there was "no segregated shelf"—was where Rodriguez found "permission to take any society, any language, any experience as mine." Recalling this, he says that nowadays he is "horrified that the price of my inclusion in America is my segregation. As a writer, in order to gain entrance into Barnes and Noble or Borders, I have to enter at the segregated counter called Latino Studies. We have tolerated a liberal agenda that has segregated the mind according to these crude categories of membership. When I was a boy, James Baldwin was not found in the Black section. He was Literature. Literature trumped everything."

By the time he left high school, Rodriguez felt "a sense of embarrassment that somehow I had betrayed my very being by exchanging my private Mexicanness for an American identity. I was a talker. Mexican men who talked a great deal were suspected of being less than full men." Nevertheless, at Stanford, which he chose not only for its academic reputation but also because "it was the school rich people went to," Rodriguez says he "didn't know how to behave. I didn't know you showered every day. I didn't have a suit. I had one tie." In his eagerness to overcome these limitations, he would take the bus to San Francisco, where he would usher at the theater, the opera, the symphony.

"Minority student—" Rodriguez writes in *Hunger of Memory,* "that was the label I bore in college at Stanford, then in graduate school at Columbia and Berkeley: a nonwhite reader of Spenser and Milton and Austen." While at first he accepted the label, it slowly became a source of unease. "Ethnic separateness: I couldn't do it. The problem with being labeled 'Hispanic' is that it wasn't like being Asian or white. It wasn't a racial designation; it was a cultural designation. The cues I gave—my knowledge of English literature, of eighteenth-century London, of Shakespeare—didn't belong to the Hispanic revival. It was a real violation of the caricature." He tells me about a day at Berkeley when an African American student asked him why he was reading a novel by the Nigerian writer Chinua Achebe. "That's when I understood that I had entered a Dark Age. That I had entered an age when we were not allowed to know each other's literature."

Rodriguez has criticized bilingualists who scorn assimilation and "romanticize public separateness." What about a parallel situation for gay people? Does he think gays have romanticized public separateness? "Yes, I do. At some level, I'm just not socialized to be around other gay men. I have lots of friends who are gay, but the notion that I would live in the Castro district is so foreign to me. I don't understand what that would be. I find men to be utterly mysterious."

After he left academia, Rodriguez moved to Los Angeles—four years from 1975 to 1979 that he calls the "lost years," a period he has yet to write about. Here he tried out a more public gay life. "I was suddenly catapulted into a very glamorous existence. For the first time, I had a body. All the lessons that I had learned in grammar school about going to big houses flowered there. I was taken on vacations, into worlds that were more glamorous, more wealthy." Was he a kept boy? "I was not a *boy*, I was a man, but I was taken care of, yes."

In this rarefied gay world—he calls it "pagan and glorious"—Rodriguez soon learned that his linguistic skills were best put aside. "It was a different game. A Nautilus body spoke more. It was not the world of Cole Porter." At swank dinner parties in Beverly Hills, he felt more comfortable with "the alcoholic daughter of the movie director than with the guy who was famous for picking up gay young men, who knew Tab Hunter, who knew everyone."

In 1979, Rodriguez moved back to San Francisco "in order," he has written, "not to be distracted by the ambitions or, for that matter, the pleasures of others." There he wrote *Hunger of Memory*. By then the AIDS epidemic had surfaced. "I saw beautiful men die, youth die. I was paralyzed by their deaths. I couldn't look at a human body anymore with desire. I saw death everywhere. I helped a lot of men die. If I were to write a sexual coming-of-age novel, it would be with a bedpan." While he does feel a responsibility to address gay issues—as an example, he mentions a piece he wrote against Proposition 8 and another on whether Abraham Lincoln was gay (Rodriguez insists he was)—Rodriguez says that he is "never brought within the circle. I've never been invited to a gay literary conference. Gay writers find that I'm not appropriate to my type."

In 2002, Rodriguez published his third book, *Brown: The Last Discovery of America*, a finalist for the National Book Critics Award. In it he declares that the "future is brown." I invite him to say more about that. "For all of my ranting and raving about exclusion, the proudest thing I have as a gay man is when I see black and white men together, when I see this willingness within homosexuality to violate custom. That outlaw aspect of it, whenever I see it, I will always applaud it. That's brown impulse."

These days, Rodriguez is thinking, and writing, a lot about religion. "Religion is the border between race and the unifier between races. And those of us who are 'complicated,' like gay Catholics, find ourselves in a real quandary. I was at one of these PEN extravaganzas, four hundred writers from around the world. The organizing theme was reason and belief. As though these are incompatible. The absolute inability of intellectuals to understand how you could believe in God! The new atheism is childish. I'm old enough to remember when the civil rights movement was animated by black Protestantism, when the Left was able to tolerate belief, when the finest rhetoric of the Left was inspired by biblical cadence. To separate ourselves from that realm of experience is death."

Rodriguez remains a practicing Catholic, one who has been invited to be the keynote speaker at the annual convention of Dignity, the organization for gay and lesbian Catholics. "What gays challenge right now is the notion of love that is disconnected to generation. Can we get past St. Augustine and imagine sexuality as nongenerative? That is the question for the Church." At the same time, Rodriguez takes pains to point out to me that he is "the wrong kind of gay."

"I don't take membership within a gay family. That's not the way it plays with me. I don't live that life. Most of my literary friends are not gay. And most of my literary friends who are gay have usually been censorious of me in print at some point. Where do they get permission to evaluate the level of my sexual candor? Where is there some tolerance for aspects or varieties of experience? Why is it that we all have to be on the same float in the Gay Day parade?"

David Sedaris

David Sedaris takes one look at the menu and laughs. "Pasta Whim. I'll have that!" We're doing our interview at Icarus, an upscale restaurant in Boston's South End, the quietest, least public place I can suggest that is near his hotel. The best-selling humorist is in town to do a reading tomorrow at Symphony Hall. But tonight he just wants to unwind after the torture of a delayed flight the day before.

"Yesterday I was really looking forward to my day off," he says, pouring himself a glass of mineral water. "Instead, I spent six hours on an airport runway. When I finally arrived, I met a friend for dinner. She said, 'I need to tell you, I really hated your last book.' I thought, Will I wake up at three in the morning thinking about this or at four? It was three. Oh, and before that, the airport 'greeter'—someone else you have to tip on the way to the limo—asked me if I wanted a cup of coffee. Six hours on the runway. There was nothing I wanted more. Well, Starbucks was out of coffee. Expectations and reality: I think I can make hay from it all, eventually."

It's a quintessential David Sedaris story, or what he would call an "incident," the raw material of daily life from which, "eventually," he might craft another hilarious, and poignant, essay. "I'm like a friendly junkman," he once wrote, "building things from the little pieces of scrap I find here and there."

Named "Humorist of the Year" by *Time* magazine in 2001, Sedaris is the author of half a dozen collections of the funniest, most trenchant essays and stories by any writer of his generation. His books have consistently appeared on the *New York Times* best-seller list. Seven million copies, in English and twenty-five other languages, are in print. He has won the Thurber Prize for American Humor, a Grammy nomination for best comedy album, and a Lambda Literary Award. The *Chicago Tribune* has knighted him "one of the greatest humorists writing today."

"People come to his work because he's funny," NPR's Ira Glass once told a reporter for *People* magazine. "But there's a complicated moral vision there." In fact, Sedaris's humor almost always dwells at the edge of disaster and chaos. His pieces, many of which are autobiographical, detail his close encounters with a less-than-perfect world: the family he inherited, the little miseries of childhood, his homosexuality, the daily brushes with foiled expectations and the dark underbelly of pretension. "Sedaris brings X-ray vision to this strip search of the human psyche," wrote *Entertainment Weekly* of his second book, *Naked*.

When our dinners arrive, he offers me a taste of his Pasta Whim. Linguini, shrimp, a hint of saffron. I demurely sample the linguini. "You want some shrimp, too?" he encourages. Suddenly, I'm feeling that I may have overprepared. I have a thousand questions, and David Sedaris just wants to share a morsel of sautéed crustacean with me. I decline and plunge in with my first question. How does he differ from a stand-up comedian?

"I have a piece of paper in front of me. That makes all the difference in the world. I've never been heckled, because I have a piece of paper. When you do stand-up, no one thinks of you as a writer; they don't ever think that you chose a specific word and not another."

Not everything in his stories, he tells me, is meant to be funny. Because he's a writer and not a stand-up, people know it's OK not to be laughing all the time. "Plus, there's that thing in stand-up comedy— 'How's everybody doing tonight?'—that relentless pacing, that nervous energy. I don't have that either. Then there's the Q & A thing I do at the end. The same eight questions. Sometimes I don't feel like answering those questions, so I'll just talk. That's the closest I come to stand-up. I just call it running my mouth."

Sedaris says that he is most often called a humorist. "And most often that's what I'm hoping for. I've never written anything that's completely serious. 'Humorist' makes me think of somebody with a cardigan sweater on, but I think it's probably the most apt word. A number of years ago, somebody wrote in *New York* magazine that I'm the wittiest New Yorker since Dorothy Parker. If I could take back one thing that was ever said about me, I'd take that. It looks very nice on a poster, but it's absolutely not true, because I'm not witty. That calls for a fierce intelligence. I'm far from the smartest guy in the world. I don't threaten smart people."

I ask him if he's aware of Kevin Kopelson's book about him and his work, *Sedaris*. In it, Kopelson writes that shame is a big theme in Sedaris's work.

"He wrote and told me he was doing the book. I told him that's fine, but I would never, ever read it. I spent some time with Kevin; I like him a lot, but I wouldn't read the book for the same reason I don't read reviews. If somebody likes something, then I think, Oh, is that what I should do? Should I do that more often?" Sedaris puts down his fork. "He says shame is a theme? It's a big theme in my life. If you asked me about the themes in my work, I wouldn't really know. Me, me, me. That's a good start."

Sedaris has peppered his essays with uproarious, and mostly true, anecdotes of his early life. When he was young, his family relocated from western New York State, where his father worked for IBM, to Raleigh, North Carolina. The South, he writes, provided opportunities galore to make "relentless fun of our neighbors and their pokey, backward way of life. . . . Along with grits and hush puppies, the abbreviated form of *you all* was a dangerous step on an insidious path leading straight to the doors of the Baptist church."

The sensibilities of a nascent gay boy are everywhere in Sedaris's stories about his boyhood. In one, he tells his mother he wants a "peach-colored velveteen blazer with matching slacks." Boys make him anxious: he has "absolutely nothing in common" with his more gregarious and athletic classmates. He doesn't get the "point" of football. At an all-boy slumber party, while the others play "titty twister," he flutters his hands in front of his face, screeching. And when he wins at strip poker, he forces the loser to sit naked on his lap. Weekends he makes banana nut muffins or dreams about a career in the arts, perhaps as a "song stylist."

Sedaris had a peripatetic college career, first at Western Carolina University and then at Kent State University, neither of which he completed. "The Bong Studies Program," he calls his time at Kent

State. But he also started writing a diary, one he has kept now for over thirty years. "A worse writer than me never existed," he tells me of his early scribbling. "Pretentious. Looking back, I guess that's normal. That's how you learn. I tried to be like Patti Smith, Joni Mitchell. And eventually I grew up and tried to be Joan Didion." After a "slumming phase," during which he became a "speed enthusiast" and tried his hand at conceptual art, Sedaris moved to Chicago to enroll in the School of the Art Institute of Chicago. He was twenty-seven.

"In painting class, we would have these critiques: people would put up their artwork and talk about it as if they were talking to a therapist. It was really boring. Nobody was getting anything out of it. The first public piece I ever read was a statement about my artwork. It was more in the form of a character. I think it was titled 'What Certain People Have Been Saying about My Work.' It was short, and people laughed. It felt great. Really, really good." After that, friends would invite him to read at their happenings or loft parties.

Sedaris found himself "more moved by things that I read than by things that I saw. But it took me about a year to take an English class. I was too afraid." The first short story he wrote in that class was "a dead-on parody of Raymond Carver." Soon he was attending literary readings, where he took note of the pitfalls and mistakes in other writers' work. He would imagine telling these writers: "You went on too long, or you didn't give your character a name: it's an interior monologue. No one *wants* anything in your story. No one's talking to anybody."

"I learned a lot by paying attention to my own mistakes and other people's mistakes as well." Even now, Sedaris says, when he is onstage in front of an audience, "I have a pencil in my pocket, making notes. Reading it out loud is the best advice there is."

After graduating from the Art Institute in 1987, Sedaris remained in Chicago, teaching writing and working other, more menial jobs. With his friends, he was also curating art shows at Links Hall, a community space for artists and performers in Boystown, the city's gay neighborhood. And he kept writing in his diary. "I couldn't see it at the time, but the writing was so bad. Now I think, No wonder I drove that boyfriend away, if this is who I was." But not so bad that he wasn't able to publish an early collection, *Origins of the Underclass, and Other Stories* (1992), with Amethyst Press, a small gay publishing house.

By now, Sedaris was also giving public readings from his worked-up diary entries. At one such reading, held at Links Hall's basement performance space, Lower Links, Ira Glass heard him. Glass, who was freelancing for NPR's *All Things Considered*, soon invited Sedaris to read another piece on *Morning Edition*. His radio debut took place on December 23, 1992, by which time Sedaris had moved to New York, working more menial jobs and "living off the cruel joke I referred to as my savings," as he later put it in *Me Talk Pretty One Day*. For the broadcast, he chose part of his "SantaLand Diaries," about working as a Christmas elf for Macy's department store.

"It aired at something like 7:15 in the morning," he tells me. "And then the phones started ringing." When the phones eventually stopped ringing, Sedaris had become a "minor phenomenon," according to the *New York Times*, and had a contract with Little, Brown. Soon he was a regular on NPR. "Ira changed my life like someone in a fairy tale. There was 'before' and 'after,' and it was immediate. I owe him everything."

Two years later, Sedaris's first big commercial success, *Barrel Fever*, a collection of stories and essays, was published. "I had been writing fiction, but when I started on the radio, things had to be true, or true enough. It had never occurred to me that I would write nonfiction. My fiction is outrageous; it doesn't take any time at all for people to be doing things that are completely unbelievable. When Ira put that Santa thing on the radio, and then he said, 'OK, they want you to do more,' I thought, Now what? It wasn't what I had imagined for myself."

Did reading for the radio change his prose style in any way? "If my tongue were cut out, it would really change my writing a lot. I wouldn't be able to look forward to reading it aloud. But I think it can affect the writing in a bad way too. The biggest laugh you can get is from looking up or rolling your eyes. Sometimes you can imitate somebody. I often worry things work better out loud. People will tell me they prefer my books on tape to reading them. On paper, you need to write all that stuff *into* the prose."

Does he look for intrinsically funny situations or situations that he knows he can render in a funny way? "Life just feels like a story. Because I write in my diary every day, I hope that I'm attentive so I know when that story moment comes along." And then he tells me a story:

"After I quit smoking, I was looking for something I could do that wouldn't make me miss smoking. I took up swimming, because you can't swim and smoke at the same time. I was in Yakima, and there was a YMCA down the street from my hotel. So I go to the YMCA, and this nine-year-old kid pops out of the water like a seal and starts talking to me. He said, 'Let's have a race.' I'm not the kind of person who's going to slow down to let a nine-year-old win, so I gave it all I had. I beat him.

"Then he said, 'Do you believe in God?' I told him no. He said, 'Well, you should, because God made you win.' I said, 'Well, if He knows I don't believe in Him, why would He be doing me any favors? Maybe instead, God made you lose. Did you ever think of that?' And then I thought, What am I doing saying this to a nine-year-old in a strange town?

"So I continued swimming, and at the next lap he stopped me and said, 'You're going to go to hell!' I said, 'Is this about me winning that race?' He said, 'No, you don't believe in God, so you're going to burn in hell for all eternity.' I said, 'Where did you learn that?' He said, 'In church.' I said, 'Which one?' He said, 'A *godly* one.'

"*That* felt like a story to me. I thought, If I engage him more, then maybe I'll have more of a story. But to have engaged him more would have ruined whatever story I'd gotten."

Sedaris tells me that he wrote down an account of the incident in his diary, taking care to include as many details as he could remember—the boy's haircut, how many lifeguards were on duty, the fact that everybody else in the pool was Mexican. "I don't know that any of that will eventually factor into a story, but it caught my notice at the time." He says that he often sits on material like that for years until he finds a way to turn the incident into something publishable. "An incident doesn't make for a story. I have to plug it in to something else." For that reason, he thinks "The SantaLand Diaries" feel "chunky and blocky," lacking the kind of counterpoint he now aims for. "I wouldn't give you two cents for it now."

As for his daily routine, Sedaris says he works "all the time" at his writing. "I never take a day off. I get to work immediately. A lot of the stuff that I've gotten done in my life I've gotten done because I'm there, sitting at the keyboard. If you're not there, it's pretty much guaranteed you're not going to get anything written. In the afternoon, I go to the movies." It wasn't always that way. Sedaris tells me that for years he would write in the evening, having primed himself beforehand with a big bottle of beer. "And then it was three beers, four beers, five beers with a scotch, and then with two scotches. All on an empty stomach. I'd get drunk and stoned. That just had to stop."

He tells me how he did it: "I was on a book tour. A friend's husband had just gotten out of a treatment center for alcoholics. I was staying with them, and I brought booze into their house. I mean, just because he had gotten out of the center *the day before*, I wasn't going to go without. I couldn't go a day without it. Well, he got into my liquor. That's the last time I had a drink. I switched to writing the first thing in the morning. At night, I'd be thinking, Shouldn't I have some booze here?"

Sedaris estimates that only about 10 percent of his audience is gay. "When I read in San Francisco, you'd think I was Amy Tan. Everyone in the audience is Chinese. In El Paso, everyone is Mexican. Sometimes I don't think I'm gay enough." Nevertheless, he says his homosexuality has, "more than anything, affected my perspective, which is to be a watcher. That may be one of the reasons why I moved to Europe. I thought, Well, I'll move to Europe because I'll still be an outsider, not part of the group. There's something about not fitting in that I like. But when I think about it, it wasn't necessary to go to any of those places, because I never changed that perspective."

Does he think of himself as an outsider? "Observer rather than outsider. If you're playing basketball, and your team is winning, you don't have time to look; but if you were never picked to begin with— if you're on the sidelines—you have to come up with a reason for why what they're doing isn't so great in the first place. A few weeks ago, these two guys came to one of my readings to get a book signed. Sixteen and nineteen, they'd met in high school, and they were a couple. I told them, 'Man, when I was your age there was *no way* to identify myself as gay, much less tell my parents, much less have my boyfriend come and spend the night. That's amazing.' It made me realize how, in a really short amount of time, so much has happened."

By now, it's dessert time—apple crisp for him—and we get to talking about his boyfriend of many years, Hugh Hamrick, an artist and designer. They divide their time between homes in Paris, Normandy, and London. Mentioning Paris reminds Sedaris of the time he heard Ed White read from his memoir, *My Lives*, at the Village Voice Bookshop in Paris. There was a man in the audience who was complaining about some of the erotic details White had revealed in the book.

"That was the best sales pitch I ever heard. I got it, read it, and admired White even more. When people say to me, 'How can you expose yourself like that?' I think, No, no, no. White's book—the way he describes himself so piteously—*that's* exposing yourself! I just give the illusion of exposing myself. I sometimes think that the people who come to hear me read don't know many homosexuals, because if they did, they'd realize I'm not that funny. Pretty much everyone in my address book is funnier."

David Sedaris

Carl Siciliano

Recent estimates put the number of homeless gay youth in America at over 600,000. Ali Forney was one of them. From age thirteen until his murder when he was twenty-two, Forney lived as a homeless person in New York City. Carl Siciliano still remembers the day he met Ali. It was the day he took over as director of Safe Space, a drop-in center in Times Square whose clientele included many gay kids. "Ali was such a loving person. His gift was his heart." Siciliano remembers the frustration of trying to get money to shelter homeless youth like Ali. And he remembers Ali's funeral. "More than a hundred people from all over the city showed up."

It was in the wake of such tragedies that Siciliano founded the agency that bears Forney's name. The Ali Forney Center provides emergency and transitional housing and support to homeless LGBTQ youth ages sixteen to twenty-four. The idea is to help these young adults get off the streets so that they can learn to lead healthy, independent lives. Since its founding in 2002, AFC has grown to become the largest and most comprehensive service provider for LGBTQ youth in the country. For his work, Siciliano has been recognized with numerous awards, including the New York City Anti-Violence Project's Courage Award. *OUT* magazine named him on its list of one hundred outstanding gay achievers.

"Don't call me a saint," Siciliano says the day I meet him. "That's how you write me off." He's quoting Dorothy Day, the founder of the Catholic Worker Movement and the person he most credits with inspiring his passion for social justice work.

He and I are seated around the dining table in one of the Ali Forney Center's bright, attractive, transitional-housing apartments. One of several AFC sites in the city, it is located on Madison Avenue's Upper East Side, not the kind of address one might associate with homeless youth. But that's the point. Siciliano's vision is to create homey, loving spaces that send these kids a message about themselves that is different from the one they've gotten from their families, on the streets, and, all too often, from the giant agencies that try to help him.

The fight for these kids, he says, is about "being allowed to be open about who they are and not treated as horrible second-class citizens. When I started working with homeless youth, I was shocked. Their options were sad and degrading."

At the time Ali Forney was murdered in 1997, services for homeless gay youth were limited to places like Covenant House. Described as "the Wal-Mart of homeless youth services" by Kai Wright in *Drifting toward Love: Black, Brown, Gay, and Coming of Age on the Streets of New York*, Covenant House had grown to become the largest privately funded agency for runaway youth.

"That kind of model of service for homeless youth is problematic," Siciliano tells me. "It was especially challenging for gay kids." He points to the huge institutional setting and a staff that was not always adequately trained to be responsive to the particular needs of queer kids. "Gay kids would be seen as the problem, as too flamboyant and therefore provoking everyone else." In the wake of an institutional culture that "froze in their presence," gay runaways often remained on the streets, where they were susceptible to prostitution, HIV infection, and drug addiction.

"When I was a teenager in the late seventies and early eighties, there was no sense that I could come out," Siciliano says. "I saw *Boys in the Band* once and was terrified. In those days, there was this real sense of isolation. Now we have a society where it's more unbearable to be in the closet. Ten times as many people under the age of seventeen are coming out now than ten years ago. Most of these kids are taking a very bold stance by saying who they are while nevertheless remaining in a state of complete dependence upon adult society to protect them. That's where things break down. There is still a repugnance about homosexuality in so many communities. These kids' honesty invites a tremendous amount of brutality upon them."

Siciliano's heritage is Italian and Slavic, which, he says, "explains my mystical nature." His parents were divorced when he was four. He grew up with his father, who "wasn't necessarily the most stable person." They moved often, finally settling in Wilton, Connecticut, where Siciliano spent his high school years.

When he was fifteen, Siciliano had what he calls "a mystical experience" that changed the course of his life. Walking down a road one spring evening, he witnessed a Canadian goose killed by a speeding car. "I had never seen a big creature die. I was overwhelmed." Agitated and overwrought, he started running down the road until he came to the local convent. Siciliano's description of the place hardly suggests the setting for a spiritual transformation: "Gaudy, tacky mosaic in front. Kitschy Italian art." But the subject of the picture, the founder of the convent with all her children in heaven, arrested him. "All of a sudden I'm having this overwhelming sense of love, peace, love throbbing and emanating through everything. I stood there transfixed. It put me in the face of—*pow!*—love."

For the next six months, Siciliano retreated into introspection and reading—Kierkegaard, Sartre, Thoreau's *Walden*—which got him "looking at things as if there was a center beyond any individual." More reading followed—ancient Chinese texts, Vedanta literature. "I was in ecstasy. Sixteen years old. I just threw myself into it."

Eventually, Siciliano discovered two Catholic writers whose lives and ideas profoundly challenged him. Having grown up with no religious affiliation, he had come to think of Christianity as "people singing bad songs on TV." But Thomas Merton's *The Seven Storey Mountain* and Dorothy Day's *The Long Loneliness*—autobiographies that chronicle each writer's conversion to Catholicism—made him rethink everything.

"I struggled with feeling, on the one hand, that Catholicism was crazy and, on the other, that Merton and Day had gone to a place that I would be lucky to go to in terms of my own sanctity." Deciding to "defer to their wisdom and experience," Siciliano began a private practice of prayer and meditation, "very ardently wanting to have mystical union with God." The question before him now was "how to connect this very private experience to a larger community in the real world. How could it be that I was in Wilton with so much

251

wealth and privilege, and ten miles away in South Norwalk it could be so terrible? I was profoundly bothered by that."

The teenager became a kind of hippie St. Francis. "I grew my hair long, I went to thrift stores and bought cast-off clothes. I taught classes in the school library. We would read stuff like the Dao De Jing and Richard Brautigan and talk about what it means." He took a part-time job as a janitor. By senior year, he was cutting classes "all the time" in order to volunteer at a soup kitchen. "Everybody thought I was the coolest person around." As to his sexual identity, Siciliano tells me that by the time he was thirteen he was aware of "what boys I had crushes on" but was "terrified" of being gay. "So I put all of my sexual stuff into this religious thing." I ask him if he feels that his religious ecstasy was a manifestation of sexual repression.

"I think about that a lot. My critique of modernity"—and here he giggles, as if someone like him has no intellectual authority to formulate a critique of modernity—"is that it flattens everything out and doesn't respect the depth of things. I would say that it was definitely repression, *and* I would also say that my ecstasy was definitely true. It was profound, joyful, rapturous. It changed my life. I still feel like the hand of God is upon me."

After high school, Siciliano went to Washington, D.C., where he volunteered for the Catholic Worker Movement, working with the poor and homeless. He joined demonstrations and protests, getting arrested several times, and traveled in Guatemala for a while as a "proto-Witness for Peace." Then, feeling that he was losing his spiritual center, he entered a Benedictine monastery but left after six months because they "weren't poor and pure enough." For two years, he managed a soup kitchen and worked as the overnight supervisor of a shelter in South Norwalk, Connecticut. As satisfying as this work was—the street people in town called him "the Good Shepherd"— Siciliano "felt ambivalent about being a service provider, always in control of the goods. I felt that Jesus was *with* the poor rather than in charge of the poor."

He decided to get his "batteries charged back up" at Bailey House, one of the Catholic Worker residences in New York. It was January 1986. He was twenty years old. The buzz at the Catholic Worker that winter was the gay rights bill being proposed for New York. "The first thing everybody wanted to know when I got there was what my stance was on homosexuality. It was the first time I had encountered so many openly gay people."

Thrown into turmoil and not ready to say he was gay, Siciliano decided to join another monastery, this time a "hardcore" one in the desert of New Mexico. Hitchhiking across the country, he was picked up by a drunk driver outside of Santa Fe. A few miles from the monastery, the car plunged off the road into a river at the bottom of a canyon. Siciliano, who ended up with forty pieces of glass in his head, credits the intervention of his favorite saint, Thérèse of Lisieux, with saving his life.

Out of the hospital and still intent on entering the monastery, Siciliano learned that Cardinal Joseph Ratzinger, later to become Pope Benedict XVI, had just released his "Letter to the Bishops of the Catholic Church on the Pastoral Care of Homosexual Persons," in which he reaffirmed the Church's teaching that the living out of a homosexual orientation is morally unacceptable. "I was so angry. I didn't know how to reconcile this hatefulness with my experience of love. I was totally struggling with my homosexuality."

On Christmas Eve, 1986, as he went to bed in his monastic cell, Siciliano prayed to St. Thérèse, asking to be made "more spiritually grounded." Instead, he awoke with "this utter conviction that I'd have to leave the monastery and go back to New York and come out of the closet and that God would lead me from there. In order to respond in some honest way to the truth of who I was, I had to put this Catholic madness aside." He flashes me a sweet, slightly disingenuous smile. "So St. Thérèse is the patron saint of my sexual liberation." He returned to New York, came out, and took a position with the Neighborhood Coalition for Shelter, helping to run a supportive residence for homeless people.

In 1994, Siciliano became director of Safe Space, a drop-in center. To his dismay, he discovered that the gay kids weren't connecting to the services there. Instead they were contracting HIV, becoming drug addicted, and falling into prostitution. "We were having funerals all the time. I was very angry and frustrated. I felt like such a failure. I was just holding their hands while they were dying."

Without success, Siciliano tried to get HUD money to open a shelter specifically targeted for homeless gay kids. After Ali Forney was killed, he found his voice as a public figure. Grief stricken and angry, he showed up at the next HUD meeting and lambasted the committee: "I'm so sick of coming here every year and saying that there's nothing for these kids and then having to bury them while you guys put the money somewhere else." After that, he says, everyone in the city knew who he was. Suddenly, HUD made homeless youth a priority, and he had money to house eighteen homeless gay kids a night. In the two years between 1999 and 2001, not one of the LGBTQ kids under the care of Safe Space died.

In 2001, Siciliano was fired after he exposed serious financial mismanagement at Safe Space. Less than a year later 90 percent of the programs he had opened were closed. As the programs were being shut down, he realized that for the gay kids there was "nothing but back to Covenant House, where they would start to die again."

He outlines the problem: "First, you had all these gay kids coming out and being rejected by their families. Two, you had a service system that was unable to protect them. Three, there was no awareness in the gay community that this was happening to so many kids. It created a perfect storm of horror for these kids. There was nobody advocating for them or protecting them. They were being revictimized."

With an initial grant of $37,000 and the free use of a church basement, Siciliano started the Ali Forney Center in 2002. "I felt in some core place of myself that it was unacceptable that these kids were being treated so badly. The day that I announced that we were going to open, I had twenty kids on a waiting list for six cots. Shortly after, we had a hundred kids on a waiting list. In those early years, we were turning away more kids than we were serving."

Having developed good relationships with many private funders, Siciliano was able to put together an additional $200,000 in funding during the first six months of the center's existence. With these initial successes he turned his attention toward getting the support of the broader community, but when he approached the agencies that were most likely to make significant financial commitments, he got nowhere. Other gay agendas—he mentions in particular gay marriage—were getting all the attention.

"I said to these people, 'What worse thing is happening in the gay community in America than that thousands of people are being deprived of economic support and thrown into the streets? Is it because they're kids that somehow it doesn't resonate?'" By the second winter, he had "this list of hundreds and hundreds of kids" who needed help. Armed with the list, Siciliano knocked on lots of doors. Eventually, the NGLTF and other organizations responded.

Under Siciliano's guidance, AFC has grown to include several transitional-housing sites, emergency housing, a center in Brooklyn that offers training and vocational skills, and a day center in

Manhattan's Chelsea neighborhood where kids new to AFC's services come to get evaluated and receive medical attention and psychiatric care. Siciliano estimates that forty to fifty new kids show up every day, often in crisis situations.

"There's now this sense of momentum that didn't exist when we started. The gay community had to wake up to this. I was in the right place at the right time. Tonight, there are a lot of kids who have a nice place to sleep, who have a job, who are going to school. I have a kid who is studying dance at NYU as an apprentice member of the Paul Moore Dance Company. Another kid spent the summer in London as part of a student exchange. Another started the first gay/straight alliance at his college. Ten years ago, the kids I was working with were dying."

Siciliano now spends a lot of time speaking to groups in other cities about how best to serve homeless LGBTQ youth. "What I still have from the Catholic Worker is a sense that small is beautiful and that there is a humanness in relationship. If you go to a scope that loses that, you really deteriorate the quality of what you do."

Whenever he represents the Ali Forney Center or works with his staff and the kids, Siciliano says he doesn't talk about God, but he thinks about God all the time. "I'm a mystical dude. I can't help it. I pray. I meditate. I've recently moved to the country with my partner of ten years, and I find being at the base of the Catskills to be rapturously beautiful. It's reconnecting me to that original experience. I spent years obsessing about Catholicism. It gave me something that helped me get somewhere. But I don't want to spend my limited life on this earth worrying so much about that anymore. I just want to love God and do what I can."

Dean Spade

The biggest stereotype is that trans people are defined by surgery," Dean Spade tells me the afternoon we meet. "I would ask that you not have that be the center of what my identity is. I'm tired of journalists thinking that my breast reduction surgery is the defining moment of my life or that it changed my gender. It's just one moment in my story. Unfortunately, that's the dominant narrative in our culture about trans people. I'm not willing to be framed that way. The fact that I have no breasts shouldn't be relevant."

Spade and I are sitting at a table in the Housing Works, a bookstore/café in New York's Soho whose proceeds fund services for people with AIDS and the homeless. The transgender lawyer, who teaches at Seattle University School of Law, is on the East Coast this weekend to attend a conference in Philadelphia. He's picked Housing Works as the locale for our conversation because the organization espouses the kind of politics he's committed to, a politics that "asks hard questions about the root causes of injustice and violence."

Spade, who tells me he identifies as "a fag," says he regrets having published what may be to date his most famous essay, "Mutilating Gender," an account of his battle with the medical establishment to be certified as "transsexual enough" to obtain a mastectomy. "It's the piece everybody loves because it has this personal narrative. And that's the problem: people want trans people to just be personal narratives. The cultural gaze around trans is around sensationalism and surgery and fascination. So the only way trans people get to be subjects is as people who disclose every 'dirty' detail of their lives. It frustrates me."

He would much rather we turn our talk to his work and ideas, ideas that he has articulated in numerous essays and lectures, "trying to influence the conversation around questions about trans rights." In fact, he stresses, his work is not just about trans rights but about locating that struggle within the larger struggle to "interrogate oppression dynamics in the world and in your own shit."

"Resistance" is a word that appears in the title of many of Spade's articles. His work is about directing the movement for social justice back toward a radical-sixties rhetoric that critiques the unexamined privileges inherent in society. Specifically within the LGBTQ community, Spade sees nonprofit gay rights organizations—"which are pleasing and easy to love and state affirming"—as incapable of getting at the root causes of injustice. He has called these mainstream groups "LGBfakeT organizations," ones that, he claims, have merely "added T to their names because that's in vogue."

Moreover, he insists, his work is about critiquing a lot more than that. "These organizations center rich white people as the subject of gay rights. They're not social justice oriented. They don't care about other marginalized people. Theirs is an incredibly narrow agenda that only benefits white gay men." In an essay he contributed to the anthology *Transgender Rights*, Spade wrote, "Sexual and gender liberation will never be meaningful if it is contingent on economic privilege, racial privilege, or genital status."

The first professor to teach a transgender law course at Harvard Law School, Spade speaks with a rapid-fire delivery, knocking out ideas at the pace of flyers from a photocopy machine. He tends to cut off a sentence midway in order to make room for the next one. It's a heady, exhausting, exhilarating hour and a half that we spend together.

Spade's assigned birth gender (he was born in 1977) was female. As Jane Goldschmidt, he spent his childhood and young adulthood in Virginia, where his mother, pretty much a single parent, was on welfare. "We cleaned houses together." It was a household, he tells me, "saturated with shame." The central struggle of his life in those years became hiding his poverty in order to "pass" and succeed.

As a young person, Spade "did not have a gender-nonconforming identity" and in fact rejects the narrative of a gender-troubled childhood. "I didn't have the narrative that everyone, including the medical literature, says trans people are supposed to have. My experience was about the class and race divisions that I saw around me, having a single mom, not being Christian, living in the South. Here I was, coded as a girl in a middle-school world. Who knows if my experience was different from that of other eleven- to fourteen-year-old girls? It's a crappy scene." When he was fourteen, Spade's mother died of cancer, and he was placed with foster families.

In an essay entitled "For Lovers and Fighters," Spade writes that his "first political inquiries came up during my teens." He says that it was a relief to discover that feminists were mounting a critique of romance. "In the world I was living in, you were defined by romantic relationships. Getting a boyfriend was the only thing to want. And sex—but not too much or you'd be labeled as a slut. All those rules for women about sexuality. Always being wrong. Always so much shame. It was so anxiety provoking." Spade hated having to pretend that he had "less capacity" than he did. His reading during this period was an eclectic mix of books, including Susan Faludi's *Backlash: The Undeclared War against American Women*, books on Wicca and earth-based religion, and a copy of *Roe v. Wade*.

Spade skipped a year of high school, attended classes at a community college, did a summer program in Columbus, Mississippi, anything he could come up with to get out of his oppressive high school environment. He chose the University of California at Santa Cruz—"the farthest away"—for college but in 1995 transferred to Barnard, where he majored in women's studies and political science. He wanted "to be in a big city where I didn't have to be with college students all the time." At this point Spade was identifying as "a dyke, and maybe as butch."

During college, he interned at Lambda Legal Defense and the Gay and Lesbian Alliance Against Defamation (GLAAD) but felt "all this dissatisfaction" that such mainstream organizations did not have a vigorous response to welfare reform. "I knew welfare reform was about me, but these places said it wasn't a gay issue."

Around this time, he started working at A Different Light Bookstore. "And the world of queer New York opened up to me. I was working with these amazing characters—trans, drag queens, other people living marginal lives, performers, intellectuals, activists."

Through these friends, Spade learned about Sex Panic! a pro-queer direct action group focused on combating Mayor Rudolph Giuliani's attempts to police immigrants, sex workers, queers, public sex, and "any other stain on the new Disneyfied city he was creating." Spade tells me, "To find a world of activists who were not in a professionalized setting, who were doing in-your-face engagement, was really exciting. I got some real mentorship from them."

He worked for Sex Panic! for about a year until he and some of his friends, "dissatisfied with age and race dynamics" in the organization, moved on and created the Fuck the Mayor Collective. In 1998, the collective mounted Gay Shame, "an event about highlighting what is wrong with the gay pride agenda and what a queer politics should look like." It was an event that went on to be replicated all over the country.

In an article he wrote for the *Harvard Gay & Lesbian Review* (co-authored with Eva Pendleton and still signed under the name of Jane Goldschmidt), Spade said that Sex Panic!'s activism "allows for a broader pro-sex agenda by seeking alliances based not on 'gayness,' but on stigmatized sexual practices." Can he elaborate?

"There is something really radical about the notion that people should be able to seek pleasure without consumerism. Sexual enjoyment is something that people have a public entitlement to. People should be able to be in a park without having to buy something, should be able to engage in public sex that has no impact on anyone else. Respecting pleasure is pretty radical in this culture."

During his time with Sex Panic! Spade fell in love with a gay man, a turn of events that brought up social and ideological challenges.

"In the circles we were in, the kind of queer politics that was being articulated was very gay and lesbian. Bisexuals were considered sellouts. A lot of people had feminist misgivings about trans people. Craig and I felt that our genders were more similar than anyone else we had ever dated, but we didn't have a way of talking about that with other people. It's interesting that our friends' politics were so radical, but there was no room for this. So we kept our relationship a secret. We had a five-year live-in partnership that no one knew about. If we had tried to explain our relationship, people would have said, 'Oh, you're straight.' That would have been such an erasure of our experience. Or 'You're bisexual.' That is not how I felt about myself."

Early on in their relationship Spade and his boyfriend attended an NGLTF conference where they heard trans men talking about their experiences. "A lot of it didn't sound like me. Stuff like, 'Oh, from my childhood, I've always wanted to be a real man.' But there were a couple of people on the panel, including Zack Sinclair, a trans guy from San Francisco, who were talking about gender in a totally different way. It wasn't about having a fixed belief in men and women and wanting to change from one to the other. And I was like, 'Holy Mother of God!' It made sense to me. What I was hearing about trans people was much more interesting, nuanced, and complicated. It made sense to me. That was a really big shift."

Spade began to develop a trans identity. "A lot of my coming to understand my trans identity was through Craig's and my talking a lot about what this gendering felt like to us. It was a wild journey. When I first came out as trans, I didn't have trans friends. I had to work through this with my friend circle."

Spade graduated summa cum laude from Barnard in December 1997. He continued living in New York until the end of the summer, then moved to L.A. with Craig to attend UCLA Law School. "In terms of class, law school was a solid upward mobility dream. I remember distinctly thinking, I need to get a job, a trade. I'm a working-class person. I was being practical."

At UCLA, transgender law was never mentioned in Spade's classes, "not even in the Sexual Orientation and Law class." During the summers, Spade and his boyfriend returned to New York, where he worked at the Drug Policy Alliance and at Housing Works. By the summer of 2000, Spade had changed his name and the gender of his pronoun. Not wanting to have to "undo a previous identity" in Los Angeles, he remained in New York for his final year in law school, finishing up at CUNY and doing an internship at the Urban Justice Center. His first job as a lawyer was as a clerk at the federal district court, "which I quit."

That year, Spade demonstrated against the World Economic Forum, which was meeting in New York. Afterward, as he and his friends were passing through Grand Central Station, he went to use the men's room and was arrested. "Craig and my friends were also arrested because they were trying to tell the cops to let me go. We spent twenty-four hours in jail." Out of that experience, Spade and transgender videomaker Tara Mateik made a documentary film called *Toilet Training*, which focuses on the discrimination and violence that trans people face in gender-defined bathrooms.

In 2002, Spade founded the Sylvia Rivera Law Project (SRLP), a nonprofit law collective that provides free legal services to transgender, intersex, and gender-nonconforming people who are low income and/or people of color. Rivera, a transgender activist who died that year, had helped to found the Gay Liberation Front, the Gay Activists Alliance, and STAR, Street Transvestite Action Revolutionaries. "She was this pain in the ass of the gay rights movement," Spade tells me. "She'd say, 'How dare you leave out people of color and trans people?' That very vigorous advocacy is what we are trying to emulate."

In addition to its direct legal services, SRLP also tackles policy reform and public education. A lot of their work, Spade says, is about "trying to influence the conversation about trans rights." He mentions problems with accessibility in homeless shelters, group homes, prisons, public bathrooms, and the juvenile justice system. In "Fighting to Win," an essay in Matt Bernstein Sycamore's *That's Revolting! Queer Strategies for Resisting Assimilation*, Spade noted that "most poverty lawyers and advocacy organizations are severely lacking in basic information about serving trans clients." What's different about the lawyers at SRLP?

"Our organization is a trans organization. Most of the people who work at SRLP are trans or closely allied. A lot of what we do is to train other lawyers on how to get over their lack of awareness and how to actually do what they're supposed to do."

Spade says that the guiding principle at SRLP is that "social justice trickles up; it doesn't trickle down." To make an impact on trans well-being, one must start with people who are in prison, in immigrant detention, who are homeless. "If you solve *their* problems, that will solve the overall problem. For example, if you solve their problem of sex-segregated facilities, trans college students will be able to go to the bathroom, too. If you solve college students going to the bathroom, that won't necessarily solve the problems of people in prison. It's about centering people who are in the most need."

To these ends, SRLP makes sure that the governance of the organization includes people in the most need. "We're always trying to improve accountability to those people. Thus we have policies about whom you ally with, whom you accept funding from, whom you make meetings accessible to, whom you hire. Even how you decorate your space. Our models were mostly women-of-color feminist organizations. We've developed these tactics to be the opposite of the white gay organizations that run businesses, with some rich lawyer on top who gets paid four times as much as everyone on the bottom, and people of color working at the front desk. We are interested in not having that sort of organizational development."

In 2006, Spade left SRLP to teach as an adjunct professor at UCLA and Harvard. In 2008, he joined the faculty at Seattle University Law School. He tells me that he feels "extremely grateful" to be doing justice work.

"It's a huge privilege and responsibility. I also feel a lot of disappointment sometimes with people who I think will be politically aligned and then aren't. When you see people who you think should get it and don't. That's sad to me, and enraging. People are in a social position sometimes where their privilege insulates them from a certain understanding. They resist hearing the message. Sometimes it's better to focus your energy on organizing people who are vulnerable rather than trying to move people who are privileged. You can work endlessly on somebody who doesn't want to get it when you could have spent your energy developing resources with the people who should be resisting."

Spade doesn't have patience for strategies that promote endless compromise, negotiation, and pacifism. "Some stuff we're going to have to take," he tells me. "They're not going to give it to us. I don't believe in the model of change where we can rely on America to do the right thing. It's going to happen because some people will force it to happen. Having these terrible disparities in our society while at the same time telling people to 'be free' is a joke."

Spade tells me that after our interview he will go to Hofstra University to give a lecture, one of the "tons and tons of speaking engagements at colleges and conferences" that he gives every year. He's pleased to note that he is hardly the only voice speaking up for radical trans justice. "These ideas are coming from everywhere," he says. "They're emerging in all kinds of ways."

George Takei

On the dot of four o'clock, I ring the doorbell of the house in a well-manicured neighborhood of Los Angeles where George Takei—*Star Trek*'s Mr. Sulu—lives with his husband, Brad Altman. I've been parked out front for half an hour, checking my watch every few minutes, anxious to comply with the instructions that Altman has sent me a few weeks before: "Kindly arrive promptly and let us know if you are going to be more than five minutes late."

Altman answers the door, greets me warmly, and leads the way into an invitingly elegant living room, where Takei, in a starched white shirt and handsome silk tie, is waiting. Having overheard his partner commenting on my punctuality, he smiles with amusement.

"Brad gets me to parties on time," he informs me in the deep, resonant voice that is his trademark. "He starts egging me on about two hours before we're supposed to be there. We always arrive so early that we have to spend half an hour sitting in the car."

For the three years of the television series and then through the first five enormously popular *Star Trek* movies, Takei, as the helmsman for the Starfleet's intergalactic craft, got his multiethnic crewmates through the vastness of outer space on time. In an era when there were few positive images of Asians on TV or in film, Mr. Sulu was an intelligent, brave, likeable, and humane character—"the antithesis," coproducer Robert Justman once said, "of the so-called expressionless-unemotional-inscrutable Asian."

Rumors that Takei was gay circulated for years among his fans, but it wasn't until 2005 that the actor publicly came out. Three years later, he made even bigger headlines when he and Altman became the first same-sex couple in West Hollywood to apply for a marriage license.

"It was heady!" Takei tells me as we settle around a large coffee table laden with his collection of crystal objets d'art. "The city hall was not able to accommodate the huge crowds, so they held it in a park. There were hordes. We spoke, and then we were ushered to the front of the line. I felt like one of those people who barge their way to the head of the check-out line."

Throughout our two hours together, Takei is witty, gracious, and surprisingly eager to talk about his love of democracy. "The ideals of democracy," he tells me, "are glorious, but it's only as good as the people who actively engage in the process of making this participatory democracy realer than it has been." He should know. Ever since his father "volunteered" him at age nineteen for Adlai Stevenson's 1956 bid for the presidency, Takei has exercised his cherished right to engage in political activism.

Nor has he slowed down as a professional actor. Since the final *Star Trek* movie was released in 1991, Takei has appeared—or been the voice-over—in numerous TV episodes and movies. He is a recurring character on NBC's *Heroes*, has been a narrator for many symphony orchestras, and is a regular guest on *The Howard Stern Show*. In 2006, he and queer comedian Margaret Cho cohosted "Crossing East," a radio documentary about Asian American immigration. That year, he also went on a nationwide speaking tour with the Human Rights Campaign (HRC) to talk about his life as a gay Japanese American.

"Change doesn't happen with pessimists," he tells me. "Change happens with people who can see beyond the travails of our time. No matter how daunting it seems, you've got to be confident that we will prevail because, well, we are on the side of right. Equality is right for all humankind."

Takei's family on both sides traced its lineage back to samurai warriors. "We have one of the great samurais in our family tree, Takeda Shingen." As the oldest child in a well-off Japanese American family, Takei remembers generally happy times growing up in L.A., playing with his best friend, a blue-eyed boy named Donald, who was "completely Caucasian." Happy, that is, until one day when Donald didn't show up anymore. The Japanese attack on Pearl Harbor changed everything for Takei and thousands of other Japanese Americans. In 1942, he and his family were rounded up and deported to an internment camp in Rohwer, Arkansas. "I remember how scary that day was. Two American soldiers with bayoneted rifles came stomping up to our front door and ordered our family out. My mother was crying. That was the first prejudice that I remember."

After eight months, the family was reassigned to another internment camp, at Tule Lake, California, a maximum-security camp for "disloyals" who, like Takei's parents, had refused to answer yes to a humiliating Loyalty Questionnaire. It was while he was interned at Tule Lake that Takei first discovered what in his 1994 autobiography *To the Stars* he called "the mind-expanding, world-extending, emotion-exhausting joy of the movies." He tells me, "The story, the setting, the romance, the terror—the escape! Camp was pretty boring. To see all that excitement on the screen." The family was finally released in March 1946. Takei was almost nine and now deeply ashamed that he was Japanese American. "I didn't even tell my parents. I just swallowed it."

Takei attended Los Angeles High School, where he began to learn about American ideals, ones that ran counter to what he and his family had experienced in the camps. "Despite everything, it's still a nation of ideals," his father told him. It was a message that kindled Takei's lifelong devotion to democracy. He joined the drama and glee clubs. After school, he would usher at the Biltmore Theater. "I endeared myself to the house manager, who let me see the plays for free." Takei was also an avid long-distance runner, an athletic interest that he has maintained. (Years later, in 1984, he jogged with the Olympic Flame in the Los Angeles Olympic Torch Relay.)

One day during his high school years, Takei met a man who acknowledged to him the tragedy and the injustice of the internment camps. Takei broke down crying, relieved to find "people who know about us." But as one stressful chapter in his life was winding down, another was just beginning.

"When I started coming out, if you will, as a Japanese American, that's when I was closeting another aspect of myself. I was hanging out with boys, acting like I was just a buddy. I knew I wanted to do a bit more. But that's not how the guys acted. I knew what I felt, and I didn't think the other guys felt the same way. I didn't tell my parents either. I knew that this was something they would not approve of. Because I had once learned to suppress my 'Japaneseness,' suppressing this other thing was a seamless transition."

In the spring of 1956, Takei entered the University of California at Berkeley as an architecture student, though his yearnings to be an actor were very much alive. After his freshman year, he took a summer acting class at UCLA, which led to his first paying job in film, dubbing Japanese sci-fi movies. Another of the dubbers was Keye Luke, the Chinese American actor who had played Charlie Chan's "Number One Son" during the thirties.

"He was an idol: a working Asian American actor making a career of it. And he was nice to me. He was masterful. You grow up thinking that they, white people, are better than us. That's why we're not the movie stars, the writers, the big businessmen. But I saw that Keye was just as good. He was holding his own."

After three terms at Berkeley, Takei transferred to UCLA to study acting, the only Asian student in the Theater Arts Department. While still in college, he made his motion picture debut with Richard Burton in *Ice Palace*. In another early film, *A Majority of One*, he played the son to Alec Guinness's "sinister, almost reptilian" Mr. Asano, a Japanese businessman.

Takei recalls that the roles available to Japanese American actors in films of that era were confined to "villains, or the buffoons, or the silent servants. My father said, 'Is this what you want to be doing for your life's work?' I said, 'Daddy, I will change it. I will go out there and educate these directors and writers. I can do it.' And I did do it. Sulu was not a villain, a buffoon, or a servant. You know, the stereotype of Asians is that we are bad drivers. Well, I was the best driver in the Galaxy!"

Takei graduated from UCLA in 1960 with a B.A. in theater arts. He spent part of that summer at the Shakespeare Institute at Stratford-upon-Avon and then toured Europe. When he returned to the States, he decided to continue at UCLA as a graduate student. He got a part in a new musical, *Fly Blackbird!*, about a group of idealistic college students during the civil rights movement. When it turned out to be a huge local success, the creators sold the rights to a New York producer, and Takei moved to Manhattan to "chase the blackbird," as he put it in the autobiography. He didn't get a part but remained in New York, moving from one temporary job to the next.

After almost a year on the East Coast, he moved back to Los Angeles, continuing his studies at UCLA and picking up some television and film work, including a couple of come-on parts in Jerry Lewis comedies, where he played "cartoon 'Oriental' characters." Takei was now twenty-five. His autobiography is silent about his romantic and sex life. What was going on during those years? I ask.

"I was living a double life. Here I am, a young actor who wants to build a career in a very public arena where image is vital. First of all, before you even get to the point of building an image, you have to get cast. You'd go to so many auditions, casting calls, lineups. And you'd be eliminated because you're either too tall, too short, too fat, too skinny, too old, too young. I didn't want to give them another 'too this.' You keep that part of your life very hidden." Takei went out with women—"genuine friends, people I enjoyed being with"—whom he would escort in order to maintain that image. "Emotional toll? Well, it's what you resign yourself to. On the side, you go to the baths, you meet people in clandestine parks."

Through the midsixties, Takei continued to get bit parts, some credited, some not, in films and television episodes. Then in 1965, he got a call from his agent, who had set up an interview for him at Desilu Studios. They were looking for actors to cast in a new space series on television, "something about the future." *Star Trek* premiered on September 8, 1966. In the autobiography, Takei notes that diversity—"infinite diversity in infinite combinations"—was the watchword of the show's creator, Gene Roddenberry.

"He used to remind us regularly that Starship *Enterprise* was a metaphor for Starship *Earth* and that the ship's strength lay in its diversity—that was the important thing—and working in concert. This was the sixties, when the civil rights movement was going full strength, when racial tension was exploding, when the Soviet Union and the United States were threatening each other with mutual annihilation." Takei points out that among the "trusted crew members" was Chekhov, who "spoke with a Russian accent and was proud of his Russian heritage—very consciously a part of Gene Roddenberry's vision."

"Gene said that TV is a powerful medium and that it was being wasted on a plethora of pap entertainment. He was a real pioneer in using science fiction as a metaphor for the various issues of the time. His confidence in our problem-solving capacity, our entrepreneurial spirit, the power of diversity was valid. And today, forty years later,

George Takei

267

look, we have an African American president. We have a space craft in space and—most astounding—Russians and Americans working side by side, when, in fact, that was the most preposterous political fiction on *Star Trek*."

In the climate of the sixties, Roddenberry's embrace of diversity could only go so far. Takei remembers a conversation he had with Roddenberry at a party once. "We were in a corner of the swimming pool. Without coming out, speaking hypothetically, I talked with him privately about the gay issue. Gene said, 'Yes, you're absolutely right. That is a part of society. But I have to recognize the fact that I'm working in TV, an enormously conservative medium. I'm getting in trouble enough by dealing with the Vietnam War or the civil rights movement. I had an interracial kiss that was blacked out in some Southern states. My concern is keeping the show on the air so that I can make the statements that I can make. I would jeopardize that by dealing with the gay issue.' I understood what he was talking about."

During these years, Takei notes, the stereotyped depiction of gay people in films was analogous to the earlier stereotyped images of Asians in the media—"inscrutable, vicious, untrustworthy, cunning, calculating." He recalls the books and plays of the time "where gay characters, when exposed, cannot face society and commit suicide."

Takei is delighted by the "enormous, unimagined advances" made in the frequency and portrayal of gay people in recent years "because of the strong advocacy that has been done by LGBT organizations, politically and in the media. The advance we have not made is to have a gay actor play a straight romantic lead. In the old days you could do it if, like Rock Hudson or Tab Hunter, you weren't publicly gay."

When, after three seasons—"dreamy halcyon times," he calls them—*Star Trek* was cancelled, Takei put more of his energies into political activism. In 1969, he worked on Tom Bradley's unsuccessful bid to become mayor of L.A. and the next year undertook the chairmanship of Asian Americans for George Brown, who was running for a U.S. Senate seat from California. He was an elected delegate to the Democratic National Convention, pledged to George McGovern for president, and in 1973 ran for the Los Angeles City Council, losing by a small percentage. When Bradley made another run for mayor, Takei again worked for his campaign, this time helping to deliver a victory for the first black mayor of a major American city.

For eleven years, from 1973 to 1984, Takei served on the board of directors of the Southern California Rapid Transit District, working strenuously on behalf of transit improvement for the city of Los Angeles. He recalls that his duties included attending transportation conferences in many parts of the country where, at various gay bars and bathhouses, he thought he might enjoy relative anonymity. It was not always the case. Mr. Sulu's face was too well known. "There was a buzz about me. Apparently, it had even reached the *Star Trek* fans." A positive buzz? A negative buzz? "Just a buzz." Nevertheless, blackmail was a concern. "I did worry about it. It was always there. I got pretty bold later on. I would bring guys home. You live with that kind of tension. You accept those kinds of risks. With AIDS, that ended."

In his autobiography, Takei notes that in both the television series and the subsequent *Star Trek* feature films made by Paramount Mr. Sulu was "still at the helm console, doing the same damn thing." I ask him why he continued to play the role.

"When you have an ensemble cast of seven people, and two strong stars elbowing each other for their place in the spotlight—and they *are* stars, so they have the powers that go with that status—it's very difficult for the second bananas, if you will, to get that opportunity. I tried to use the *Star Trek* ideal on the writers, directors, and producers. When I went into meetings, I reminded them that *Star Trek* is supposed to be a meritocracy. I said the promotions had to be met with more leadership roles. I kept lobbying for that." With *Star Trek VI: The Undiscovered Country* (1991), Takei's efforts to get Sulu promoted finally paid off. He became Captain Sulu. "I thought that would be the launching pad to a Captain Sulu series. Didn't happen. It could have happened if the powers that be at Paramount and NBC were more adventuresome."

By the time *Star Trek VI* came out, Takei had known his future husband for eight years. They met at a Frontrunners run around Silver Lake reservoir. "He was gorgeous. Thin as a rail, muscled—a runner's muscles—the best runner in the L.A. Frontrunners. I knew that joining the Frontrunners was another step in coming out. In fact, the first run I did with them, some of the runners recognized me. I heard whispers—'Sulu, Sulu!'—that sibilant sound. But they were cool. When I saw Brad, I ran alongside of him." Altman and Takei pursued a long courtship that culminated in their moving in together in 1987.

Seven years later, when he published his *To the Stars*, Takei was still "very mute" about the gay aspect of his life. "What really got me to come out publicly was Arnold Schwarzenegger's veto of the same-sex marriage bill. That really stuck in my craw." A month later, in October 2005, *Frontiers*, a gay magazine out of L.A., published an interview with Takei. It was his official, public coming out. "It's not really coming out," he told interviewer Alex Cho, "which suggests opening a door and stepping through. It's more like a long, long walk through what began as a narrow corridor that starts to widen."

Takei and Altman were married in a Buddhist ceremony at the Democracy Forum of the Japanese American National Museum on September 14, 2008. "I find my peace and inspiration in Buddhism. Because our adversaries tend to be faith-based people who use their religious beliefs against us, we wanted to have a religious ceremony to make the point that California is a diverse state, not just ethnically and culturally but religiously as well. No one faith group—whether it be Christians, Jews, Hindus, Muslims, or Buddhists—should have the right to write their beliefs into civil law. Those Mormons who supported Prop 8 to the tune of seventeen million dollars, how would they feel if we wrote Buddhist beliefs into civil law and made them live by it and abide by it?"

In 2009, Takei and Altman appeared in a short documentary, directed by Academy Award–nominated filmmaker Jessica Sanders, entitled *George & Brad in Bed*. "She was looking for a hook, and Brad came up with the idea of filming us in bed, doing our usual morning ritual, tea and the newspaper."

As our conversation comes to a close, Altman appears with a tea tray—green tea, Takei's favorite. "I've got a little story to tell you about the Oscars this year," Takei tells me as we relax with our refreshments.

"Every year, when we would attend, Brad always used to enter through the 'noncelebrity' entrance. He's kind of shy about public appearances. Well, we got married last year, so this year I grabbed his hand and said, 'Come on, we're legal now,' and pulled him with me onto the red carpet. People in the grandstands were shouting, 'Brad! Brad!' He started blowing kisses to everybody. He was in seventh heaven. And then we looked around, and there were Angelina and Brad!"

Rachel Tiven

No raw fish for me," a very pregnant Rachel Tiven says as we survey our menus. We are in a sushi restaurant near Exchange Place, the street address of Immigration Equality, where Tiven is executive director. She and her partner of ten years, Sally Gottesman, are expecting their second child in less than two months. After we both order soba noodles and vegetables, Tiven lays out the cold, hard reality that her clients face.

According to the 2000 census, an estimated forty thousand same-sex binational couples are living in the United States. Their relationships, whether legalized by marriage or not, do not qualify the non-citizen for immigration benefits. These couples face antigay laws that effectively say, You may not be a couple at all.

"The only way for such couples to stay together in the United States," Tiven says, "is almost exclusively through employer sponsorship. People call our office crying. They say, 'Men in black came to our house at five a.m. and took my boyfriend away. What do I do?' These are things that would not happen if they were a straight couple."

Tiven lays down her chopsticks. "There are lots of privations that gay couples suffer. But many of them have workarounds, however unfair or expensive or cumbersome they may be. My partner and I just completed a second-parent adoption for our daughter. Should we have had to spend a year's worth of paperwork and four thousand dollars so that I could adopt my own kid? No! But it was available to us. For a binational same-sex couple that is facing permanent physical separation, there may be no country in the world where they can live together."

And that's what Immigration Equality does: find legal solutions—in some cases, precedent-setting judgments—for the most hopeless of situations.

Tiven, who was born in Atlanta, says what is most significant about her early years was that she grew up in a family of very committed Jews. "We were not Orthodox, but we were very connected to a liberal Jewish community in every place we lived. The idea that you have an obligation that grows out of your communal identity was very clear." She says that message—"the obligation to participate in the communal welfare of your identity group"—became a lens through which she looked at the rest of the world.

Tiven entered Harvard in 1992, thinking she would do a lot of journalism, but aside from a few reviews she published in the *Crimson*, Harvard's student daily, and some pieces for the student gay and lesbian magazine *HQ*, she was far more involved in the lively student theater scene in Cambridge. She also helped to start Harvard Hillel's queer Jewish group, BAGELS.

Tiven is almost gleeful as she recalls working on a "terrific protest" against Harvey Mansfield, a professor of government at Harvard who, in October 1993, testified as a paid expert witness on a constitutional amendment in Colorado that sought to prohibit cities in that state from enacting gay rights laws. The gay and lesbian students on campus, appalled by Mansfield's remarks about gay sex being "shameful" and homosexuals contributing to the downfall of civilization, met to consider their response.

"We printed posters on neon-pink paper. They said, 'Harvey Mansfield thinks'—and then there was the name of a famous LGBT person, like James Baldwin or Eleanor Roosevelt—'undermines civilization.' We must have had thirty names. We delivered a full set of the posters to his office. I remember some sweet, nerdy-looking kid came up to me and said how much it meant to him that we had included Alan Turing. Quite a few years later, *Boston Magazine* did a profile of Mansfield, and the whole lead was the story of our protest."

After her sophomore year, Tiven took a year off in order to be a full-time theater techie. When that work didn't satisfy her, she interned at Bloomberg News. Evenings and weekends, she continued to do theater work in Manhattan. During the summer of 1995, on assignment in Israel, she took a dog with her. She now quips that it's easier for an American to bring a dog in and out of a country than it is to bring one's same-sex partner.

Back at Harvard, Tiven volunteered for the Boston chapter of NOW. "I got very interested in legal remedies for discrimination. Working with NOW, I figured out that the law might be good for something." By the time she graduated in 1997, with a degree in comparative religion, Tiven knew she wanted to be a lawyer. She went to India for six months "to figure out if I was interested in international human rights law." She was aware that every human rights cause that she had so far become involved in was connected to her identity as a lesbian or a Jew. But was she interested in human rights for its own sake? She concluded that she was not. Her future in the law would be tied to gay and lesbian causes. She came back to the States and worked for a year at Lambda Legal Defense Fund.

Tiven attended Columbia Law School. There she met a woman who had been the first staff person for Immigration Equality, then known as the Lesbian and Gay Immigration Rights Task Force (LGIRTF), a friendship that eventually inspired Tiven to become a board member of that organization. After she graduated, she joined the immigration law unit of the Legal Aid Society of New York. The next year, in addition to clerking for a federal judge, Tiven chaired the committee searching for LGIRTF's first executive director. When after seven months no viable candidate emerged, she was encouraged to consider the position herself. "I had to endure many Dick Cheney jokes: hiring myself." She began as executive director in the fall of 2005.

According to Tiven, between fifteen hundred and two thousand people a year contact Immigration Equality for help in one of three areas of the organization's expertise: same-sex relationships among binational couples, persecution in a client's home country, or HIV status as it relates to immigration. Most of the inquiries (over a third, she estimates) come from couples trying to figure out how they can stay together, "whereas if they were straight, the American would have no trouble sponsoring the person he or she loves for immigration benefits." Asylum seekers account for an additional 25 percent.

"We won a terrific case for a lesbian from Uganda. In high school she had a girlfriend, but a cousin ratted her out, and the family brought a man into the house to rape her in front of the rest of the family. Then they disowned her in case she missed the point. She left Uganda and ended up in Minneapolis. She had been represented by a private attorney who didn't frame the case very well. The kind of violence lesbians suffer is often a private family matter. You have to argue that in an asylum claim. She had lost her case and called us with her appeal due in two weeks.

"We were so compelled by the story that we took the case the next day. We got pro bono counsel from Holland and Knight, a firm that we've worked with for many years. They won a terrific decision: a published decision from the Eighth Circuit Court, not a liberal court, that affirmed the line of argument that we had been pushing about lesbian asylum cases and the validity of family violence, which the government cannot or will not protect people from." The Ugandan woman went on to be granted asylum.

Tiven is quick to point out that while Immigration Equality manages to effect some important "impact litigation"—building a field of LGBTQ asylum law so that it will be a stable source of law for LGBTQ asylum seekers in the future—it also serves individual clients every day. "We take lots of gay men from, say, Jamaica whose cases are not going to be procedurally or factually that different from the case of the gay Jamaican we argued the week before. But for that person it's still lifesaving."

A small but significant percentage of IE's cases involve transgender issues. Immigration questions for transgender couples are not entirely the same as for gay and lesbian couples, Tiven points out. In coordination with the Transgender Law Center in San Francisco, Immigration Equality is in the process of writing the first ever transgender immigration manual to be published by American Immigration Lawyers Association, the first LGBTQ publication that association has ever put out.

Tiven notes that while Immigration Equality has had "fabulous" success with asylum seekers, the binational cases are "very, very tough. If you call us and say, 'I am from Zimbabwe. I cannot go back because it is not safe for me to live as a gay person in Zimbabwe, and I'm madly in love with my American partner, and I cannot bear to be separated from him,' we can help you! We have thirty national firms doing six million dollars of pro bono legal work a year. And you'll probably win."

274

Sadly, the same is not the case for gay people from most of the countries of the First World—France or the Netherlands, for example. In those cases, Tiven soberly tells me, IE has "almost nothing to offer you."

"What we can do is to tell you to get involved in the campaign to pass the Uniting American Families Act. You can talk to your member of Congress, talk to your senators, you can write letters to the local paper, join our spokescouples bureau, and be featured in your local press to try to put pressure on your local legislators. You can throw a house party to encourage your friends to give money."

Tiven says that IE helps people in those situations evaluate what their options are. "We make sure that you won't be taken for a ride by an unscrupulous immigration lawyer. Your marriage in Massachusetts or Canada is not going to qualify you for immigration benefits, which are federal. And don't let anybody tell you different. We help you figure out if there is an employment visa or student visa that you might want to pursue, and then we refer you to gay or gay-friendly counsel in your area."

In 1996, Congress passed the Defense of Marriage Act. The law gives states the right not to recognize a same-sex marriage, even if that relationship is considered a marriage in another state, and further allows the federal government not to treat same-sex relationships as marriages for any purpose, even if concluded or recognized by one of the states. In effect, then, gay people are the only people whose marriages are categorically not recognized by the Immigration and Naturalization Service.

Four years after DOMA, Rep. Jerrold Nadler (D-NY) introduced the Uniting American Families Act into Congress, a bill that would permit gay Americans in a committed relationship with a foreign national to bring their permanent partners into the United States. Since 2000, the bill has been introduced into every session of Congress. Technically, Tiven explains, the bill is not a challenge to DOMA. Rather, in the same way that a new visa category might be established, the bill creates another immigration category.

"It doesn't say that couples who get civil unions or couples who get married will receive permanent partner status. It says that permanent partners, which are defined in a very specific way, meet the INS requirements."

Sounds reasonable. So why hasn't the bill passed?

"We are in the middle of a vicious upswing in xenophobia. If you look at American history, you see anti-immigrant fervor at every point. Everybody we meet who says they are not ready to support the Uniting American Families Act attributes it to skittishness about immigration on the part of their constituents, not reluctance to support gay couples."

Tiven says that so far the bill's greatest success has been to raise visibility. "The bill is something that the LGBT mainstream is now aware of. When Nadler introduced the bill, HRC hadn't even heard of the issue. We were renegades. Now we are more visible in the gay rights universe." She is sanguine about the ultimate success of the bill. "The opportunity to amend the law in Congress will come about sooner than the judiciary, especially the conservative judiciary we have today. In the long term, there is no question that you have to recognize these marriages. Because the only alternative is to say we are dismantling the American system of domestic relations law. If they are really prepared to go that far because their hatred of gay people is that deep . . ." She laughs in disbelief.

Tiven says her proudest accomplishment with Immigration Equality is the growth of the organization itself. "Now we're nine full-time staff. In less than three years we've doubled the staff, doubled the budget."

As we wrap up, she reminds me that until 1990 gay people were not even allowed to enter the United States. "There was a commitment to excluding 'sexual deviants' and 'psychopathic personalities.' Since that law was repealed—and Barney Frank had a lot to do with it—you can now enter the country as an individual gay person. But you still can't act gay! You can't bring anyone with you, and you can't fall in love with anyone while you're here."

The incredulity in her voice suggests that she's confident lawmakers will eventually come to see the ridiculousness of this Catch-22. With Tiven at the helm of Immigration Equality, that day may come sooner than anyone would have imagined even a few years ago.

Urvashi Vaid

In 1996, having finished her book *Virtual Equality: The Mainstreaming of Gay and Lesbian Liberation*, Urvashi Vaid was thinking about starting a progressive think tank, which, only somewhat facetiously, she wanted to call CPR. "Because the Left needs it," she tells me the afternoon we talk. "Center for Progressive Renewal."

When the National Gay and Lesbian Task Force, headquartered in Washington, D.C., called her up to say that they had started their own think tank and would she consider heading it up, Vaid was intrigued, but, she told them, only if she could work out of New York, where she had recently moved with her partner, lesbian comedian Kate Clinton. NGLTF gave her the OK.

"I got a room that I rented from Bella Abzug and her group, the Women's Environment and Development Organization." Vaid chuckles as she recalls the story. "I went to Bella. She was wearing the big hat. She said, 'Awright, You'washee. What can I do for you, You'washee?'" Vaid's imitation of Abzug's gutsy New York Jewish accent is pitch perfect. "'Ya need an office? So, what can you pay?' I told her, nothing. I got a great space on Lexington Avenue."

It's a quintessential Urvashi Vaid story: the brainy idea, the chutzpah, the networking with influential people, the success at juggling multiple commitments, the humor, the pluralism.

Vaid is currently the director of the Arcus Foundation, a grant-giving organization whose mission is to achieve social justice that is "inclusive of sexual orientation, gender identity and race, and to ensure conservation and respect of the great apes." The foundation gives out more money than any other similar organization for the advancement of LGBTQ rights. Arcus's New York branch is on West Twenty-fourth Street in space owned by the Gay Men's Health Crisis. As she ushers me into her ninth-floor office, I comment on the activity that I witnessed as I entered the building.

"Man, it is such a busy place," she agrees. "The epidemic is far from over. That's what you remember every day—all the communities that are still affected. All the people we've lost." She points to a photograph on her wall. "This guy, for example—Daniel Sotomayor, an amazing guy, an activist from ACT UP Chicago. I think about all the guys I worked with in those actions in the eighties. Mark Kostopoulos, Michael Callen—beautiful, progressive, fearless men. The list just goes on and on."

Over the course of our two-hour conversation, Vaid will rattle off the names of dozens of LGBTQ, and straight, activists—big players and lesser knowns, politicos and writers, entertainers and scholars, radicals, leftists and moderates, men and women. She seems to have met everyone, worked with everyone, *remembered* everyone. In the more than twenty-five years that she has been involved in progressive causes, Vaid has been a tireless advocate for the "politics of intersection." Through her work, she has consistently sought to create a more just society by forging connections among various struggles. "I want a movement," she once told a lesbian summit at the National Organization for Women, "that is not just focused on identity but that is engaged in defining what kind of society we will have in the next century."

While her brand of activism has not met with universal favor in the gay and lesbian community (Bruce Bawer once called her an "ideological extremist"), nevertheless, now in her early fifties, Vaid is recognized as one of the most important movers and shakers in the LGBTQ and progressive movements. Over the years, the number of awards she has received amounts to a catalog of notable honors. In April 2009, *Out* magazine numbered Vaid among its fifty most influential men and women in America.

"I am a pluralist to the core," she tells me, "a radical pluralist. That's what I think the difference is between an equal rights movement and a true liberation movement. The liberation movement wants to achieve human rights and social justice for all people. It wants to fundamentally reconfigure the reallocation of the pie. It wants to rebuild the table."

Vaid was born in India and moved to the United States in 1966, when she was eight. "I bring to everything I do an immigrant consciousness, a double consciousness." As a teenager, Vaid "tried actively to assimilate. I didn't want to stand out with my thick Indian accent and my thick black hair and the big Coke bottle glasses that I had as a geeky Indian kid."

She says that though she is not an observant religious person, her Indian heritage "infuses everything I do. That connects to my love of social movements. I have always seen the work I've done as part of something that is way bigger than me, that preceded me, that will follow me. Not that I am insignificant—that's not what Hinduism teaches us, nor what I believe about each individual's responsibility—but there is a sense of being that is greater than the moment that I really appreciate about the philosophy with which I was raised."

At a young age, Vaid became politically interested. "I was raised to be questioning, to interrogate things. We were surrounded by books. I used to poke around my father's library. I read all of Thomas Hardy by the time I was twelve." She chuckles. "My brooding Hardy phase. Reading the newspaper was something you did every day. We watched the news together every night. When I was ten years old, what was on the news was the antiwar movement, Bobby Kennedy, Stokely Carmichael, the civil rights struggles. Those are the images I saw as a kid. They were very motivating for me."

At Vassar, Vaid double majored in English and political science. Passionate about the Romantic poets (her thesis was on Blake), she says what was most significant about college was her discovery of social movements, especially the women's movement, reproductive rights, and the antiapartheid movement, which prompted her to do "a lot of organizing." She got involved in challenging the college to divest its holdings in companies doing business with South Africa and worked with neighborhood groups in Poughkeepsie on community and poverty issues. Her primary activism took place on campus, where she helped to produce conferences, cultural events, and workshops, "great training," she says, that exposed to her to "great people." It was also at Vassar that Vaid became immersed in women's music and the women's "political culture" movement.

279

"From college on, that was woven into the lesbian feminist work I did."

After she graduated—and aware that she was a lesbian—Vaid went off to Boston to join the women's movement. Already at age twenty-one, she was operating in a large number of arenas—Lesbians United in Non-Nuclear Action, the Boston Food Co-op Feminist Caucus, the Lesbian Mobilization Force. She also volunteered at Boston's gay and lesbian newspaper, *Gay Community News*, which, in *Virtual Equality*, Vaid called "the most important political group in my life."

"I loved *GCN*," she tells me. "The people who were putting their intellectual and emotional energies into *GCN* were amazing people. Everybody came through there. We were all approaching our queerness from a progressive, social justice vantage point. We influenced each other, and we saved each other."

Vaid says the community newspapers as well as the independent feminist rags "were so influential to people like me. They were putting out ideas that I couldn't access in any other way. They made you think about issues you had never thought of before. It's indescribable how fresh and exciting it was in the early eighties to read that stuff."

In 1980, she entered Northeastern University School of Law. "I wanted to learn how the system worked in order to be a more effective community organizer. I didn't think I could get a job in social change, so I thought I would get a job in public interest law and do the gay and lesbian work on the side."

Inspired by what was happening in cities like San Francisco, Washington, and Los Angeles, where lobbying groups like David Mixner's MECLA (Municipal Elections Committee of Los Angeles) were successful in getting LGBTQ-friendly candidates elected to public office, Vaid and other "scruffy street radicals" decided to form a similar organization in Boston. The result was the Greater Boston Lesbian/Gay Political Alliance. Through such connections, she met John Ward, one of the first gay rights lawyers in the country. "John was the expert on representing people arrested by the cops at rest stops. He realized there was a larger civil rights issue, persecution." Out of those concerns, Ward founded GLAD, the Gay and Lesbian Advocates and Defenders. Vaid signed on for that, too.

"It's a miracle I made it through law school. That was my *part-time* job. *GCN*, GLAD, Boston Pride. I had a blast. I worked on the Green Light Safehouse Network, which was committed to stopping violence against women. We organized lesbian and gay buses to the El Salvador demo. We picketed the movie *Windows*; we picketed *Cruising*. We had an initiative to start the Lesbian and Gay Media Alliance."

After law school, Vaid moved to Washington, D.C., where she worked as a staff attorney for the National Prisons Project of the ACLU. Because HIV was spreading, Vaid recognized that the disease might create particular problems in penal communities. She conducted a survey to gather information about HIV in prisons, the results of which were published in the *Journal of the National Prison Project*, one of the first data sets of such information. She also wrote the chapter on prisons for Harlon L. Dalton's groundbreaking book *AIDS and the Law.*

In 1986, eager to do more gay rights work, Vaid went to work for the National Gay and Lesbian Task Force as its media director. Emphasizing that NGLTF was and is all about "grassroots empowerment," she tells me about several projects and direct actions that she worked on: media strategies against mandatory HIV testing, the passage of the Hate Crimes Statistics Act, the 1987 March on Washington, direct action at the Supreme Court to protest the Hardwick decision and a subsequent project to repeal the country's sodomy laws, the 1988 shutdown of the FDA. In 1989, she became the executive director of NGLTF.

Vaid helped organize the 1993 March on Washington; took an active role in insuring the gay and lesbian community's presence at the 1988, 1992, and 1996 political conventions; and generally increased coverage of the gay and lesbian rights movement. She also cofounded the Creating Change Conference, to this day the only national LGBTQ political convention.

Vaid left NGLTF in 1993 and moved to Provincetown, where she spent three years writing *Virtual Equality*. In the book's opening chapter, she debunked the myth that homosexuality had already been mainstreamed, citing numerous examples. How about now, over a decade later? Would she still adhere to the idea that the liberties that queer people have achieved are, as she said then, "incomplete, conditional, and ultimately revocable"?

"I still think that the underlying resistance to LGBT acceptance has not been fully dislodged. We're still seeing this moral opposition based on the notion that we're sinful and immoral. And based on the mainstream's resistance to seeing gender as a spectrum. Those two realities are what keeps LGBT people down. What's changed since 1996 is that our legal rights have advanced, our visibility has advanced, our communities have gotten bigger. But it still feels very marginal in a lot of places. There is a distinction between real, full acceptance as a healthy, natural, normal, moral human being and this kind of provisional 'Yeah, you can have your civil rights, but you're not fully human.' The marriage issue with all of its flaws exposes that in a deep way.

"When we say our symbol is the equal sign, there is a part of me that thinks, No, the 'greater than' sign should be our symbol. Not that we are better than anybody else, but we should aspire to greater than what we find at the current table. Entering the table doesn't mean that we are in a world that is rooted in equality. It just means we've been let into the room because we've demanded and pushed our way into the room and gotten a seat at the table. But the table itself is constructed on unequal conditions."

So what are some ways to enroll ordinary, concerned, decent LGBTQ and straight people into this more pluralist movement for shared progressive politics?

"The development of gay/straight alliances is a brilliant model for school-based activism. I can't tell you how many young people I've met—how many *straight* kids—who have cut their teeth on gay/straight alliances, who have completely learned from that experience about injustice. It's an incredible model. You don't need a lot of formality or bureaucracy. It's people organizing themselves for local needs, around local issues, with local control.

"A friend of mine in Chicago told me about his seventeen-year-old daughter who led a campaign against a school policy about dress codes at graduation because she said it adversely affected trans people. That is so amazing, that she is even thinking about stuff like that. That's how we engage people. You make it possible for them to see the expression of an issue locally."

After her stint (1997–2001) with NGLTF's think tank, the Policy Institute (out of which in 2000 she coedited a book of essays about the movement, *Creating Change: Public Policy, Civil Rights, and Sexuality*), Vaid went to work for the Ford Foundation as deputy director for the Governance and Civil Society Unit. In 2005, she joined the Arcus Foundation.

As a person of color and a lesbian, Vaid once wrote, "My skin and gender seemed barriers." Have things changed? Does she still feel the same way?

"Again and again, in many situations, I am still among the few women at the table. That has to change in our movement. And more often I'm the only person of color in the leadership room. There are so many talented LGBT people of color, but they're taking their energies into their professional lives, into other interests. They're not putting it into the gay movement because the gay movement doesn't speak to the issues that they care about. They should have the ability to be engaged in our own community because it's working on issues that they care about, too. It's that broader frame I've been stressing."

Now that she's in her fifties, has Vaid mellowed? "My political thinking hasn't mellowed. I'm still as intense as ever. Still as driven as ever. I'm still involved in forty-five things we don't even have time to talk about. No, I haven't mellowed. I'm still an unreconstructed progressive. I believe in a fairer system. I believe that the social benefits of our society should be shared more equitably. I believe education should be free, health care should be free. I feel confident that those are pretty mainstream values. If you look globally, the kinds of things I believe are what European governments espouse as the centrist position."

Remarkably, in spite of her years of national leadership, Vaid maintains that "the story of my life is a life not in the headlines. Despite the fact that I may have achieved some measure of notoriety, the 'text' that informs who I am, the experiences that have shaped me, are these hundreds of little encounters and grassroots moments— working with people that no one else will remember except the people in their community. That's where change is happening. Those are the heroes who are making it real. The headlines? That's not history to me."

Finally, I ask a question that she herself raised at the end of *Virtual Equality:* What are queer people for? What's the queer role in the human community?

"I used to think that queer people represented a glue that could bring a new unity. Because we were so dispersed in so many segments of society, we could bring a lot of fabrics together. In fact, that hasn't happened. Gay communities and the gay movement are just as fragmented as any other part of society by race, class, gender. I continue to believe that we represent an opening up and a freeing of oppressive, *oppressive* gender roles. The shaming and humiliation of men is the source of so much violence in the world. We haven't begun to speak to that."

Urvashi Vaid

Modesto "Tico" Valle

"People can make a difference," Modesto Valle tells me. It's a sentiment that he'll articulate more than once during the hour we spend together at the Center on Halsted, Chicago's new twenty-million-dollar LGBTQ community center, which opened in 2007. As executive director, Valle oversees what he calls "the most comprehensive LGBTQ community center in the country," one that boasts a staff of sixty full- and part-time members and a budget of over five million dollars. But the impressive statistics are not what Valle wants to talk about. For him, it's all about people: the people who helped to build the Center, the people they serve, and the people—many of whom may never utilize the Center's formal services—who simply stop by for a cup of coffee in the attractive lobby/café lounge.

"We were fortunate," he tells me as we settle into his memorabilia-festooned office. "A lot of other LGBTQ community centers were built or inherited their space at a time when people had to be closeted. We built with glass."

In fact, the glass and the brilliant light streaming in are what immediately struck me on my arrival at the Center. The ground-floor lobby, a two-story, sun-filled atrium, overlooks North Halsted Street, the city's gay thoroughfare. If architecture says something about the people who inhabit a building, then the initial impression that the Center makes is one of relaxation, conversation, openness, and inclusion.

"We wanted that. There were many donors who didn't think they would ever use the Center themselves. We wanted to create the Center for them, too. You don't need a reason to come here. Regardless of your sexual orientation, you can just drop in for a cup of coffee. We want to be known as a community center with a mission focused on the LGBTQ community *and* one that breaks down those barriers of bigotry and hatred." The formula is working. Fifteen hundred people a day pass through the Center's lobby.

Valle is not shy about describing his work, and his entire life, as a kind of ministry. "To serve, to make a difference. I didn't aspire to become executive director but to make a difference."

Born in Puerto Rico in 1964, Vale came to the States with his family when he was young. His mother had only one year of formal education; his father completed school through the eighth grade. "They were very poor, but not knowing they were poor. That's a special kind of simplicity. My parents came to the States for opportunity and to give their kids a good education. They wanted to break the cycle of poverty."

The family settled in Chicago's Old Town, at the time a melting pot of hippies and Latinos. Although his parents were Pentecostal Christians, they took an apartment close to St. Michael's Church, a Roman Catholic parish that ran a good parochial grammar school. The neighborhood was going through gentrification. Valle remembers blocks and blocks being torn down. Despite having to move several times, his parents did not quit Old Town. "They wanted to remain where there was education and safety. They didn't want us to be exposed to violence and gangs."

Valle attended Holy Trinity High School, a private Catholic school run by the Holy Cross Brothers. He has high praise for Holy Trinity, calling it a "welcoming, embracing community" with a non-judgmental ethic. The all-male student body was predominantly first-generation Latino. Valle knew he was gay but was only out to a few friends. Some of his gay classmates were out to the school, which didn't cause a problem, he says. "The beauty of the high school, the common thread, was that all the boys were intent on bettering their lives. At St. Michael's, which was very conservative, you'd burn in hell for being gay. At Holy Trinity, no one was going to hell."

When I ask him what values he picked up during his high school years, Valle immediately shoots back, "Respect. The brothers taught us to respect one another and to respect the community. There was a lot of talk about community. I use that philosophy here in the Center."

Valle led a kind of double life in high school, unobtrusively pursuing his academics while also enjoying something of a gay life under the aegis of a group of adults who took him under their wing. "We hung out together. Every Friday night there was a group—about twelve of us, gay and straight—who went out to dinner. The conversation went all over the place. I was known as a gay boy in the circle. They saw it as an opportunity to mentor individuals along their journey because they hadn't had that opportunity. It was my extended family. Because of them, I wasn't looking for other young people to hang out with. I was always thinking about the future. How do I change society?"

Valle attended the University of Notre Dame, which he's quick to point out was also run by the Holy Cross Brothers. He went as a seminarian. "I was going to be one of the brothers. I knew I was gay. They knew. But they didn't care. They were not there to judge but to serve. I wanted to be part of this larger organization that was serving and making a difference in peace and justice."

After two years at Notre Dame, Valle decided to drop out of the seminary. "It was because of the hierarchy of the Church. They weren't making a fast-enough difference." He finished his college education at DePaul University, graduating in 1986 with a degree in marketing, whereupon he immediately returned to his old high school as assistant dean of students. He worked there for the next nine years, helping to foster a culture of greater tolerance among the students and faculty and developing the school's recruiting and fund-raising efforts.

In 1987, Valle saw the AIDS Memorial Quilt on the Mall in Washington, D.C., a transforming moment for him. "This epidemic was devastating the gay community, but it was there that I saw moms and dads, grandmas, straight and gay, black and white, Asian, deaf, transgender coming together to grieve and let go of their pain. The Quilt was a way for them to display their anger but to continue their love for someone, to take something ugly and make something beautiful."

Inspired by the experience, Valle reinvigorated the Chicago NAMES Project, which, under his leadership, brought the Quilt to the Midwest for the first time. "In a lot of cities, the Quilt was just an awareness tool. I immediately said, We can do something better with this. We need to bus kids in." Valle wrote a curriculum, later funded by the CDC, to bring the Quilt to the schools. Chicago was the first city to bus in "hundreds and hundreds of kids, from the suburbs, the city—even from the borders of Indiana and Wisconsin—into this display." He created reflection exercises for the kids to talk about AIDS and the stigma surrounding it. Eventually, he brought in elementary school kids as well.

"I remember this seven-year-old kid, a second grader, who came up to me and said, 'This person was only seven years old when he died. That's my age. That can't be fun.' Later in the evening, that boy returned with his parents. That's how we opened those eyes back then."

The Chicago NAMES Project ended up being one of the strongest chapters in the country. "In every way you can measure that, "Valle stresses. "The volume of quilts we sent, the number of volunteers, the quilt displays, the money we raised. We were the first chapter to have a strategic plan, a storefront, a professional staff. A lot of people thought Chicago was the headquarters." For a while, Valle also sat on the National Board for the NAMES Project.

Out of his experiences with the Quilt, Valle volunteered at the Test Positive Awareness Network and Chicago House, an agency that served homeless, HIV-positive Chicagoans, where he became the first volunteer services director. From 1995 to 1998, he was employed by Open Hand Chicago, an agency that provides nutritious meals for people living with HIV/AIDS.

What particular skills does he identify as having served him well in all this service work?

"Listening, embracing all points of view, but moving people to action. There had been many opportunities to bring the Quilt to Chicago, but the leadership wasn't there. One of the things that you need is to be able to inspire people, galvanize them, and believe in them so that they can be empowered."

In 1996, Valle helped organize the Quilt display in Washington, an experience he calls breathtaking. "It was a renewed sense of spirit for me, because the movement had grown. AIDS was not just gay but mainstream. You stood there with seas of people in tears. And to hear, finally, a president—Clinton—who acknowledged that AIDS was among us."

Valle was working again at Holy Trinity when, in 2000, he was recruited to serve on the board of Gay Horizons, at that time Chicago's gay community services agency. A task force had been assembled to look into the viability of building a new LGBTQ community center. Tapped for his skills in fund-raising, he officially joined the staff two years later as director of development. Six months later—"surprise, surprise," he chuckles—he became acting executive director.

"A lot of hard decisions needed to be made. Year after year, the organization had debt. It was very kumbaya. Gay Horizons existed because of the goodwill of people. But if we were going to undertake this building project, we needed to professionalize." Valle got to work reducing the debt and gaining greater credibility in the community at large. He created strategic plans, job descriptions, all the things necessary to position the organization to launch a serious effort to build a new center.

The Center on Halsted, which replaced Gay Horizons, was five years in the making. "It was such a humbling moment the day we broke ground. We did so much work to get the buy-in of the community, not just LGBTQ but straight friends and allies."

One key to the success of the Center was its partnership with Whole Foods Market. The natural and organic foods company wanted a store in the area, and the Center wanted a tenant in the building to help generate income. Valle says that when Whole Foods was persuaded to sign a ninety-nine-year lease for the retail space, "they helped make this dream a reality."

Chicago's straight community also contributed significantly. Indeed, much of the initial seven million dollars raised during the "leadership phase" of the fund-raising campaign was given by straight donors. "It was important for us to be a civic center that would be respected in Chicago, not just in the gay ghetto. We wanted to be a prominent institution in the city."

The Center offers eight distinct programs, including mental health services, a Sexual Orientation and Gender Institute, an AIDS/HIV and STD hotline, and a community technology center. There are two art galleries, a gym, rentable conference rooms, a theater/auditorium, and a kitchen for catering and cooking classes. The rooftop garden, with a view over Boystown, is dedicated to Mayor Richard M. Daley, whom Valle calls "an honorary gay man."

Valle says that the two populations that have particularly taken to the Center are young people and elders. The staff see over 225 youth a week, predominantly youth of color. Thirty percent of them are homeless. "They come from violent homes, they've been thrown out. It's pretty awakening." At first, the Center hosted after-school programs for these kids, but it quickly became apparent that a morning-to-evening model was needed to respond to the multitude of needs—Valle calls them "opportunities"—that the young people presented. While some of the kids come for socializing and arts programs, others come for more intensive programming around mentorship, career development, job readiness, harm reduction, and housing referrals. "We are not the end-all, but we are a beginning, and with the community we can provide the resources that our young people need."

The Center's program for seniors, SAGE, is based on the holistic wellness model and includes health, social and cultural programs, and a Friendly Visitor program. SAGE has been so popular that it has already outgrown its space. "We have a log-in sheet for them. Many won't give the real name because they've lived in the closet for so many years that they are still in fear. Those who are in institutional care are not out either. Can you imagine being out your whole life and then going into supportive living and having to go back into the closet?"

The Center tests more people for HIV than any other test site in the state of Illinois. "People love coming to be tested because we don't feel like a clinic. We're testing a lot of straight people, too." Aside from HIV, Valle says the biggest challenge that the Chicago LGBTQ community faces these days is self-esteem. "When you look at substance abuse, HIV, STDs, it all goes to self-esteem. How do we conquer that?" He's proud that the Center, with its huge plate-glass windows, is "transparent" and sends a message of "no more sneaking in the back door."

Does Valle see a time when LGBTQ community centers will no longer be necessary? "That's sort of like the perfect world, when we don't need gay institutions because there are no labels anymore. We're far away from that."

My final question: what does he love about being gay? Valle's answer is as clear, simple, and heartfelt as everything he has said during our time together. "That I see the world differently and that I am able to appreciate differences in our world."

Russell van Kraayenburg

Russell van Kraayenburg says that "initiative" is one of his favorite words. The University of Texas senior who at the time we meet is doing a fifth year—"a victory lap," he calls it—is the cofounder of one of the first gay fraternities in the South. "A small piece of history at UT," he says on his Web site. We sit down over lattes on a Saturday morning at the end of Rush Week, during which van Kraayenburg, a boyish radio-television-film major, has been busy hosting socials and conducting interviews all week.

"I was completely blown away. We had twenty-eight interviews. I was expecting at most fifteen." He laughs. "I had a paper due yesterday. But class is not my priority at the moment. This fraternity is. I don't mind going from an A to a B if I'm doing something I love."

As a kid van Kraayenburg was not the most likely candidate for future activism. He grew up in northwest Houston ("very conservative, typically Republican," he tells me), a place where his high school was once voted one of the ten snobbiest in the country. His father, who grew up under apartheid in South Africa, "was not into homosexuality at all." That didn't stop van Kraayenburg from playing "house and dolls" with a little girl on his block instead of roughhousing with the boys. When he and his mother made trips to department stores, he would run off to the men's underwear section. "I just knew I liked looking at these boys on the underwear packages. I had no idea what it meant." The idyllic world of this childhood innocence came crashing down in junior high school, where van Kraayenburg suffered "some pretty horrible shit" because of what he calls his flamboyancy. He was frequently made fun of. It got so bad that two girls in his class were expelled for taunting him.

"I assumed things just happened that way. I was called 'gay' a lot. I knew what it was, but I didn't think I was. I thought I was just going through a phase." But by sophomore year he had it figured out. "I was pissed off. Why me? In my entire grade—there were a thousand—no one was out. There were two girls who would hold hands. That was it. And those girls didn't take shit from anyone. They were bad ass. I wished I were like them, but I didn't get to know them." In fact, through most of his high school career, van Kraayenburg withdrew from the social swing, preferring to spend most of his free time in his room. Filmmaking became his major emotional and creative outlet.

"I took a course called Public Speaking, which was really film-making, for three years. It was awesome. I devoted all my time to it. It was an escape. That's how I would express myself." When friends said they would "be cool with it" if he told them he was gay, van Kraayenburg denied his sexuality. "I didn't want to accept it." Despite the fact that being in the closet felt "sucky, horrible," he balked at the idea of coming out.

During senior year, he and another student made a zombie film for their filmmaking project. "In preparation, I watched fourteen zombie films. The best homework I did in my life! The process of making it was so much fun. We staged a zombie attack through the cafeteria and parking lot." A gay subtext here, I ask—the revenge of the outsider? "I wasn't purposely pushing a subtext. But, yeah, the first guy attacked was the jock in the high school."

After he enrolled at the University of Texas, van Kraayenburg decided to remain in the closet. "Because I wanted a public career, I figured it was not really smart for me to come out. My freshman year was High School, Part 2. I spent a lot of nights in. But at least there wasn't any judgment being passed. No one cared if I was gay or not."

During the second semester of his freshman year, van Kraayenburg met a guy who was to become his best friend. "Wade was the first really out gay person I met. He was very attractive, a little more flamboyant than the typical gay person. I was fascinated that he could be so publicly out and not catch any flak for it." The two started going to parties together. At one party toward the end of his freshman year—"pretty much a gay party"—van Kraayenburg had his first drink. And his first kiss with a guy.

"That night I decided I liked alcohol and *really* liked kissing boys. I was like, 'Russell, remember that time you said you weren't going to be with anyone? Well, that's not going to happen. You need to change something.' I pretty much welcomed it with open arms." Within a few days, van Kraayenburg had come out to everyone he knew, including his mother.

"Coming out was amazing. I felt like I could fly. People always ask—well, except straight guys, who never ask—'If you had it to do all over again, would you still be gay?' Absolutely! I would never want to be straight. Once I decided to come out, it was very rewarding. I don't want anyone to have to feel that alone or left out, or feel that their friends really weren't their friends because they were living a lie. Back in junior high and high school, that wasn't me."

By the time sophomore year rolled around, van Kraayenburg was a new person—a 180-degree shift, he says, "from this guy who just liked to hang out to one of the busiest students on campus. I fell in love with being with people." And he made a three-minute film about it, *Liam from 4:57 to 5:00*, about a guy running away from his female prom date to reconnect with the guy he loves, who is anxiously waiting for him at a train station. "I wanted to tell a story that I knew would be a little different from everyone else's in the class."

Soon van Kraayenburg was also running for and getting elected to campus government councils. "I got more involved in trying to push minority rights. I definitely was that voice. I fell in love with being involved." It was during the summer after his fourth year at UT, facing the prospect of returning for a fifth year and wanting a project to sink his newly honed activist teeth into, that van Kraayenburg and two friends, Ryan Yezak and Mike LaCour, cooked up the idea of starting a gay fraternity.

"Over the years, I had never wanted to be a part of Greek life, but through student government and meeting some super activists on campus I realized that there were minority groups whose needs weren't being met. I wanted to do something progressive and big. And at the same time I wanted to do something practical."

Van Kraayenburg knew that there were "a lot of queer organizations on campus." But he also knew that the fraternities at UT could be "pretty homophobic. Yes, frats accept gay members, but my friends would never feel comfortable in them. The hazing, too. I saw the Greek system at UT as irresponsible. I hate to put it that way because I know some groups are trying to change, but most aren't."

That summer, van Kraayenburg did some research and discovered Delta Lambda Phi, the national parent fraternity for gay, bisexual, and progressive men founded in 1986. "We had to prove to them that we were going to be a chapter worth their time. I devoted myself 100 percent to it." The UT "colony," as fledgling chapters are called, was started in the fall of 2008 with seven members.

"We wanted to found a brotherhood where young gay men could find a mentor. It boiled down to the idea that coming out is such a difficult process, especially at a university of fifty-four thousand people. It's so daunting. We wanted to give students a place to come out, a place to hear those stories, a place where people can make a friend for life and share those deepest thoughts."

For van Kraayenburg, it's all about brotherhood. "For me, brotherhood is a chance to make friends, to make a best friend with 100 percent no worry." He notes that when gay pledges from racial minority groups had a chance to join a black, Latino, or Asian fraternity, many of them chose the gay fraternity instead because "they're all here for the same reason."

In the long run, van Kraayenburg hopes to encourage traditional fraternities to see "how valuable gay men, bisexual men, progressive men are. Our plan is that we'll become big enough and do so many amazing things that the other fraternities at UT will realize that they should be more active in pursuing the gay community. I would like to see our Greek system so welcoming that there wouldn't be a need for gay fraternities." At the same time, he thinks that there will always be a need for fraternities like DLP, which can provide "a comfort place for those guys who are having issues coming out."

What would be the particular benefits of having gay men in a traditional fraternity?

Only somewhat jokingly, van Kraayenburg says, "We work harder, we're socially smarter, more well rounded. Honestly, gay guys have an opportunity to help enlighten the straight guys as to how tough things can be. The guys at typical white Greek fraternities are privileged, they don't have that exposure to differences."

In fact, after a rush event earlier in the week, he reports that some of the guys were harassed, called "faggot," and doused with beer and water balloons as they were walking home. "I know that in Texas it's going to be more difficult than in other places."

Unlike some of the million-dollar frat houses along Rio Grande Street or at West Campus, DLP still has no house of its own. The brothers hold their weekly meetings in van Kraayenburg's apartment or in a room on campus. In addition to hosting socials, they plan service projects and fund-raisers. Van Kraayenburg says he wants the fraternity to be "slightly different. I try to push activism and community service." Members of the fraternity have lobbied at the Texas State House for Equality Texas. Most are participating in the upcoming Hill Country Ride for AIDS. Van Kraayenburg and some of his fraternity brothers have also guest lectured for a class in human sexuality.

And how about dating among the brothers? "National has a hands-off policy: no brother or neophyte can do anything with a pledge. You're not allowed to enter into any relationship; nothing sexual, nothing lovey-dovey. We make it clear to rushes that we are not a dating service. We go a step further: we encourage the brothers themselves to avoid relationships with each other. Obviously you can't restrict the way people are going to meet. We're a whole bunch of gay guys. You might meet the guy you'll fall in love with, but relationships in organizations can get messy."

As van Kraayenburg finishes up his years at UT, he is already turning his attention to a new project. In January 2009, he co-founded the Out and Educated Foundation, a nonprofit aimed at giving scholarships to homeless and in-need queer youth in Texas. He's building a board of directors and starting to raise money. "We're hoping it becomes our fraternity's philanthropy in the future. Next year, I'll be doing the day-to-day operations."

Van Kraayenburg says that coming out has matured him in many ways. "I'm a lot more sensitive, caring, more open, less quick to pass judgment. I have straight friends who say, 'You're really cool for a gay guy.' I love and hate hearing that. I'm just glad they got to know me. I'm changing someone's life."

Russell van Kraayenburg

LIVING OUT
Gay and Lesbian Autobiographies

David Bergman, Joan Larkin, and Raphael Kadushin
SERIES EDITORS

Secret Places: My Life in New York and New Guinea
Tobias Schneebaum

Wild Man
Tobias Schneebaum

Sex Talks to Girls: A Memoir
Maureen Seaton

Outbound: Finding a Man, Sailing an Ocean
William Storandt